AMERICAN ACCENT TRAINING

A guide to speaking and pronouncing colloquial American English

Ann Cook
FOURTH EDITION

Illustrated by Holly Forsyth, Nathalie Jean-Barth, Randy Gossman, Erik Scott, and Nelson Afian
Audio by Voice Trax Studios with Marcus Harwell

BARRON'S

Get access to the downloadable audio for *American Accent Training* **at:**

http://barronsbooks.com/media/AAT8934

All inquiries should be addressed to:
Barron's Educational Series, Inc.
250 Wireless Boulevard
Hauppauge, NY 11788
www.barronseduc.com

ISBN 978-0-4380-1035-9

Library of Congress Control Number: 2016954217

PRINTED IN THE UNITED STATES OF AMERICA
9 8 7 6 5 4 3 2 1

Table of Contents

Read This First

Welcome to *American Accent Training*. This book and audio is designed to get you started on your American accent. We'll follow the book and go through the 17 lessons and all the exercises step by step. Everything is explained, and a complete Answer Key is in the back of the text. The audio can be found at http://barronsbooks.com/media/AAT8934.

WHAT IS ACCENT?

Accent is a combination of four main components: *voice quality*, *intonation* (speech music), *liaisons* (word connections), and *pronunciation* (the spoken sounds of vowels, consonants, and combinations). As you go along, you'll notice that you're being asked to look at accent in a different way. You'll also realize that the grammar you studied before and this accent you're studying now are completely different.

Part of the difference is that grammar and vocabulary are systematic and structured—the *letter* of the language. Accent, on the other hand, is free form, intuitive, and creative—more the *spirit* of the language. So, thinking of music, feeling, and flow, let your mouth relax into the American accent.

CAN I LEARN A NEW ACCENT?

Can a person actually learn a new accent? Many people feel that after a certain age, it's just not possible. Can classical musicians play jazz? If they practice, of course they can! For your American accent, it's just a matter of learning and practicing techniques this book will teach you. It is up to you to use them or not. How well you do depends mainly on how open and willing you are to sounding different from the way you have sounded all your life.

A very important thing you need to remember is that you can use your accent to say what you mean and how you mean it. Word stress conveys meaning through tone or feeling, which can be much more important than the actual words that you use. We'll cover the expression of these feelings through intonation in the first lesson.

You may have noticed that I talk fast and often run my words together. You've probably heard enough "English-teacher English" where . . . everything . . . is . . . pronounced without having to listen too carefully. We're going to talk just like the native speakers that we are, in a normal conversational tone.

Native speakers often tell people who are learning English to "slow down" and to "speak clearly." This is meant with the best of intentions, but it is exactly the opposite of what a student really needs to do. If you speak fairly quickly, with strong intonation and good voice quality, you will be understood more easily. To illustrate this point, you will hear a Chinese gentleman first trying to speak slowly and carefully and then repeating the same two sentences quickly and with clear intonation. The difference makes him sound like a completely different person.

▶ Please listen. You will hear the same words twice.

Hello, my name is Raymond Choon.

You may have to listen a couple of times to catch everything. To help you, every word is also written in the book. By seeing and hearing simultaneously, you'll learn to reconcile the differences between the appearance of English (spelling) and the sound of English (pronunciation and the other aspects of accent).

The audio leaves a rather short pause for you to repeat into. The point of this is to get you responding quickly and without spending too much time thinking about your response.

ACCENT VERSUS PRONUNCIATION

Many people equate *accent* with *pronunciation*. I don't feel this to be true at all. America is a big country, and while the pronunciation varies from the East Coast to the West Coast, from the southern to the northern states, two components that are uniquely American stay basically the same—the speech music, or *intonation*, and the word connections, or *liaisons*. Throughout this program, we will focus on them. In the latter part of the book we will work on pronunciation concepts, such as Cat? Caught? Cut? and Betty Bought a Bit of Better Butter; we also will work our way through some of the difficult sounds, such as TH, the American R, the L, V, and Z.

"WHICH ACCENT IS CORRECT?"

American Accent Training was created to help people "sound American" for lectures, interviews, teaching, business situations, and general daily communication. Although America has many regional pronunciation differences, the accent you will learn is that of standard American English as spoken and understood by the majority of educated native speakers in the United States. Don't worry that you will sound slangy or too casual, because you most definitely won't. This is the way a professor lectures to a class, the way a national newscaster broadcasts, the way that is most comfortable and familiar to the majority of native speakers.

"WHY IS MY ACCENT SO BAD?"

Learners can be seriously hampered by a negative outlook, so I'll address this very important point early. First, your accent is *not* bad; it is nonstandard to the American ear. There is a joke that goes: What do you call a person who can speak three languages? *Trilingual.* What do you call a person who can speak two languages? *Bilingual.* What do you call a person who can only speak one language? *American.*

Every language is equally valid or good, so every accent is *good.* The average American, however, truly does have a hard time understanding a nonstandard accent. George Bernard Shaw said that the English and Americans are two people *divided* by the same language!

Some students learn to overpronounce English because they naturally want to say the word as it is written. Too often an English teacher may allow this, perhaps thinking that colloquial American English is unsophisticated, unrefined, or even incorrect. Not so at all! Just as you don't say the T in *listen,* the TT in *better* is pronounced D, *bedder.* Any other pronunciation will sound foreign, strange, wrong, or different to a native speaker.

LESS THAN IT APPEARS . . . MORE THAN IT APPEARS

As you will see in the "Squeezed-Out Syllables" section, some words appear to have three or more syllables, but all of them are not actually spoken. For example, *business* is not (*bi•zi•*ness), but rather (*biz•*ness).

Just when you get used to eliminating whole syllables from words, you're going to come across other words that look as if they have only one syllable, but really need to be said with as many as three! In addition, the inserted syllables are filled with letters that are not in the written word. I'll give you two examples of this strange phenomenon. *Pool* looks like a nice, one-syllable word, but if you say it this way, at best, it will sound like *pull,* and at worst will be unintelligible to your listener. For clear comprehension, you need to say three syllables (pu/wuh/luh). Where did that W come from? It's certainly not written down anywhere, but it is there just as definitely as the P is there. The second example is a word like *feel.* If you say just the letters that you see, it will sound more like *fill.* You need to say (fee/yuh/luh). Is that really a Y? Yes. These mysterious semivowels are explained under Liaisons. They can appear either inside a word, as you have seen, or between words, as you will learn.

LANGUAGE IS FLUENT AND FLUID

Just like your own language, conversational English has a very smooth, fluid sound. Imagine that you are walking along a dry riverbed with your eyes closed. Every time you come to a rock, you trip over it, stop, continue, and trip over the next rock. This is how the average foreigner speaks English. It is slow, awkward, and even painful. Now imagine that you are a great river rushing through that same riverbed—rocks are no problem, are they? You just slide over and around them without ever breaking your smooth flow. It is *this* feeling that I want you to capture in English.

Changing your old speech habits is very similar to changing from a stick shift to an automatic transmission. Yes, you continue to reach for the gearshift for a while, and your foot still tries to find the clutch pedal, but this soon phases itself out. In the same way, you may still say "telephone **call**" (kohl) instead of (kahl) for a while, but this too will soon pass.

You will also have to think about your speech more than you do now. In the same way that you were very aware and self-conscious when you first learned to drive, you will eventually relax and deal with the various components simultaneously.

A new accent is an adventure. Be bold! Exaggerate wildly! You may worry that Americans will laugh at you for putting on an accent, but I guarantee you, they won't even notice. They'll just think that you've finally learned to "talk right." Good luck with your new accent!

A FEW WORDS ON PRONUNCIATION

Track 2

I'd like to introduce you to the pronunciation guide outlines in the following chart. There aren't too many characters that are different from the standard alphabet, but just so you'll be familiar with them, look at the chart. It shows eight *tense* vowels and six *lax* vowels and semivowels.

Tense Vowels? Lax Vowels?

In some books, tense vowels are called *long* and lax vowels are called *short*. Since you will be learning how to lengthen vowels when they come before a voiced consonant, it would be confusing to say that *hen* has a long, short vowel. It is more descriptive to say that it has a lax vowel that is doubled or lengthened.

Tense Vowels				Lax Vowels			
Symbol	Sound	Spelling	Example	Symbol	Sound	Spelling	Example
ā	εi	take	tāk	ε	eh	get	gεt
ē	ee	eat	ēt	i	ih	it	it
ī	äi	ice	īs	ü	ih + uh	took	tük
ō	ou	hope	hōp	ə	uh	some	səm
ū	ooh	smooth	smū<u>th</u>				
ä	ah	caught	kät		**Semivowels**		
æ	ä + ε	cat	kæt	ər	er	her	hər
æo	æ + o	down	dæon	ᵊl	ul	dull	dəᵊl

Although this may look like a lot of characters to learn, there are really only four new ones: **æ, ä, ə,** and **ü.** Under Tense Vowels, you'll notice that the vowels that say their own name simply have a line over them: **ā, ē, ī, ō, ū.** There are three other tense vowels. First, **ä** is pronounced like the sound you make when the doctor wants to see your throat, or when you loosen a tight belt and sit down in a soft chair—*aaaaaaah*! Next, you'll find **æ,** a combination of the tense vowel **ä** and the lax vowel **ε.** It is similar to the noise that a goat or a lamb makes (*half, last, chance*). The last one is **æo,** a combination of **æ** and **o.** This is a very common sound, usually written as *ow* or *ou* in words like *down* or *round*.

A *tense vowel* requires you to use a lot of facial muscles to produce it. If you say **ē,** you must stretch your lips back; for **ū** you must round your lips forward; for **ä** you drop your jaw down; for **æ** you will drop your jaw far down and back; for **ā** bring your lips back and drop your jaw a bit; for **ī** drop your jaw for the *ah* part of the sound and pull it back up for the *ee* part; and for **ō** round the lips, drop the jaw, and pull back up into **ū.** An American **ō** is really **ōū.**

▶ Now you try it. Repeat after me. **ē, ū, ā, æ, ä, ī, ō.**

A *lax vowel,* on the other hand, is very reduced. In fact, you don't need to move your face at all. You only need to move the back of your tongue and your throat. These sounds are very different from most other languages.

Under Lax Vowels, there are four reduced vowel sounds, starting with the Greek letter epsilon **ε**, pronounced *eh*; **i** pronounced *ih*, and **ü** pronounced *ü*, which is a combination of *ih* and *uh*, and the schwa, **ə**, pronounced *uh*—the softest, most reduced, most relaxed sound that we can produce. *It is also the most common sound in English.* The semivowels are the American **R** (pronounced *er*, which is the schwa plus R) and the American **L** (which is the schwa plus L).

Voiced Consonants? Unvoiced Consonants?

A consonant is a sound that causes two points of your mouth to come into contact, in three locations—the *lips,* the *tip of the tongue,* and the *throat.* A consonant can either be *unvoiced* (whispered) or *voiced* (spoken), and it can appear at the beginning, middle, or end of a word. You'll notice that for some categories, a particular sound doesn't exist in English.

Beginning		Middle		End	
Whispered	Spoken	Whispered	Spoken	Whispered	Spoken
parry	bury	apple	able	mop	mob
ferry	very	afraid	avoid	off	of
stew	zoo	races	raises	face	phase
sheet		pressure	pleasure	crush	garage
two	do	petal	pedal	not	nod
choke	joke	gaucho	gouger	rich	ridge
think	<u>th</u>at	ether	ei<u>th</u>er	tooth	smoo<u>th</u>
come	gum	bicker	bigger	pick	pig
		accent	exit	tax	tags
	yes		player		day
	wool		shower		now
his		ahead			
	late		collect		towel
	rate		correct		tower
	me		swimmer		same
	next		connect		man
			finger		ring

Pronunciation Points

In many dictionaries, you may find a character that looks like an upside-down *V* (**ʌ**) and another character that is an upside-down *e* (**ə**), the *schwa.* There is a linguistic distinction between the two, but they are *pronounced* exactly the same. Since you can't hear the difference between these two sounds, we'll just be using the upside-down *e* to indicate the schwa sound. It is pronounced *uh.*

The second point is that we do not differentiate between **ä** and **ɔ**. The **ä** is pronounced *ah.* The backwards *C* (**ɔ**) is more or less pronounced *aw.* This *aw* sound has a "back East" sound to it, and as it's not common to the entire United States, it won't be included here.

R can be considered a semivowel. One characteristic of a vowel is that nothing in the mouth touches anything else. **R** definitely falls into that category. So in the exercises throughout the book it will be treated not so much as a consonant, but as a vowel.

The *ow* sound is usually indicated by **äu**, which would be *ah + ooh*. This may have been accurate at some point in some locations, but the sound is now generally æo. *Town* is *tæon*, *how* is *hæo*, *loud* is *læod*, and so on.

Besides *voiced* and *unvoiced*, there are two words that come up in pronunciation. These are *sibilant* and *plosive*. When you say the *s* sound, you can feel the air sliding out over the tip of your tongue—this is a sibilant. When you say the *p* sound, you can feel the air popping out from between your lips—this is a plosive. Be aware that there are two sounds that are sometimes mistakenly taught as sibilants, but are actually plosives: *th* and *v*.

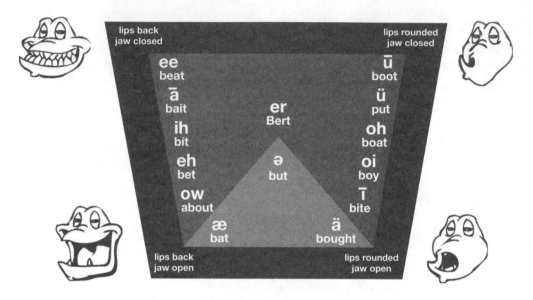

For particular points of pronunciation that pertain to your own language, refer to the Nationality Guides on page 188.

WE DON'T HAVE SOME OF THOSE SOUNDS IN MY LANGUAGE . . .

Track 3

This is undoubtedly true, but you can see that you only need to pick up a limited number of new sounds (**ä, æ, ɛ, ə, ü**). Given what you've already accomplished in life, this is not a big deal. A Chinese speaker was once bemoaning how hard it was for him to say the **R**. When asked if he went to college, he said "Of course, I have a PhD in physics from Caltech." After a beat, he realized that compared to that . . . the **R** is not harrrrrrrrd.

Other Characters

If you use one of these character sets, compare it with English.

American Phonics	ä	bä	chä	dä	fä	gä	hä	jä	kä	lä	mä	nä	pä	rä	sä	shä	tä	thä	vä	wä	yä	zä
Japanese	あ	ば	ちゃ	だ		が	は	じゃ	か		ま	な	ぱ		さ	しゃ	た			わ	や	ざ
Chinese	啊	八	茶	大	伐	嘎	蛤	家	卡	拉	馬	拿	怕		洒	沙	他			哇	壓	匝
Korean	아	바	차	다		가	하	자	카		마	나	파		사		타			와	야	
Vietnamese	a	ba	cha	đa	pha	ga	ha	tra	ca	la	ma	na	pa		xa	sa	ta		va	oa	ia	da
Arabic	١	ب		ذ	ف		ﻉ	ﻍ	ك	ﻝ	م	ن			س	ش	ت	ث ذ.		و	ي	ز
Russian	а	ба	ча	да	фа	га	ха	джа	ка	ла	ма	на	па		са	ша	та		ва*	ува	я	за

*ва is much softer than the American V

Let me give a quick explanation of why we're using these sounds. When you come in through your own language, you are coming from a place of total and absolute confidence. You *know* that sound. So, we're taking something you know and doing a lateral transference to a set of letters in English. If, on the other hand, you start from scratch, you'll be wondering if you're doing it right, and this will drain your confidence and your energy.

Now that you've worked hard and successfully imitated the sounds, you're going to go on to the next step, which is regular spelling.

Throughout this text, we will be using three symbols to indicate three separate actions:

▶ Indicates a command or a suggestion.

◀ Indicates the beep tone.

✗ Indicates that you need to turn the audio on or off, back up, or pause.

VOWEL & CONSONANT OVERVIEW: NONSENSE SYLLABLES

Track 4

The first column is **ä** because it's going to be easy for you. I'm going to say that again. Ready? It's going to be **easy** for you. Why? Because as far as I can tell, every language on Earth has an *ah* sound. Some of the consonants may be a little tricky (**TH** and **R** spring to mind), but listen and repeat, repeat, repeat . . . in a deep voice. (Final consonants, diphthongs, and consonant blends such as **BL** and **CR** are covered in later chapters.)

Track 5

	ä	æ	ɛ	i	ə	ü	ē	ō	ū	ā	ī
b	bä	bæ	bɛh	bih	bə	bü	bē	bō	bū	bā	bī
ch	chä	chæ	chɛh	chih	chə	chü	chē	chō	chū	chā	chī
d	dä	dæ	dɛh	dih	də	dü	dē	dō	dū	dā	dī
f	fä	fæ	fɛh	fih	fə	fü	fē	fō	fū	fā	fī
g	gä	gæ	gɛh	gih	gə	gü	gē	gō	gū	gā	gī
h	hä	hæ	hɛh	hih	hə	hü	hē	hō	hū	hā	hī
j	jä	jæ	jɛh	jih	jə	jü	jē	jō	jū	jā	jī
k	kä	kæ	kɛh	kih	kə	kü	kē	kō	kū	kā	kī
l	lä	læ	lɛh	lih	lə	lü	lē	lō	lū	lā	lī
m	mä	mæ	mɛh	mih	mə	mü	mē	mō	mū	mā	mī
n	nä	næ	nɛh	nih	nə	nü	nē	nō	nū	nā	nī
p	pä	pæ	pɛh	pih	pə	pü	pē	pō	pū	pā	pī
r	rä	ræ	rɛh	rih	rə	rü	rē	rō	rū	rā	rī
s	sä	sæ	sɛh	sih	sə	sü	sē	sō	sū	sā	sī
sh	shä	shæ	shɛh	shih	shə	shü	shē	shō	shū	shā	shī
t	tä	tæ	tɛh	tih	tə	tü	tē	tō	tū	tā	tī
th	thä	thæ	thɛh	thih	**the***	thü	thē	thō	thū	thā	thī
v	vä	væ	vɛh	vih	və	vü	vē	vō	vū	vā	vī
w	wä	wæ	wɛh	wih	wə	wü	wē	wō	wū	wā	wī
y	yä	yæ	yɛh	yih	yə	yü	yē	yō	yū	yā	yī
z	zä	zæ	zɛh	zih	zə	zü	zē	zō	zū	zā	zī

*Most commonly used word in English

As you go through this chart, pronouncing all the sounds, deepen your voice and make the vowels a little longer than you are inclined to. Some of these will sound like real words, but most of them are just fragments. Observe that for **ä**, you drop your jaw, for **ē**, you stretch your lips back a bit, and for **ū**, you round your lips. There are only five new characters: **ä, æ, ɛ, ə, ü**. Listen carefully and repeat this whole chart at least five times in columns, and five times across. Record yourself, listen back, and compare.

VOWEL & CONSONANT OVERVIEW: REAL WORDS

Track 6

Apply the *phonetic* sound to the entire column, no matter what the *spelling* is. Then, read each row across, making the vowel distinctions.

	ä	æ	ɛ	i	ü	ə	ē	ō	ū	ā	ī
	ought	at	etch	it	■	um	eat	oat	oops	ate	I'm
b	Bob	bat	bet	been	book	but	beat	boat	boot	bait	bite
ch	chop	chat	check	chin	■	chuck	cheat	choke	choose	chase	child
d	Don	Dad	dead	did	■	done	deal	don't	do	day	die
f	fawn	fat	fetch	fit	foot	fun	feet	phone	food	fail	find
g	gone	gap	get	give	good	gun	geese	go	ghoul	gate	guy
h	hot	had	head	his	hood	hut	he	hold	who	hey	hi
j	jaw	Jack	Jeff	gin	■	jump	jeans	joke	jewel	jail	giant
k	call	cat	Ken	kid	could	come	key	cold	cool	cane	kite
l	law	laugh	left	lick	look	luck	lead	load	lose	lay	lie
m	Mom	mad	men	mix	■	much	me	most	moon	make	mine
n	not	Nan	net	knit	nook	none	need	note	new	name	knife
p	pot	pat	pet	pick	put	putt	peak	pole	pool	pay	pie
r	raw	ran	red	rib	rook	rub	reed	row	room	raise	rise
s	saw	sat	said	sin	soot	such	see	so	suit	say	sigh
sh	shawl	shack	shed	shill	should	shut	she	show	shoe	shape	shine
t	tall	tack	ten	tin	took	tub	tea	toe	tube	take	try
th	thought	that	then	this	■	the*	these	though	through	they	thigh
v	Von	vat	vex	vim	■	vug	veal	voice	voodoo	veil	vie
w	walk	wax	when	with	would	was	we	won't	woo	whales	why
y	yawn	yap	yes	yip	you'll	young	yield	yo-yo	you	Yale	yikes
z	czar	zap	zen	zig	■	zug	zeal	Zoey	zoo	zany	zygote

Most commonly used word in English

Telephone Tutoring

PRELIMINARY DIAGNOSTIC ANALYSIS

This is a speech analysis to identify the strengths and weaknesses of your American accent. If you are studying *American Accent Training* on your own, contact toll-free (800) 457-4255 or go to *AmericanAccent.com* for a referral to a qualified telephone analyst. The diagnostic analysis is designed to evaluate your current speech patterns to let you know where your accent is standard and nonstandard.

Hello, my name is _____. I'm taking American Accent Training. There's a lot to learn, but I hope to make it as enjoyable as possible. I should pick up on the American intonation pattern pretty easily, although the only way to get it is to practice all of the time.

1. walk, all, long, caught	5. ice, I'll, sky	9. tuck, fun, medicine, indicate	13. out, house, round
2. cat, matter, laugh	6. tick, fill, will	10. too, fool, wooed	14. loyal, choice, oil
3. take, say, fail	7. teak, feel, wheel	11. took, full, would	
4. get, any, says, fell	8. work, first, learn, turn	12. woke, told, so, roll	

A	B	C	D	E	F
1. pit	1. bit	1. staple	1. stable	1. cap	1. cab
2. fear	2. veer	2. refers	2. reverse	2. half	2. have
3. sue	3. zoo	3. faces	3. phases	3. race	3. raise
4. sheer	▆	4. cashew	4. casual	4. rush	4. rouge
5. tin	5. din	5. metal	5. medal	5. hat	5. had
6. chin	6. gin	6. catcher	6. cadger	6. rich	6. ridge
7. thin	7. then	7. ether	7. either	7. bath	7. bathe
8. cut	8. gut	8. bicker	8. bigger	8. tack	8. tag
9. yellow	9. race	9. million	9. correction	9. say	9. sore
10. would	10. breed	10. coward	10. surprise	10. how	10. peeper
11. him	11. man	11. reheat	11. summer	11. soul	11. palm
12. lace	12. name	12. collection	12. runner	12. people	12. can
13. bleed	▆	13. supplies	13. kingdom	13. sink	13. sing

1. Make him get it.
2. Let her get your keys.
3. You've got to work on it, don't you?
4. Soup or salad?

1. Maykim **ged**dit.
2. Ledder getcher **keez**.
3. Yoov gädda **wr** kä nit, doan choo?
4. Super **salad**?

1. Betty bought a bit of better butter.

2. Beddy bada bida bedder budder.

3. Italian	Italy
4. attack	attic
5. atomic	atom
6. photography	photograph

7. bet	bed

1

The American Sound

Deepen your voice, project it out!

LET'S START AT THE BEGINNING

Track 8

As the philosophers say, start with yourself and define your terms. What are the parts of your mouth? How do they interact? What is a consonant? What is a vowel? Let's take a tour of the mouth, starting with the most basic sound.

Exercise 1-1: The Starting Point—Mmmm . . .

Let's start with the mmmm sound. It's super easy to do. All you do is put your lips together and hum. You'll notice a couple things here. Your lips are touching and the air is coming out through your nose in a continuous stream. Put your hand on your throat and say mmmm, and observe that you can feel a vibration in your fingertips. This means that the M sound is spoken and not whispered.

Mmmmmm . . .

This exercise tells you four important things about the consonant **M**:

1. Point of contact (*lips*)
2. Where the air comes out (*nose*)
3. How the air comes out (*glide*)
4. If the sound is spoken or whispered (*spoken*)

Exercise 1-2: Combining Sounds

 Track 9

Now that you know where things are, let's turn it into something. In a deep voice, say the following out loud. We're adding two more consonants at the lip position: P & B.

Mmm   Ah

1. mah
2. mah-mah
3. pah
4. pah-pah
5. bah
6. bah-bah

Exercise 1-3: Pronunciation & Cadence

 Track 10

In your deepest voice, repeat these syllables. To get the physical experience of intonation, either stretch a rubber band, snap your fingers, or tap the table. Repeat this ten times.

1. **MAH**-mah   2. mah-**MAH**   3. **PAH**-pah   4. pah-**PAH**   5. **BAH**-bah   6. bah-**BAH**

Exercise 1-4: Pure Sound Track 11

Let's put this in context. Using the äh sound, repeat the following sounds. Don't worry about what it means, just repeat the sounds in a deep, confident voice. That little upside-down e sounds like uh.

    1. bä bläs diz jäb   2. skät tädə lät   3. dän bädə bäik

At this point, you may be thinking, *What the heck is this? It's nonsense! It doesn't even look like English! I really need to know what I'm saying, and I don't know what this means! This is gibberish, and I might just sound like a fool, here! I need the confidence of understanding what I'm saying. I'm afraid I'll sound completely foolish! I'm not confident with this because it's so different from what I've been taught. I just want to see what it looks like in regular English.*

Exercise 1-5: Regular English Track 12

OK, go ahead and decipher it into regular English, as best as you can. Listen to the audio in the previous section to make sure you're getting all the words. (Check Answer Key on page 216.)

1. _____   2. _____   3. _____

Exercise 1-6: Pure Sound Track 13

This time, listen and imitate the speaker while reading the first line. Notice that in the second line, it's spelled out for you. Match the sounds with the new letters, including the T that turns into a D. (This is only a temporary transition, and once you've really learned the sounds, you'll go back to regular spelling.) The intonation is marked for you, so continue with the physical tapping and snapping.

    1. bä bläs diz jäb   2. skät tädə lät   3. dän bädə bäik
      Bob lost his job.   Scott taught a lot.   Don bought a bike.

YOU'RE VISUAL

If you *see* it, you've *got* it, and it's hard to catch sounds if you can't get a look at them. Now that you've seen the sentences in proper English, you can imprint with the visual representation (a fancy way of saying *spelling*).

> What is Beethoven's favorite fruit?

> Ba-na-na-na

VOICE QUALITY

Track 14

You know how you hear a voice across a crowded room and you can just tell that it's American? What's at play there? To answer that question, let's first define our terms: What *is* voice quality and the American sound? It's a combination of vocal placement and cadence. This means a throaty sound and a stairstep intonation.

Listen to British comedian Eddie Izzard imitate the American accent. Notice how his voice moves back in his throat and down in his chest when he's imitating the American accent. This throaty quality is an essential characteristic. There's even a fancy word to describe it—*rhoticity*—which is that solid **R** as in *hard* and *far*. There are regional dialects that are notable for lacking rhoticity, such as the classic Bostonian *Pahk yah cah in Hahvahd Yahd* for *Park your car in Harvard Yard*, but the overwhelming majority of Americans growl out the **R**.

Intonation, voice quality, and phrasing all contribute to the uniquely American voice, along with a casual, relaxed attitude. This relaxation causes American English to differ from the crisper sounds of British English. Within voice quality, you'll be adjusting your volume (a little louder vs. muted or murmured), pitch (high pitched vs. a deeper register), air flow (popped, hissed, or buzzed), and where the voice is generated (throat and chest vs. head and nose).

Americans tend to be a little louder than you're accustomed to. The stereotypical American is louder, a little brasher, more boisterous, immediately friendly, informal, and slightly jokey. It's important to project your voice out with more force than usual, and you'll need more breath to push it out. Kids are loud, right? Things stick in their heads because they yell them out. Yell this out! In the privacy of your home, car, or mountaintop, get out and yell some of these sounds and practice sentences so that you can get it really in your head. Don't be afraid to exaggerate and go way further than you think the American accent actually is. This will help you embrace the sound.

MUSIC

Track 15

Even if you can't sing, you'll recognize the correlation between song and speech music. We're going to listen to a range from high to low.

The singer's natural voice is in the middle range, so for him the highs and lows don't feel natural, just as deepening your voice won't feel natural for you in the beginning. You'll have to practice and get comfortable with it.

PITCH / SOUND

Track 16

Let's transition from song to speech. Interestingly, languages are spoken at different pitches, so it's important to recognize the pitch you're coming from as well as the pitch you're heading toward. Even though there are millions of English speakers, both male and female, there is a general pitch range into which English falls. Listen to this audio clip, ranging from a Japanese woman speaking at a very high pitch, to an Arabic man speaking in a much deeper register. You'll notice that English is in the middle.

Generally speaking, to Americans a higher pitch indicates stress or tension, and they will respond accordingly, even if you are not stressed. Of course, speaking in a second language can be stressful, so make a conscious effort to match your speaking voice in English to your deepest voice in your own language.

THE DADDY VOICE

Track 17

Americans are culturally programmed to trust the deep voices of authority. In a study from McMaster University in Canada, published in the *Journal of Evolution and Human Behavior*, researchers found that men with lower-pitched voices are found to be more dominant and attractive than are men with higher-pitched voices. They found that lower-pitched voices are associated with favorable personality traits more often than are higher-pitched voices. Listeners were asked to assess the attractiveness, honesty, leadership potential, and intelligence—among other qualities—of the speakers. For nearly every attribute they were asked to rate, participants were significantly more likely to prefer the deeper voice.

Think of national broadcasters and the deep, mellifluous tones they use. If you deepen your voice, you'll find that Americans become more respectful and attentive. To capture this voice, hark back to when your dad would call you in for dinner (even if this was never the case). Put your shoulders back, your chest out, take a deep breath and say, *Hey! Get in here!* Notice how that feels physically and mentally. If you come in through the Daddy Voice, you'll probably have a less negative reaction than just by deepening your voice randomly, to which we've had people say, *I sound like a monster! I sound like a gangster!* This is not the direction we want to push you in, but rather the calm, reassuring voice of an authority figure. Shoulders back, chin up, chest out, project from your diaphragm, and relax your throat.

THE AMERICAN SPEECH MUSIC: CHANGE PITCH ON IMPORTANT INFORMATION

Track 18

What to Do with Your Mouth to Sound American

One of the main differences between the way an American talks and the way the rest of the world talks is that we don't really move our lips. (So, when an American says "Read my lips!" what does he really mean?) We create most of our sounds in the throat, using our tongue very actively. If you hold your fingers over your lips or clench your jaws when you practice speaking American English, you will find yourself much closer to native-sounding speech than if you try to pronounce every . . . single . . . sound . . . very . . . carefully.

If you can relate American English to music, remember that the indigenous music is jazz. Listen to their speech music, and you will hear that Americans have a melodic, jazzy way of producing sounds. Imagine the sound of a cello when you say, *Beddy bada bida bedder budder* (Betty bought a bit of better butter) and you'll be close to the native way of saying it.

Because most Americans came from somewhere else, American English reflects the accent contributions of many lands. The speech music has become much more exaggerated than British English, developing a strong and distinctive intonation. If you use this intonation, not only will you be easier to understand, but you will sound much more confident, dynamic, and persuasive.

Intonation, or speech music, is the sound that you hear when a conversation is too far away to be clearly audible but close enough for you to tell the nationality of the speakers. The American intonation dictates liaisons and pronunciation, and it indicates mood and meaning. Without intonation, your speech would be flat, mechanical, and very confusing for your listener. What is the American intonation pattern? How is it different from other languages? *Foa egzampuru, eefu you hea ah Jahpahneezu pahsohn speakingu Ingurishu*; the sound would be very choppy, mechanical, and unemotional to an American. *Za sem vey vis Cheuman pipples*; it sounds too stiff. *A mahn frohm Paree ohn zee ahzer ahnd, eez intonashon goes up at zee end ov evree sentence* and has such a strong intonation that he sounds romantic and highly emotional, but this may not be appropriate for a lecture or business meeting in English.

AMERICAN INTONATION DO'S AND DON'TS

▶ **Do not speak word by word.**
If you speak word by word, as many people who learned "printed" English do, you'll end up sounding mechanical and foreign. You may have noticed the same thing happens in your own language: When someone reads a speech, even a native speaker, it sounds stiff and stilted, quite different from a normal conversational tone.

Bob... is... on... the... phone

▶ **Connect words to form sound groups.**
This is where you're going to start doing something completely different than what you have done in your previous English studies. This part is the most difficult for many people because it goes against everything they've been taught. Instead of thinking of each word as a unit, think of sound units. These sound units may or may not correspond to a word written on a page. Native speakers don't say Bob is on the phone, but say bäbizän the foun. Sound units make a sentence flow smoothly, like peanut butter—never really ending and never really starting, just flowing along. Even chunky peanut butter is acceptable. So long as you don't try to put plain peanuts directly onto your bread, you'll be OK.

bä bizän the foun

▶ **Use staircase intonation to stress important information.**
Let those sound groups floating on the wavy river in the figure flow downhill and you'll get the staircase. Staircase intonation not only gives you that American sound, it also makes you sound much more confident. Not every American uses the downward staircase. A certain segment of the population uses rising staircases—generally, teenagers on their way to a shopping mall: "Hi, my name is Tiffany. I live in La Cañada. I'm on the pep squad."

Bä
bi
zän
the
foun.

Start a new staircase
when you want to emphasize
that information, generally a *noun*.

WHAT EXACTLY IS STAIRCASE INTONATION?

In saying your words, imagine that they come out as if they were bounding lightly down a flight of stairs. Every so often, one jumps up to another level and then starts down again. Americans tend to stretch out their sounds longer than you may think is natural. So, to lengthen your vowel sounds, put them on two stairsteps instead of just one.

We're here.

Too Flat

We
're
he
re.

Well-Modulated

   The sound of an American speaking a foreign language is very distinctive, because we double sounds that should be single. For example, in Japanese or Spanish, the word *no* is, to our ear, clipped or abbreviated.

When you have a word ending in an *unvoiced consonant*—one that you "whisper" (t, k, s, x, f, sh)—you will notice that the preceding vowel is said quite quickly, and on a single stairstep. When a word ends in a vowel or a *voiced consonant*—one that you "say" (b, d, g, z, v, zh, j), the preceding vowel is said more slowly, and on a double stairstep.

There are two main consequences of not doubling the second category of words: Either your listener will hear the wrong word or, even worse, you will always sound upset. Consider that the words *curt, short, terse, abrupt,* and *clipped* all literally mean *short.* When applied to a person or to language, they take on the meaning of *upset* or *rude.* For example, the expressions *"His curt reply . . . ," "Her terse response . . ."* or *"He was very short with me"* all indicate a less than sunny situation.

THREE WAYS TO MAKE INTONATION

About this time, you're coming to the point where you may be wondering, what exactly are the mechanics of intonation? What changes when you go to the top of the staircase or when you put stress on a word? There are three ways to stress a word.

▶ The first way is to just get louder, or raise the volume. This is not a very sophisticated way of doing it, but it will definitely command attention.
▶ The second way is to streeeeetch the word out, or lengthen the word that you want to draw attention to (which sounds very insinuating).
▶ The third way, which is the most refined, is to change pitch. Although pausing just before changing the pitch is effective, you don't want to do it every time, because then it becomes an obvious technique. However, it will make your audience stop and listen because they think you're going to say something interesting.

Exercise 1-7: Rubber Band Practice with Nonsense Syllables	🔊 Track 19

Take a rubber band and hold it with your two thumbs. Every time you want to stress a word by changing pitch, pull on the rubber band. Stretch it out gently; don't jerk it sharply. Make a looping ∞ figure with it and do the same with your voice. Use the rubber band and stretch it out every time you change pitch. Read first across, then down.

A	B	C	D
1. **duh** duh **duh**	1. **la** la **la**	1. **mee** mee **mee**	1. **ho** ho **ho**
2. duh duh **duh**	2. la la **la**	2. mee mee **mee**	2. ho ho **ho**
3. duh **duh** duh	3. la **la** la	3. mee **mee** mee	3. ho **ho** ho
4. **duh** duh duh	4. **la** la la	4. **mee** mee mee	4. **ho** ho ho

Read each column down, keeping the same intonation pattern.

A	B	C	D
1. **duh** duh **duh**	1. duh duh **duh**	1. duh **duh** duh	1. **duh** duh duh
2. **ABC**	2. impre**cise**	2. con**dition**	2. **al**phabet
3. **123**	3. a hot **dog**	3. a **hot** dog	3. **hot** dog stand
4. **Dogs** eat **bones.**	4. They eat **bones.**	4. They **eat** them.	4. **Give** me one.

THE AMERICAN SPEECH MUSIC

Track 20

All cultures gesture, and recently a developmental physiologist at University of Wisconsin, Dr. Alibali, put forth that gestures accompany speech because our mouths and hands are closely linked in the brain. You may have noticed babies saying *ga-ga-ga* and moving their hands to the beat. It's not necessary for you to gesticulate wildly, but it **is** important to integrate the rhythm of your speech music with physical gestures. To this end, you'll be tapping the table, snapping your fingers, and maybe even stretching a rubber band.

NOT IN MY LANGUAGE

A Pakistani database analyst said, "I didn't think about my own language in this way before. There is intonation when we speak, but not as much as in American English. Now that I've analyzed it, I found my language to be rhythmic too. In many places, we do the same up and down intonation. I must not have realized it because I speak without thinking about the language itself! It's really interesting to compare both language styles and then to extract certain resemblances from them. I never thought of it in that way."

STAIRCASE INTONATION

Track 21

So, what is intonation in American English? What do Americans do? We go up and down staircases. We start high and end low.

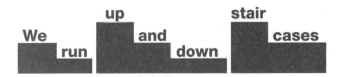

Every time we want to stress a word or an idea, we just start a new staircase. That sounds simple enough, but when and where do you start a new staircase?

STATEMENT INTONATION WITH NOUNS

Intonation, or pitch change, is primarily used to introduce *new information.* This means that when you are making a statement for the first time, you will stress the *nouns.*

The underlying hum is always here.

Exercise 1-8: Noun Intonation   Track 22

Practice the noun stress pattern after me, using pitch change. Add your own examples.

1. **Dogs** eat **bones.**	11. **Jerry** makes **music.**
2. **Mike** likes **bikes.**	12. **Jean** sells some **apples.**
3. **Elsa** wants a **book.**	13. **Carol** paints the **car.**
4. **Adam** plays **pool.**	14. **Bill** and I fix the **bikes.**
5. **Bobby** needs some **money.**	15. **Ann** and **Ed** call the **kids.**
6. **Susie** combs her **hair.**	16. The **kids** like the **candy.**
7. **John** lives in **France.**	17. The **girls** have a **choice.**
8. **Nelly** teaches **French.**	18. The **boys** need some **help.** ·
9. **Ben** writes **articles.**	19. _____
10. **Keys** open **locks.**	20. _____

▶ Practice the patterns five more times on your own, using your rubber band.

STATEMENT INTONATION WITH PRONOUNS
Track 23

When you replace the nouns with pronouns (i.e., *old information*), stress the verb.

As we have seen, *nouns* are *new* information; *pronouns* are *old* information. In a nutshell, these are the two basic intonation patterns.

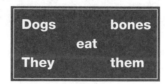

Exercise 1-9: Noun and Pronoun Intonation Track 24

In the first column, stress the nouns. In the second column, stress the verb. Fill in your own examples at the bottom.

1. **Bob** sees **Betty**.	1. He **sees** her.
2. **Betty** knows **Bob**.	2. She **knows** him.
3. **Ann** and **Ed** call the **kids**.	3. They **call** them.
4. **Jan** sells some **apples**.	4. She **sells** some.
5. **Jean** sells **cars**.	5. She **sells** them.
6. **Bill** and I fix the **bikes**.	6. We **fix** them.
7. **Carl** hears **Bob** and me.	7. He **hears** us.
8. **Dogs** eat **bones**.	8. They **eat** them.
9. The **girls** have a **choice**.	9. They **have** one.
10. The **kids** like the **candy**.	10. They **like** it.
11. The **boys** need some **help**.	11. They **need** something.
12. **Ellen** should call her **sister**.	12. She should **call** someone.
13. The **murderer** killed the **plumber**.	13. He **killed** a man.
14. The **tourists** went **shopping**.	14. They **bought** stuff.
15. _____	15. _____
16. _____	16. _____
17. _____	17. _____
18. _____	18. _____
19. _____	19. _____
20. _____	20. _____

STATEMENT VERSUS QUESTION INTONATION

Track 25

You may have learned at some point that questions have a rising intonation. They do, but usually a question will step upward until the very end, where it takes one quick little downward step. A question rises a little higher than a statement with the same intonation pattern.

EMOTIONAL OR RHETORICAL QUESTION INTONATION

If you know that your car is parked outside, however, and someone doesn't see it and asks you where it is, you might think that it has been stolen, and your emotion will show in your intonation as you repeat the question. As your feelings rise in an emotional situation, your intonation rises up along with them.

Underline or highlight the words that you think should be stressed. (Check Answer Key on page 216.)

1. Sam sees Bill.
2. She wants one.
3. Betty likes English.
4. They play with them.
5. Children play with toys.
6. Bob and I call you and Bill.
7. You and Bill read the news.
8. It tells one.
9. Bernard works in a restaurant.
10. He works in one.
11. He sees him.
12. Mary wants a car.
13. She likes it.
14. They eat some.
15. Len and Joe eat some pizza.
16. We call you.
17. You read it.
18. The news tells a story.
19. Mark lived in France.
20. He lived there.

Depending on the situation, a word may be stressed for any of the following reasons:

New Information	Opinion	Contrast	"Can't"

1. New Information
*It sounds like **rain.***
Rain is the new information. It's the most important word in that sentence, and you could replace everything else with *duh-duh-duh. Duh-duh-duh **rain*** will still let you get your point across.

▶ Repeat: *Duh-duh-duh **rain** / It sounds like **rain.***

▶ Make *rain* very musical and put it on two notes: *ray-ayn.*
*Duh-duh-duh **ray-ayn** / It sounds like **ray-ayn.***

2. Opinion
*It **sounds** like rain, but I don't think it is.*
In this case, intonation makes the meaning the opposite of what the words say: *It **looks** like a diamond, but I think it's a **zircon**. It **smells** like Chanel, but at that price, it's a **knock**-off. It **feels** like . . . It **tastes** like . . .* These examples all give the impression that you mean the *opposite* of what your senses tell you.

▶ Practice the intonation difference between *new information* and *opinion*:

*It sounds like **rain.*** (It's rain.)
*It **sounds** like rain,* (but it's not).

3. Contrast
*He **likes** rain, but he **hates** snow.*

Like and *hate* are contrasted and are the stronger words in the sentence.

4. Can't

*It **can't rain** when there're no **clouds**.*

Contractions *(shouldn't, wouldn't)* and negatives *(no, not, never)* are important words since they totally negate the meaning of a sentence, but they are not usually stressed. *Can't* is the exception.

Exercise 1-12: Pitch and Meaning Change	Track 28

Practice saying the four sentences after me. Pay close attention to the changes in pitch that you must make to convey the different meanings intended. The words to be stressed are indicated in bold face.

1. It sounds like **rain**.
2. It **sounds** like rain.

3. He **likes** rain, but he **hates** snow.
4. It **can't rain** on my **parade**! He **can't do** it. *(See also Exercise 1-23 for negatives.)*

Exercise 1-13: Individual Practice	Track 29

Practice saying the sentences after the suggestion and the beep tone. You will be given only a short time in which to reply so that you won't have the leisure to overthink. Start speaking as soon as you hear the tone, because I'll be saying the sentence only a few seconds later.

1. Convey the information that it really does sound as if rain is falling. ◀
2. Convey the opinion that although it has the sound of rain, it may be something else. ◀
3. Convey the different feelings that someone has about rain and snow. ◀
4. Convey the fact that rain is an impossibility right now. ◀

▶ Practice the four sentences on your own ten times.

✗ Once you're familiar with moving the stress around and feeling how the meaning changes, turn the audio on to continue with the next exercise.

Exercise 1-14: Meaning of "Pretty"	Track 30

*Native speakers make a clear distinction between pretty **easily** (easily) and **pretty** easily (a little difficult). Repeat the answers after me, paying close attention to your stress.*

Question: How did you like the movie?
Answer: 1. *It was pretty **good**.* (She liked it.)
                   2. *It was **pretty** good.* (She didn't like it much.)

Question: How was the show?
Answer: 1. *It was kinda **funny**.* (It was funny.)
                   2. *It was **kinda** funny* (but kinda juvenile, too).

Question: How'd the process go?
Answer: 1. *It was sorta **confusing**.* (It was confusing.)
                   2. *It was **sorta** confusing* (but I figured it out).

Exercise 1-15: Inflection   Track 31

Notice how the meaning changes while the actual words stay the same.

1. I didn't say he stole the money. Someone **else** said it.
2. I **didn't** say he stole the money. **That's** not true at **all.**
3. I didn't **say** he stole the money. I only **suggested** the **possibility.**
4. I didn't say **he** stole the money. I think someone **else** took it.
5. I didn't say he **stole** the money. Maybe he just **borrowed** it.
6. I didn't say he stole **the** money, but rather some **other** money.
7. I didn't say he stole the **money**. He may have taken some **jewelry.**

I	I didn't say he stole the money. Someone **else** said it.
	It's true that somebody said it, but I wasn't that person.
Didn't	I **didn't** say he stole the money. **That's** not true at **all.**
	Someone has accused me and I'm protesting my innocence.
Say	I didn't **say** he stole the money. I only **suggested** the **possibility**.
	Maybe I hinted it. Maybe I wrote it. In some way, I indicated that he stole the money, *but* I didn't say it.
He	I didn't say **he** stole the money. I think someone **else** took it.
	I think someone stole the money, only not the person you suspect did it.
Stole	I didn't say he **stole** the money. Maybe he just **borrowed** it.
	I agree that he took it, but I think his motive was different.
The	I didn't say he stole **the** money, but rather some **other** money.
	We agree that he stole some money, but I don't think it's this money.
Money	I didn't say he stole the **money**. He may have taken some **jewelry**.
	We agree that he's a thief, but we think he stole different things.

Notice that in the first half of these sentences nothing changes but the intonation.

▶ Repeat after me.

Exercise 1-16: Individual Practice   Track 32

Now, let's see what you can do with the same sentence just by changing the stress around to different words. I'll tell you which meaning to express. When you hear the tone ◀, say the sentence as quickly as you can, then I'll say the sentence for you. To test your ear, I'm going to repeat the sentences in random order. Try to determine which word I'm stressing. The answers are given in parentheses, but don't look unless you really have to. Here we go:

1. Indicate that he borrowed the money and didn't steal it. (5) ◀
2. Indicate that you are denying having said that he stole it. (2) ◀
3. Indicate that you think he stole something besides money. (7) ◀
4. Indicate that you were not the person to say it. (1) ◀
5. Indicate that you don't think that he was the person who stole it. (4) ◀
6. Indicate that you didn't say it outright, but did suggest it in some way. (3) ◀
7. Indicate that he may have stolen a different amount of money. (6) ◀

Exercise 1-17: Sticky Note Exercise 🔊 **Track 33**

Imagine that you are being held hostage by a mad bomber and the only way to communicate with the outside is with notes stuck to the bank window.

If you give each word of your plea equal value, the message will be lost in the barrage of information.

To clearly convey your message, you'll need to empha- size the most important words. This way, any random passerby can, at a glance, immediately catch your meaning.

This is the same with intonation. Repeat the sentence, clearly stressing the marked words.

Please **help** me! I'm being held **captive** by a mad **bomber**!

OVERDO IT

Track 34

Practice these sentences on your own, really exaggerating the word that you think should be stressed. In the beginning, you're going to feel that this is ridiculous. *(Nobody stresses this hard! Nobody talks like this! People are going to laugh at me!)* Yet, as much as you may stress, you're probably only going to be stressing about half as much as you should.

✘ Practice the sentences from Exercise 1-16 in random order ten times.

Another reason you must overexaggerate is because when you get tired, emotional, or relaxed, you will stop paying attention. When this happens, like a rubber band, you're going to snap back to the way you originally were sounding (10%, which is the extent to which you are exaggerating the intonation). So, if you just stretch yourself to the exact position where you ideally want to be, you'll go back almost completely to the old way when you relax. For practice, then, stretch yourself far *beyond* the normal range of intonation (150% or so), so when you relax, you relax back to a standard American sound (100%).

WE ALL DO IT

Possibly about this time you're thinking, *Well, maybe you do this in English, but in **my** language, I just really don't think that we do this.* I'd like you to try a little exercise.

Take the sentence **I didn't say he stole the money** *and translate it into your native language. Write it down below, using whatever letters or characters you use in your language.*

_____

Track 36

Now that you have written your sentence down, try shifting the stress around in your own language by going through the stress patterns. Don't try to put on a particularly American or other accent; just concentrate on stressing a different word in the sentence each time you say it.

For example, if your language is German, *Ich habe nicht gesagt daß er das Geld gestohlen hat,* you would change the stress to: **Ich** *habe nicht gesagt daß er das Geld gestohlen hat,* or *Ich habe* **nicht** *gesagt daß er das Geld gestohlen hat.*

If you translated it into French, you would say, *Je* **n'ai pas** *dit qu'il a volé l'argent,* or *Je n' pas dit qu'il a* **volé** *l'argent.*

In Japanese, many people think that there are no intonation changes, but if you hear someone say, *wak**ka**nai,* you'll realize that it has similarities to every other language. *Watashi wa* **kare** *ga okane o nusunda to wa iimasen deshita.* Or perhaps, *Watashi wa kare ga okane o nusunda to wa* **iimasen** *deshita.*

No matter how strange it may sound to you, stress each different word several times in your language. You may notice that with some words it sounds perfectly normal, but with other words it sounds very strange. Or you may find that in your language, rather than stressing a word, you prefer to change the word order or substitute another word. Whatever you do is fine, as long as you realize where your language patterns are similar to and different from the American English intonation patterns. Then, when you do it again in English, it will be much easier.

Note *An excellent exercise is to practice speaking your native language with an American accent. If you can sound like an American speaking your native language, imagine how easy it would be to speak English with an American accent.*

✗ Practice shifting the stressed words in your native language.

INTONATION CONTRAST

Track 37

Below are two sentences—the first is stressed on the most common, everyday word, *book.* Nine times out of ten, people will stress the sentence in this way. The second sentence has a less common, but perfectly acceptable, intonation, since we are making a distinction between two possible locations.

Normal intonation   Where's the **book**? It's on the **table.**

Changed intonation   Is the book **on** the table or **under** it? It's **on** the table.

✗ Repeat the sentences.

Write a short sentence and indicate where you think the most normal intonation would be placed. Then, change the meaning of the sentence slightly and change the intonation accordingly.

Normal intonation   _____

Changed intonation   _____

Track 39

QUESTION TYPES

There are three types of questions:

1. Yes / No
2. Either / Or
3. The Five W Questions

They each have a different inflection pattern, so even if you don't catch all of the words, you can still tell what type of question it was. The Five W Questions are *Who?*, *What?*, *Where?*, *When?* and *Why?* (and *How?*).

    As you heard in the question and response above, "Where's the book? It's on the table.", the inflection goes up on the question and down on the statement. A query like "Would you like tea or coffee?" could be an **Either/Or** question (Tea? Coffee?) or a **Yes/No** question (Hot beverage?).

A classic, probably apocryphal, story spells out the consequences of misinterpreting the question type. An immigrant was passing through Ellis Island and was asked the then-standard question, "Are you planning to overthrow the United States by force or violence?"

    The man pondered deeply for a moment and tentatively replied, "By force?" Of course, he was not let in, as the only acceptable answer was, "No."

Exercise 1-20: Variable Stress   🔊 **Track 40**

Notice how the meaning of the following sentence changes each time we change the stress pattern. You should be starting to feel in control of your sentences now.

1. **What would you like?**
   This is the most common version of the sentence, and it is just a simple request for information.

2. **What would you like?**
   This is to single out an individual from a group.

3. **What would you like?**
   You've been discussing the kinds of things he might like and you want to determine his specific desires:
   "*Now that you mention it, what **would** you like?*"
   or
   He has rejected several things and, a little exasperated, you ask, "*If you don't want any of these, what **would** you like?*"

4. **What would you like?**
   You didn't hear and you would like the speaker to repeat herself.
   or
   You can't believe what you heard: "*I'd like strawberry jam on my asparagus.*"—"***What** would you like?*"

◀ Repeat the four sentences.

Exercise 1-21: Make a Variable Stress Sentence Track 41

Now you decide which words should be emphasized. Write a normal, everyday sentence with at least seven words and put it through as many changes as possible. Try to make a pitch change for each word in the sentence and think about how it changes the meaning of the entire sentence.

1. _____
2. _____
3. _____
4. _____
5. _____
6. _____
7. _____

Exercise 1-22: Yes, You *Can* or No, You *Can't*? Track 42

Next, you use a combination of intonation and pronunciation to make the difference between can and can't. Reduce the positive can to k'n and stress the verb. Make the negative can't (kæn⁽ᵗ⁾) sound very short and stress both can't and the verb. This will contrast with the positive, emphasized can, which is doubled—and the verb is not stressed. If you have trouble with can't before a word that starts with a vowel, such as open, put in a very small ⁽ᵈ⁾—The keys kæn⁽ᵈ⁾ open the locks. Repeat.

I can **do** it.	I k'n **do** it	positive
I **can't do** it.	I **kæn**⁽ᵗ⁾**do** it	negative
I **can** do it.	I **kææn** do it	extra positive
I **can't** do it.	I **kæn**⁽ᵗ⁾do it	extra negative

Exercise 1-23: Can or Can't Quiz Track 43

Listen to how each sentence is said and select positive, negative, extra positive, or extra negative. (Answer Key on page 216.)

1. I can see it. ◀
☐ A. positive
☐ B. negative
☐ C. extra positive
☐ D. extra negative

2. I can't see it. ◀
☐ A. positive
☐ B. negative
☐ C. extra positive
☐ D. extra negative

3. I can see it. ◀
☐ A. positive
☐ B. negative
☐ C. extra positive
☐ D. extra negative

4. I can't see it. ◀
☐ A. positive
☐ B. negative
☐ C. extra positive
☐ D. extra negative

5. He can try it. ◀
☐ A. positive
☐ B. negative
☐ C. extra positive
☐ D. extra negative

6. I can't understand him. ◀
☐ A. positive
☐ B. negative
☐ C. extra positive
☐ D. extra negative

7. We can call you. ◀
☐ A. positive
☐ B. negative
☐ C. extra positive
☐ D. extra negative

8. She can't buy one. ◀
☐ A. positive
☐ B. negative
☐ C. extra positive
☐ D. extra negative

9. She can do it. ◀
☐ A. positive
☐ B. negative
☐ C. extra positive
☐ D. extra negative

Track 44

APPLICATION OF INTONATION

There is always at least one stressed word in a sentence, and frequently you can have quite a few if you are introducing a lot of new information or if you want to contrast several things. Take a pencil and mark every word that you think should be stressed or sound stronger than the words around it. I'd like you to make just an accent mark (') to indicate a word you think should sound stronger than others around it.

Reminder: The three ways to change your voice for intonation are:

1. **Volume** (speak louder)

2. **Length** (stretch out a word)

3. **Pitch** (change your tone)

✗ Work on the paragraph in Exercise 1-24.

Exercise 1-24: Application of Stress	Track 45

Now, read each sentence of the paragraph after the speaker. Use your rubber band, give a clear pitch change to the marked words, and think about the meaning that the pitch is conveying.

Héllo, **my**' name is _____. I'm taking American Accent Training. There's a lot to learn, but I hope to make it as enjoyable as possible. I should pick up on the American intonation pattern pretty easily, although the only way to get it is to practice all of the time. I use the up and down, or peaks and valleys, intonation more than I used to. I've been paying attention to pitch, too. It's like walking down a staircase. I've been talking to a lot of Americans lately, and they tell me that I'm easier to understand. Anyway, I could go on and on, but the important thing is to listen well and sound good. Well, what do you think? Do I?

▶ Listen and make any corrections. After you've put in the accent marks where you think they belong, take a highlighter and, as I read very slowly, mark the words that I stress. I am going to exaggerate the words far more than you'd normally hear in a normal reading of the paragraph. You can mark either the whole word or just the strong syllable, whichever you prefer, so that you have a bright spot of color for where the stress should fall.

Note *If you do the exercise only in pencil, your eye and mind will tend to skip over the accent marks. The spots of color, however, will register as "different" and thereby encourage your pitch change. This may strike you as unusual, but trust me, it works.*

✗ Practice reading the paragraph out loud three times on your own.

HOW YOU TALK INDICATES TO PEOPLE HOW YOU ARE

Beware of "Revealing" a Personality that You Don't Have!

There is no absolute right or wrong in regard to intonation, because a case can be made for stressing just about any word or syllable, but you actually reveal a lot about yourself by the elements you choose to emphasize. For example, if you say, *Hello,* this intonation would indicate doubt. You say, *Hello?* when answering the telephone because you don't know who is on the other end, or when you go into a house and you don't know who's there because you don't see anyone. But if you're giving a speech or making a presentation and you stand up in front of a crowd and say, *Hello,* the people would probably laugh because it sounds so uncertain. This is where you'd confidently want to say *Hello,* **my** *name is* **So***-and-so.*

A second example is, **my** *name is*—as opposed to *my* **name** *is.* If you stress *name,* it sounds as if you are going to continue with more personal information: *My* **name** *is So-and-so, my* **address** *is such-and-such, my* **blood** *type is O.* Since it may not be your intention to give all that information, stay with the standard—*Hello,* **my** *name is* **So***-and-so.*

If you stress *I* every time, it will seem that you have a very high opinion of yourself. Try it: *I'm taking American Accent Training.* *I've been paying attention to pitch, too.* *I think I'm quite wonderful.*

An earnest, hard-working person might emphasize words this way: *I'm* **taking** *American Accent Training* (Can I learn this stuff?). *I hope to* **make** *it as enjoyable as possible* (I'll force myself to enjoy it if I have to). *Although the only way to get it is to practice* **all** *of the time* (24 hours a day).

A Doubting Thomas would show up with: *I* **should** *pick up on* (but I might not) *the American intonation pattern* **pretty** *easily* (but it looks pretty hard, too). *I've been talking to a lot of Americans lately, and they* **tell** *me that I'm easier to understand* (but I think they're just being polite).

Exercise 1-25: Paragraph Intonation Practice	Track 47

▶ *From your color-marked copy, read each sentence of the paragraph (Exercise 1-24) after me. Use your rubber band, give a clear pitch change to the highlighted words, and think about the meaning that the pitch is conveying.*

✗ *Practice this paragraph three times.*

INTONATION & ATTITUDE

There are certain sounds in any language that are considered nonsense syllables, yet impart a large amount of information to the informed listener. Each language has a different set of these sounds, such as *eto ne* in Japanese, *em* in Spanish, *eu* in French, and *um* in English. In this particular case, these are the sounds that a native speaker makes when he is thinking out loud—holding the floor, but not yet committing to actually speaking.

Exercise 1-26: Nonverbal Intonation Track 49

The top eight are the most common non-word communication sounds. They can all be nasalized or not, and said with the mouth open or closed. Intonation is the important factor here. Repeat after me.

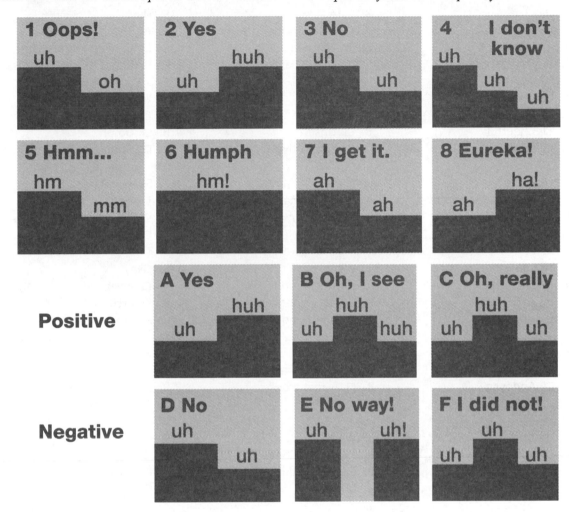

Exercise 1-27: Sounds of Empathy Track 50

Let's see how well you interpret emotionally meaningful words.

1. Okay
A. ☐ Got it!
B. ☐ Uneasy
C. ☐ Depressed

2. Okay
A. ☐ Surprised
B. ☐ Cheerful
C. ☐ Impatient

3. Okay
A. ☐ What a good idea!
B. ☐ Whatever
C. ☐ Doubtful

4. Thanks
A. ☐ Sarcastic
B. ☐ Appreciative
C. ☐ Unsure

5. Fine
A. ☐ Great!
B. ☐ Annoyed
C. ☐ I don't care . . .

6. Uh huh
A. ☐ Sure, no problem
B. ☐ I do, too!
C. ☐ Really?

7. No
A. ☐ Absolutely not!
B. ☐ How ridiculous
C. ☐ Defensive

8. Sure
A. ☐ Disbelieving
B. ☐ Worried
C. ☐ Quickly agreeable

9. Yeah
A. ☐ Positive
B. ☐ Unsure
C. ☐ Supportive

10. Sooo
A. ☐ Expecting more info
B. ☐ Impatient
C. ☐ Uneasy

11. What
A. ☐ That's funny
B. ☐ Not caring
C. ☐ Uh-oh, not again

12. Really
A. ☐ Barely attentive
B. ☐ Is that true?
C. ☐ Bored

13. Well
A. ☐ Sorta/ kinda
B. ☐ Annoyed
C. ☐ Happy

14. I don't know
A. ☐ Curious
B. ☐ Casual
C. ☐ Why ask me?!

15. Hey
A. ☐ Shy
B. ☐ Canned enthusiasm
C. ☐ Bored

16. Yes
A. ☐ Confused
B. ☐ Go on . . .
C. ☐ Great joy

17. Sorry
A. ☐ Not sorry at all
B. ☐ Apologetic
C. ☐ Perky

18. Okay
A. ☐ Resigned
B. ☐ Excited
C. ☐ Sure, why not?

19. Hmmm
A. ☐ What?!
B. ☐ Not so sure
C. ☐ Thinking

20. I know
A. ☐ Nonchalant
B. ☐ Knowing
C. ☐ Defensive

21. Oh
A. ☐ Happy
B. ☐ Disappointed
C. ☐ Confused

WARM UP WITH RUN-UP PHRASES

Track 51

Another trick to oil the joints is to pick some general intro phrases and string them all together with as strong an American accent as possible, without ever actually saying anything, just focusing on creating that rich round deep American sound . . . **Well, you know, I was just thinking, and it kinda seems like, uhh, what do you think about** . . .

Variety also applies to active listening, so instead of having one phrase and over-using it, have at least 5–10 different responses that you've practiced.

Track 52

1. Ah, I see . . .	6. Really?	11. Is that a fact?
2. Oh, that's interesting!	7. Oh, yeah!	12. You don't say.
3. Hmm, tell me more.	8. Right.	13. Wow, that's weird!
4. Got it!	9. Fair enough.	14. Oh, no!
5. Gotcha!	10. Good point, I can see that.	15. That's too bad.

Exercise 1-28: Reading with Staircase Intonation   **Track 53**

Read the following with clear intonation where marked.

Hello, **my** name is _____. I'm taking American **Accent** Training. There's a **lot** to **learn**, but I **hope** to make it as **enjoyable** as possible. I should pick **up** on the American **intonation** pattern pretty **easily**, although the **only** way to **get** it is to **practice** all of the time. I use the **up** and down, or **peaks** and valleys, **intonation** more than I **used** to. I've been paying attention to **pitch, too**. It's like **walking** down a **staircase**. I've been **talking** to a lot of **Americans** lately, and they tell me that I'm **easier** to **understand**. **Anyway,** I could go **on** and on, but the **important** thing is to **listen** well and sound **good**. **Well,** what do you **think**? **Do I?**

Just as there is stress in words or phrases, there is intonation in spelling and numbers. Americans seem to spell things out much more than other people. In any bureaucratic situation, you'll be asked to spell names and give all kinds of numbers—your phone number, your birth date, and so on. There is a distinct stress and rhythm pattern to both spelling and numbers—usually in groups of three or four letters or numbers, with the stress falling on the last member of the group. Acronyms (phrases that are represented by the first letter of each word) and initials are usually stressed on the last letter. Just listen to the words as I say them, then repeat the spelling after me.

Acronym	Pronunciation	Spelling	Pronunciation
IBM	Eye Bee **Em**	Box	Bee Oh **Ex**
MIT	Em Eye **Tee**	Cook	See Oh Oh **Kay**
Ph.D.	Pee Aitch **Dee**	Wilson	Dubya You Eye **El**, Ess Oh **En**
MBA	Em Bee **ɛi**		
LA	Eh **Lay**		
IQ	Eye **Kyu**	**Numbers**	**Pronunciation**
RSVP	Are Ess Vee **Pee**	Area Code	2**13**
TV	Tee **Vee**	Zip Code	916**04**
USA	You Ess **ɛi**	Date	9/6/**62**
ASAP	ɛi Ess ɛi **Pee**	Phone Number	**1**(800) **457-4255**
CIA	See Eye **ɛi**		
FBI	Eff Bee **Eye**		
USMC	You Ess Em **See**	**Time**	**Pronunciation**
COD	See Oh **Dee**	Nine-fifteen	9:**15**
SOS	Ess Oh **Ess**	Two-thirty	2:**30**
X, Y, Z	Ex, Why, **Zee**	Names	**mid**night, after**noon**

Intonation is powerful. It can change meaning and pronunciation. Here you will get the chance to play with the sounds. Remember, in the beginning, the meaning isn't that important—just work on getting control of your pitch changes. Use your rubber band for each stressed word.

my **tie**	mai-tai	**Might** I?	How many **kids** do you have?	I have **two**.
my **keys**	Mikey's	My **keys**?	I've been to **Europe**.	I have, **too**.
inn **key**	in **key**	**inky**	Why do you **work** so hard?	I **have** to.
my **tea**	**mighty**	My **D**		
I have **two**.	I have, **too**.	I **have** to.		

Exercise 1-31: Squeezed-Out Syllables Track 56

Intonation can also completely get rid of certain entire syllables. Some longer words that are stressed on the first syllable squeeze weak syllables right out. Cover up the regular spelling and read the phonetics.

accidentally	æk•sə•**dent**•lee	favorite	**fāv**•rit
actually	**æk**•chully	finally	**fyn**•lee
aspirin	**æ**sprin	general	**jɛn**r'l
average	**æ**vr'j	groceries	**gross**reez
bakery	**bā**•kree	history	**hiss**tree
basically	**ba**•sə•klee	interest	**in**tr'st
beverage	**bev**•r'j	jewelry	**jool**ree
boundary	**bound**•ree	liberal	**lib**r'l
broccoli	**brä**klee	mathematics	mæth**mæ**dix
business	**biz**ness	memory	**mɛm**ree
cabinet	**cæb**•net	natural	**næch**•rul
camera	**kæm**ruh	Niagara	**nyæ**•grə
catholic	**cæth**•l'k	nursery	**nr**•sree
chocolate	**chäkl**'t	onion	**ə**ny'n
comfortable	**k'mf**•t'bl	opera	**äp**rə
conference	**cän**frns	orange	**ornj**
corporal	**cor**pr'l	preference	**pref**•rənce
coverage	**c'vr**'j	probably	**präb**lee
desperate	**dɛ**spr't	realize	**ri**•lize
diamond	**däi**m'nd	restaurant	**rɛ**stränt
diaper	**däi**per	separate	**sɛp**r't
different	**diff**r'nt	several	**sɛv**r'l
emerald	**ɛm**r'ld	theory	**thi**ree
emory	**ɛm**ree	threatening	**thrɛt**ning
every	**ɛv**ree	vegetable	**vej**•t'bl
family	**fæm**lee	victory	**vic**•tree

Note *The –cally ending is always pronounced –klee; –tory turns into –tree.*

In the list below, change the stress from the first syllable for nouns to the second syllable for verbs. This is a regular, consistent change. Intonation is so powerful that you'll notice that when the stress changes, the pronunciation of the vowels do, too.

Nouns		Verbs	
an accent	**æk**s'nt	to accent	æks**ɛnt**
a concert	**kän**sert	to concert	k'n**sert**
a conflict	**kän**flikt	to conflict	k'n**flikt**
a contest	**kän**test	to contest	k'n**test**
a contract	**kän**trækt	to contract	k'n**trækt**
a contrast	**kän**træst	to contrast	k'n**træst**
a convert	**kän**vert	to convert	k'n**vert**
a convict	**kän**vikt	to convict	k'n**vict**
a default	**dee**fält	to default	d'**fält**
a desert*	**dɛz**'rt	to desert	d'**z'rt**
a discharge	**dis**chärj	to discharge	d'**schärj**
an envelope	**änv**'lop	to envelop	envel**'p**
an incline	**in**kline	to incline	in**kline**
an influence	**influ**⁽ʷ⁾'ns	to influence	influ⁽ʷ⁾ns†
an insert	**in**sert	to insert	in**sert**
an insult	**in**s'lt	to insult	ins**əlt**
an object	**äb**ject	to object	əb**ject**
perfect	**prf**'ct	to perfect	prf**ekt**
a permit	**pr**mit	to permit	pr**mit**
a present	**prɛz**'nt	to present	pr'**zɛnt**
produce	**pro**duce	to produce	pr'**duce**
progress	**prägr**'s	to progress	pr'**grɛss**
a project	**präj**ect	to project	pr'**jɛct**
a pronoun	**pro**noun	to pronounce	pr'**nounce**
a protest	**pro**test	to protest	pr'**test**
a rebel	**rɛb**əl	to rebel	r'**bɛl**
a recall	**ree**käll	to recall	r'**käll**
a record	**rɛk**'rd	to record	r'**cord**
a reject	**re**ject	to reject	r'**jɛct**
research	**res**'rch	to research	r'**srch**
a subject	**s'b**jekt	to subject	s'**bjekt**
a survey	**s'r**vei	to survey	s'**rvei**
a suspect	**s's**pekt	to suspect	s's**pekt**

*The *désert* is hot and **dry**. A *dessért* is ice cream. To *desért* is to abandon.
†*Pronunciation symbols (w) and (y) represent a glide sound. This is explained on page 49.*

Exercise 1-33: Regular Transitions of Adjectives and Verbs Track 58

*A different change occurs when you go from an adjective or a noun to a verb. The stress stays in the same place, but the -**mate** in an adjective is completely reduced to -m't, whereas in a verb it is a full ā sound: -mɛit.*

Nouns/Adjectives		Verbs	
advocate	**æd**v'k't	to advocate	**æd**v'kɛit
animate	**æn**'m't	to animate	**æn**'mɛit
alternate	**äl**tern't	to alternate	**äl**ternɛit
appropriate	ə**pro**pre(y)'t	to appropriate	ə**pro**pre(y)ɛit
approximate	ə**präks**'m't	to approximate	ə**präks**' mɛit
articulate	är**ti**cyul't	to articulate	är**ti**cyəlɛit
associate	ə**sso**sey't	to associate	ə**sso**seyɛit
deliberate	d'**libr**'t	to deliberate	d'**libe**rɛit
discriminate	d'**skrim**'n't	to discriminate	d'**skrim**'nɛit
duplicate	**dup**l'k't	to duplicate	**dup**l'kɛit
elaborate	e**læb**r't	to elaborate	ə**læb**erɛit
an estimate	**ɛst**'m't	to estimate	**ɛst**'mɛit
graduate	**græ**jyu(w)'t	to graduate	**græ**jyu(w)ɛit
intimate	**int**'m't	to intimate	**int**' mɛit
moderate	**mä**der't	to moderate	**mä**derɛit
predicate	**prɛd**'k't	to predicate	**prɛd**'kɛit
separate	**sɛp**r't	to separate	**sɛp**erɛit

Exercise 1-34: Regular Transitions of Adjectives and Verbs Track 59

Mark the intonation or indicate the long vowel on the boldfaced word, depending on which part of speech it is. Mark the proper syllables. Check Answer Key on page 216.

1. You need to **insert** a paragraph here on this newspaper **insert**.
2. How can you **object** to this **object**?
3. I'd like to **present** you with this **present**.
4. Would you care to **elaborate** on his **elaborate** explanation?
5. The manufacturer couldn't **recall** if there'd been a **recall**.
6. The religious **convert** wanted to **convert** the world.
7. The political **rebels** wanted to **rebel** against the world.
8. The mogul wanted to **record** a new **record** for his latest artist.
9. If you **perfect** your intonation, your accent will be **perfect**.
10. Due to the drought, the fields didn't **produce** much **produce** this year.
11. Unfortunately, City Hall wouldn't **permit** them to get a **permit**.
12. Have you heard that your **associate** is known to **associate** with gangsters?
13. How much do you **estimate** that the **estimate** will be?
14. The facilitator wanted to **separate** the general topic into **separate** categories.

SYLLABLE STRESS

When there's more than one syllable, stress the next to last.

Syllable Count Intonation Patterns

Track 60

In spoken English, if you put the emphasis on the wrong syllable, you totally lose the meaning, when you need to put the emphasis on the right syllable.

At this point, we won't be concerned with *why* we are stressing a particular syllable—that understanding will come at the end of this chapter.

Exercise 1-35: Syllable Patterns 🔊 Track 61

In order to practice accurate pitch change, repeat the following columns. Each syllable will count as one musical note. Remember that words that end in a vowel or a voiced consonant will be longer than ones ending in an unvoiced consonant (p, f, s, t, k, x, sh, th, ch).

	A	B	C
1 Syllable			
Pattern 1a	la!	get	stop
	cat	quick	which
	jump	choice	bit
	box	loss	beat
Pattern 1b	**la**-a	law	bid
	dog	goes	bead
	see	choose	car
	plan	lose	know
2 Syllables	la-**la**	Bob **Smith**	for **you**
Pattern 2a	a **dog**	my **car**	Who **knows**?
	a **cat**	some **more**	cas**sette**
	des**troy**	red **tape**	bal**let**
	a **pen**	en**close**	va**let**
	pre**tend**	con**sume**	to **do**
	your **job**	my **choice**	to**day**
	pea **soup**	How's **work**?	to**night**
Pattern 2b	**la**-la	**wrist**watch	**phone** book
	hot dog	**text**book	**door**knob
	icy	**book**shelf	**note**book
	suitcase	**sun**shine	**house** key
	project	**place**mat	**bal**lot
	sunset	**stap**ler	**val**id
	Get one!	**mo**dern	**dog** show
	Do it!	**mo**dem	**want** ad

A hot **dog** is an overheated canine 🐕, while a **hot** dog is a frankfurter 🍴.

Exercise 1-35: Syllable Patterns *continued*   🔊 Track 61

3 Syllables	A	B	C
Pattern 3a	la-la-**la**	**Worms** eat **dirt**.	**Joe** has **three**.
🎵🎵🎵	**Bob's** hot **dog** 🐕	**Inchworms inch**.	**Bob** has **eight**.
	Bob won't **know**.	**Pets** need **care**.	**Al** jumped **up**.
	Sam's the **boss**.	**Ed's** too **late**.	**Glen** sat **down**.
	Susie's nice.	**Paul** threw **up**.	**Tom** made **lunch**.
	Bill went **home**.	**Wool** can **itch**.	**Kids** should **play**.
	Cats don't **care**.	**Birds** sing **songs**.	**Mom** said, "**No!**"
	Stocks can **fall**.	**Spot** has **fleas**.	**Mars** is **red**.
	School is **fun**.	**Nick's** a **punk**.	**Ned** sells **cars**.
Pattern 3b	la-la-**la**	Make a **cake**.	IBM
🎵🎵🎵	a hot **dog** 🐕	He for**got**.	a good **time**
	I don't **know**.	Take a **bath**.	Use your **head**!
	He's the **boss**.	We're too **late**.	How are **you**?
	We cleaned **up**.	I love **you**.	We came **home**.
	in the **bag**	over **here**	on the **bus**
	for a **while**	What a **jerk**!	engi**neer**
	I went **home**.	How's your **job**?	She fell **down**.
	We don't **care**.	How'd it **go**?	They called **back**.
	It's in **March**.	Who'd you **meet**?	You goofed **up**.
Pattern 3c	la-**la**-la	per**cen**tage (%)	O**hi**o
🎵🎵🎵	a **hot** dog 🍴	ad**van**tage	his **foot**ball
	I **don't** know!	It's **star**ting.	They're **leav**ing.
	Jim **killed** it.	Let's **try** it.	How **are** you?
	to**mor**row	fi**nan**cial	em**phat**ic
	a **fruit**cake	I **thought** so.	Dale **planned** it.
	the **en**gine	on **Wednes**day	You **took** it.
	a **wine**glass	in **April**	ex**ter**nal
	po**ta**to	I **love** you.	a **bar**gain
	what**ev**er	Let's **tell** him.	Don't **touch** it.
Pattern 3d	**la**-la-la	**al**phabet	**phone** number
🎵🎵🎵	**hot** dog stand	**pos**sible	**think** about
	I **don't** know.	**Show** me one.	**com**fortable
	analyze	**ar**ea	**wait**ing for
	article	**punc**tuate	**pit**iful
	dinnertime	**em**phasis	**ev**erything
	digital	**syl**lable	**or**chestra
	analog	**Post**It note	**ig**norant
	cell structure	**Ro**lodex	**Rub**bermaid

4 Syllables	A	B	C
Pattern 4a	la-la-la-**la**	**Nate** needs a **break**.	**Max** wants to **know**.
	Spot's a hot **dog**. 🐕	**Ed** took my **car**.	**Al's** kitchen **floor**
	Jim killed a **snake**.	**Jill** ate a **steak**.	**Bill's** halfway **there**.
	Joe doesn't **know**.	**Spain's** really **far**.	**Roses** are **red**,
	Nate bought a **book**.	**Jake's** in the **lake**.	**Violets** are **blue**,
	Al brought some **ice**.	**Sam's** in a **bar**.	**Candy** is **sweet**,
			and *so* are *you*.
Pattern 4b	la-la-la-**la**	She asked for **help**.	I want to **know**.
	It's a hot **dog**. 🐕	We took my **car**.	the kitchen **floor**
	He killed a **snake**.	We need a **break**.	We watched **TV**.
	He doesn't **know**.	It's really **far**.	She's halfway **there**.
	We came back **in**.	I love you, **too**.	We played all **day**.
	He bought a **book**.	They got a**way**.	Please show me **how**.
Pattern 4c	la-la-**la**-la 🍴	**Boys** ring **door**bells.	**Phil** knows **mail**men.
	Bob likes **hot** dogs.	**Bill** ate **break**fast.	**Joe** grew **egg**plants.
	Ann eats **pan**cakes.	**Guns** are **le**thal.	**Hump**ty **Dump**ty
	Cats eat **fish** bones.	**Inch**worms **bug** me.	**Hawks** are **vicious**.
	Bears are **fuzz**y.	**Rag**tops **cost** more.	**Home**work **bores** them.
	Planets **ro**tate.	**Sales**men **sell** things.	**Mike** can **hear** you.
Pattern 4d	la-la-**la**-la	an a**larm** clock	He said "**light**bulb."
	It's my **hot** dog. 🍴	I don't **need** one.	What does "**box**" mean?
	imi**ta**tion	Ring the **door**bell.	Put your **hands** up.
	ana**ly**tic	What's the **mat**ter?	Where's the **mail**man?
	We like **science**.	intro**duc**tion	an as**sem**bly
	my to-**do** list	my re**port** card	defi**ni**tion
Pattern 4e	la-**la**-la-la	po**ta**to chip	What **time** is it?
	a **hot** dog stand	Whose **turn** is it?	my **phone** number
	Jim **killed** a man.	We **worked** on it.	Let's **eat** something.
	a**nal**ysis	How **tall** are you?	How **old** are you?
	in**vis**ible	in**san**ity	un**touch**able
	a **plat**ypus	a**bil**ity	a **ma**niac
Pattern 4f	la-la-la-la	**su**pervisor	**light**house keeper
	permanently	**win**dow cleaner	**cough** medicine
	demonstrated	**race** car driver	**bus**iness meeting
	category	**Jan**uary (jæn•yə•wery)	**Feb**ruary (feb•yə•wery)
	office supplies	**pro**gress report	**ba**by-sitter
	educator	**thing**amajig	**dic**tionary

Syllable Stress

The good news is that most of the words used in English are only one syllable.
Rule of Thumb: Stress **nouns** on the **first** syllable and **verbs** on the **second** syllable.

Exercise 1-36: Syllable Stress	Track 63

When in doubt, stress the next-to-last syllable.

2 Syllables	3 Syllables	1 Syllable Suffix	2 Syllable Suffix	Multiple Syllable Suffix
paper	po**ta**to	econ**om**ic ic	**poss**ible ible	**crit**ically i+cal+ly
napkin	com**pu**ter	ad**mon**ish ish	**syll**able able	**ver**ifying i+fy+ing
hotdog	per**sua**sive	**vis**ion ion	com**mun**ity ity	astro**nom**ical nom+i+cal
contest	con**di**tion	**cru**cial ial	bi**ol**ogy logy	edu**ca**tionally tion+al+ly
angry	di**ver**sion	**pho**tograph graph	pho**tog**raphy graphy	photo**graph**ically ic+al+ly

Exercise 1-37: The 5% Rule—Stress the Last Syllable	Track 64

*Most **two-syllable verbs** stress the **last** syllable, as do words starting with the prefixes **a-** and **be-**, and words that end in **French suffixes**.*

2-Syllable Verbs	Prefixes a- and be-	French Suffixes
be**gin**	a**bove**	refe**ree**
con**test**	be**low**	engi**neer**
de**ny**	a**bout**	clien**tele**
con**tain**	be**neath**	bal**let**
re**fuse**	a**cross**	ga**rage**

Exercise 1-38: Intonation Shifts	Track 65

Practice the following intonation shifts.

1st to 3rd	1st to 4th	1st to 2nd to 3rd	2nd to 3rd
accident	**quan**tity	**an**alyze	con**demn**
acci**den**tal	**quan**tify	a**nal**ysis	con**dem**natory
acci**den**tally	quantifi**ca**tion	ana**lyt**ic	condem**na**tion
president	**max**imum	**cat**alyze	re**volve**
presi**den**tial	**max**imize	ca**tal**ysis	re**vol**ver
presi**den**tially	maximi**za**tion	cata**lyt**ic	revo**lu**tionary
de**vel**op*	**or**igin	**real**	cre**ate**
de**vel**opment	o**rig**inal	**real**ize	cre**a**tive
develop**men**tal	o**rig**inate	re**al**ity	cre**a**tion
develop**men**tally	origi**na**tion	reali**za**tion	crea**tiv**ity

*This is a key word-stress issue for Indians, who tend to stress the first syllable, **de**velop, instead of the second, de**vel**op. This is the same situation in com**po**nent and be**gin**ning.

COMPLEX INTONATION

When in doubt, stress the noun.

This is the beginning of an extremely important part of spoken American English—the rhythms and intonation patterns of the long streams of nouns and adjectives that are so commonly used. These exercises will tie in the intonation patterns of **adjectives** *(nice, old, best, etc.)*, **nouns** *(dog, house, surgeon, etc.)*, and **adverbs** *(very, really, amazingly, etc.)*.

One way of approaching sentence intonation is not to build each sentence from scratch. Instead, use patterns, with each pattern similar to a mathematical formula. Instead of plugging in numbers, however, plug in words. (In Exercise 1-8, we looked at simple noun•verb•noun patterns, and on pages 26–29, the syllable-count intonation patterns were covered. Here, we'll examine intonation patterns in two-word phrases.)

It's important to note that there's a major difference between *syllable stress* and *compound noun stress* patterns. In the syllable-count exercises, each *syllable* was represented by a single musical note. In the noun phrases, each individual *word* will be represented by a single musical note—no matter how many total syllables there may be.

At times, what appears to be a single-syllable word will have a "longer" sound to it—*seed* takes longer to say than *seat* for example. (This was introduced on page 5, where you learned that a final voiced consonant causes the previous vowel to double.)

Exercise 1-39: Single-Word Phrases 🔊 Track 67

Repeat the following noun and adjective sentences.

Noun	Adjective
1. It's a **nail**.	It's **short**.
2. It's a **cake**.	It's **chocolate**. (chäkl't)
3. It's a **tub**.	It's **hot**. (hät)
4. It's a **drive**.	It's **härd**.
5. It's a **door**.	It's in **back**. (bæk)
6. It's a **cärd**.	There are **four**.
7. It's a **spot**. (spät)	It's **smäll**.
8. It's a **book**. (bük)	It's **good**. (güd)

Write your own noun and adjective sentences below. You will be using these examples throughout this series of exercises.

9. It's a _____ It's _____

10. It's a _____ It's _____

11. It's a _____ It's _____

Two-Word Phrases

Descriptive Phrases

Track 68

Nouns are "heavier" than adjectives; they carry the weight of the new information. An adjective and noun combination is called a *descriptive phrase,* and in the absence of contrast or other secondary changes, the stress will always fall naturally on the noun. In the absence of a noun, you will stress the adjective, but as soon as a noun appears on the scene, it takes immediate precedence—and should be stressed.

Exercise 1-40: Sentence Stress with Descriptive Phrases   **Track 69**

Repeat the following phrases.

Adjective	Noun/Adjective
1. It's **short**.	It's a short **nail**.
2. It's **chocolate**.	It's a chocolate **cake**.
3. It's **good**.	It's a good **plan**.
4. It's **guarded**.	It's a guarded **gate**.
5. It's **wide**.	It's a wide **river**.
6. There're **four**.	There're four **cards**.
7. It was **small**.	It was a small **spot**.
8. It's the **best**.	It's the best **book**.

Write your own adjective and noun/adjective sentences. (Use the same words from Exercise 1-39.)

    9. It's _____   It's a _____

10. It's _____   It's a _____

11. It's _____   It's a _____

Exercise 1-41: Two Types of Descriptive Phrases Track 70

Repeat.

Adjective / Noun	Adverb / Adjective
1. It's a short **nail**.	It's really **short**.
2. It's a chocolate **cake**.	It's dark **chocolate**.
3. It's a hot **bath**.	It's too **hot**.
4. It's a hard **drive**.	It's extremely **hard**.
5. It's the back **door**.	It's far **back**.
6. There are four **cards**.	There are only **four**.
7. It's a small **spot**.	It's laughably **small**.
8. It's a good **book**.	It's amazingly **good**.

Write your own adjective/noun and adverb/adjective sentences.

9. It's a _____ It's _____
10. It's a _____ It's _____
11. It's a _____ It's _____

Exercise 1-42: Descriptive Phrase Story—The Ugly Duckling Track 71

The following well-known story has been rewritten to contain only descriptions. Stress the second word of each phrase. Repeat after me.

There is a *mother duck*. She lays *three eggs*. Soon, there are three *baby birds*. Two of the birds are *very beautiful*. One of them is *quite ugly*. The *beautiful ducklings* make fun of their *ugly brother*. The *poor thing* is *very unhappy*. As the *three birds* grow older, the *ugly duckling* begins to change. His *gray feathers* turn *snowy white*. His *gangly neck* becomes *beautifully smooth*.

　　In *early spring*, the *ugly duckling* is swimming in a *small pond* in the *back yard* of the *old farm*. He sees his *shimmering reflection* in the *clear water*. What a *great surprise!* He is no longer an *ugly duckling*. He has grown into a *lovely swan*.

Set Phrases

Track 72

A Cultural Indoctrination to American Norms

When I learned the alphabet as a child, I *heard* it before I *saw* it. I heard that the last four letters were *dubba-you, ex, why, zee*. I thought that *dubba-you* was a long, strange name for a letter, but I didn't question it any more than I did *aitch*. It was just a name. Many years later, it struck me that it was a *double U*. Of course, a **W** is really **UU**. I had such a funny feeling, though, when I realized that something I had taken for granted for so many years had a background meaning that I had completely overlooked. This "funny feeling" is exactly what most native speakers get when a two-word phrase is stressed on the wrong word. When two individual words go through the cultural process of becoming a set phrase, the original sense of each word is more or less forgotten and the new meaning completely takes over. When we hear the word ***pain**killer,* we think *anesthetic.* If, however, someone says *pain**killer,*** it brings up the strength and almost unrelated meaning of *kill.*

When you have a two-word phrase, you have to stress either on the first word or the second word. If you stress both or neither, it's not clear what you are trying to say. Stress on the first word is more noticeable and is one of the most important concepts of intonation that you are going to study. At first glance, it doesn't seem significant, but the more you look at this concept, the more you are going to realize that it reflects how we Americans think, what concepts we have adopted as our own, and what things we consider important.

Set phrases are our "cultural icons," or word images; they are indicators of a *determined use* that we have internalized. These set phrases, with stress on the first word, have been taken into everyday English from descriptive phrases, with stress on the second word. As soon as a descriptive phrase becomes a set phrase, the emphasis shifts from the *second* word to the *first.* The original sense of each word is more or less forgotten, and the new meaning takes over.

Set phrases indicate that we have internalized this phrase as an *image,* that we all agree on a concrete idea that this phrase represents. A hundred years or so ago, when Levi Strauss first came out with his denim pants, they were described as *blue **jeans**.* Now that we all agree on the image, however, they are ***blue** jeans.*

A more recent example would be the descriptive phrase *He's a real party animal.* This slang expression refers to someone who has a great time at a party. When it first became popular, the people using it needed to explain (with their intonation) that he was an *animal* at a *party.* As time passed, the expression became cliché and we changed the intonation to *He's a real **party** animal* because "everyone knew" what it meant.

Clichés are hard to recognize in a new language because what may be an old and tired expression to a native speaker may be fresh and exciting to a newcomer. One way to look at English from the inside out, rather than always looking from the outside in, is to get a feel for what Americans have already accepted and internalized. This starts out as a purely language phenomenon, but you will notice that as you progress and undergo the relentless cultural indoctrination of standard intonation patterns, you will find yourself expressing yourself with the language cues and signals that will mark you as an insider—not an outsider.

When the interpreter was translating for the former Russian President Gorbachev about his trip to San Francisco in 1990, his pronunciation was good, but he placed himself on the outside by repeatedly saying, *cable **car**.* The phrase ***cable** car* is an image, an established entity, and it was very noticeable to hear it stressed on the second word as a mere description.

An important point that I would like to make is that the "rules" you are given here are not meant to be memorized. This discussion is only an introduction to give you a starting point in understanding this phenomenon and in recognizing what to listen for. Read it over; think about it; then listen, try it out, listen some more, and try it out again.

As you become familiar with intonation, you will become more comfortable with American norms, thus the cultural orientation, or even cultural indoctrination, aspect of the following examples.

Note *When you get the impression that a two-word description could be hyphenated or even made into one word, it is a signal that it could be a set phrase—for example, **flash** light, **flash**-light, **flash**light. Also, stress the first word with Street (**Main** Street) and nationalities of food and people (**Mexican** food, **Chinese** girls).*

Exercise 1-43: Sentence Stress with Set Phrases   Track 73

Repeat the following sentences.

Noun	Noun/Adjective	Set Phrase
1. It's a **finger**.	It's a **nail**.	It's a **finger**nail.
2. It's a **pan**.	It's a **cake**.	It's a **pan**cake.
3. It's a **tub**.	It's **hot**.	It's a **hot** tub. (Jacuzzi)
4. It's a **drive**.	It's **hard**.	It's a **hard** drive.
5. It's a **bone**.	It's in **back**.	It's the **back**bone. (spine)
6. It's a **card**.	It's a **trick**.	It's a **card** trick.
7. It's a **spot**.	It's a **light**.	It's a **spot**light.
8. It's a **book**.	It's a **phone**.	It's a **phone** book.

Write your own noun and set-phrase sentences. Remember, when you use a noun, include the article (a, an, the); when you use an adjective, you don't need an article.

9. It's a _____ It's a _____ It's a _____
10. It's a _____ It's a _____ It's a _____
11. It's a _____ It's a _____ It's a _____

Exercise 1-44: Making Set Phrases   Track 74

Add a noun to each word as indicated by the picture. (Check Answer Key on page 216.)

1. a chair   a **chair**man
2. a phone   _____
3. a house   _____
4. a base   _____
5. a door   _____
6. The White   _____
7. a movie   _____
8. The Bullet   _____
9. a race   _____
10. a coffee   _____

11. a wrist   _____
12. a beer   _____
13. a high   _____
14. a hunting   _____
15. a dump   _____
16. a jelly   _____
17. a love   _____
18. a thumb   _____
19. a lightning   _____
20. a pad   _____

Exercise 1-45: Set-Phrase Story—The Little Match Girl Track 75

The following story contains only set phrases (as opposed to the descriptive story in Exercise 1-42, The Ugly Duckling*). Stress the first word of each phrase.*

The little *match girl* was out in a *snowstorm.* Her feet were like *ice cubes* and her *fingertips* had *frostbite.* She hadn't sold any matches since *daybreak,* and she had a *stomachache* from the *hunger pangs,* but her *stepmother* would beat her with a *broomstick* if she came home with an empty *coin purse.* Looking into the bright *living rooms,* she saw *Christmas trees* and warm *fireplaces.* Out on the *snowbank,* she lit a match and saw the image of a grand *dinner table* of food before her. As the *matchstick* burned, the illusion slowly faded. She lit *another one* and saw a room full of happy *family members.* On the last match, her *grandmother* came down and carried her home. In the morning, the *passersby* saw the little *match girl.* She had frozen during the *nighttime,* but she had a smile on her face.

Contrasting a Description and a Set Phrase

We now have two main intonation patterns—*first word stress* and *second word stress.* In the following exercise, we will contrast the two.

Exercise 1-46: Contrasting Descriptive and Set Phrases Track 76

Repeat after me.

Descriptive Phrase	Set Phrase
1. It's a short **nail**.	It's a **finger**nail.
2. It's a chocolate **cake**.	It's a **pan**cake.
3. It's a hot **bath**.	It's a **hot** tub.
4. It's a long **drive**.	It's a **hard** drive.
5. It's the back **door**.	It's the **back**bone.
6. There are four **cards**.	It's a **card** trick.
7. It's a small **spot**.	It's a **spot**light.
8. It's a good **book**.	It's a **phone** book.

Rewrite your descriptive phrases (Exercise 1-40) and set phrases (Exercise 1-43).

9. It's a _____   It's a _____
10. It's a _____   It's a _____
11. It's a _____   It's a _____

Repeat the following pairs.

Descriptive Phrase	Set Phrase
a light **bulb**	a **light** bulb
blue **pants**	**blue** jeans
a cold **fish**	a **gold**fish
a gray **hound**	a **grey**hound
an old **key**	an **inn** key
a white **house**	The **White** House
a nice **watch**	a **wrist**watch
a sticky **web**	a **spider** web
a clean **cup**	a **coffee** cup
a sharp **knife**	a **steak** knife
a baby **alligator**	a **baby** bottle
a shiny **tack**	**thumb**tacks
a wire **brush**	a **hair**brush
a new **ball**	a **foot**ball
a toy **gun**	a **machine** gun
a silk **bow**	a **Band**-Aid
a bright **star**	a **fire**cracker
Mary **Jones**	a **mail**box
Bob **Smith**	a **spray** can
foreign **affairs**	a **wine**glass
down **payment**	a **foot**print
New **York**	a **straw**berry
Social **Security**	a **fig** leaf
City **Hall**	an **ice** cream

Summary of Stress in Two-Word Phrases

Track 78

First Word	set phrases	*light bulb*
	streets	*Main Street*
	Co. or Corp.	*Xerox Corporation*
	nationalities of food	*Chinese food*
	nationalities of people	*French guy*
Second Word	descriptive phrases	*new information*
	road designations	*Fifth Avenue*
	modified adjectives	*really big*
	place names and parks	*New York, Central Park*
	institutions, or Inc.	*Oakland Museum, Xerox Inc.*
	personal names and titles	*Bob Smith, Assistant Manager*
	personal pronouns and possessives	*his car, Bob's brother*
	articles	*the bus, a week, an hour*
	initials and acronyms	*U.S., IQ*
	chemical compounds	*zinc oxide*
	colors and numbers	*red orange, 26*
	most compound verbs	*go away, sit down, fall off*
	percent and dollar	*10 percent, 50 dollars*
	hyphenated nationalities	*African-American*
	descriptive nationalities	*Mexican restaurant*

Nationalities

Track 79

When you are in a foreign country, the subject of nationalities naturally comes up a lot. It would be nice if there were a simple rule that said that all the words using nationalities are stressed on the first word. There isn't, of course. Take this preliminary quiz to see if you need to do this exercise. For simplicity's sake, we will stick with one nationality—American.

Exercise 1-48: Nationality Intonation Quiz   ◀))) **Track 80**

Stress one word in each of the following examples. Repeat after me.

1. an American guy
2. an American restaurant
3. American food
4. an American teacher
5. an English teacher

When you first look at it, the stress shifts may seem arbitrary, but let's examine the logic behind these five examples and use it to go on to other, similar cases.

1. an American guy

The operative word is *American; guy* could even be left out without changing the meaning of the phrase. Compare *I saw two **American** guys yesterday,* with *I saw two **Americans** yesterday.* Words like *guy, man, kid, lady, people* are de facto pronouns in an anthropocentric language. A strong noun, on the other hand, would be stressed—*They flew an American **flag**.* This is why you have the pattern change (in Exercise 1-35: (4e) *Jim **killed** a man;* (4b) *He killed a **snake***).

2. an American restaurant

Don't be sidetracked by an ordinary descriptive phrase that happens to have a nationality in it. You are describing the restaurant: *We went to a good **restaurant** yesterday* or *We went to an American **restaurant** yesterday.* You would use the same pattern where the nationality is more or less incidental in *I had French **toast** for breakfast. **French** fry,* on the other hand, has become a set phrase.

3. American food

Food is a weak word. *I never ate **American** food when I lived in Japan. Let's have **Chinese** food for dinner.*

4. an American teacher

This is a description, so the stress is on *teacher.*

5. an English teacher

This is a set phrase. The stress is on the subject being taught, not the nationality of the teacher: *a **French** teacher, a **Spanish** teacher, a **history** teacher.*

Exercise 1-49: Contrasting Descriptive and Set Phrases Track 82

Repeat the following pairs.

Set Phrase	Descriptive Phrase
An **English** teacher . . .	An English **teacher** . . .
. . . teaches English.	. . . is from England.
An **English** book . . .	An English **book** . . . is on any subject,
. . . teaches the English language.	but it comes from England.
An **English** test . . .	An English **test** . . . is on any subject,
. . . tests a student on the English language.	but it deals with or comes from England.
English food . . .	An English **restaurant** . . .
. . . is kippers for breakfast.	. . . serves kippers for breakfast.

Intonation can indicate completely different meanings for otherwise similar words or phrases. For example, an ***English** teacher* teaches English, but an *English **teacher*** is from England; ***French** class* is where you study French, but *French **class*** is Gallic style and sophistication; an ***orange** tree* grows oranges, but an *orange **tree*** is any kind of tree that has been painted orange. To have your intonation tested, call (800) 457-4255.

Exercise 1-50: Contrast of Compound Nouns Track 83

In the following list of words, underline the element that should be stressed. (Check Answer Key on page 216.) Repeat after me.

1. The White House	21. convenience store	41. a doorknob
2. a white house	22. convenient store	42. a glass door
3. a darkroom	23. to pick up	43. a locked door
4. a dark room	24. a pickup truck	44. ice cream
5. Fifth Avenue	25. six years old	45. I scream.
6. Main Street	26. a six-year-old	46. elementary
7. a main street	27. six and a half	47. a lemon tree
8. a hot dog 🐕	28. a sugar bowl	48. Watergate
9. a hot dog 🌭	29. a wooden bowl	49. the back gate
10. a baby blanket	30. a large bowl	50. the final year
11. a baby's blanket	31. a mixing bowl	51. a yearbook
12. a baby bird	32. a top hat	52. United States
13. a blackbird	33. a nice hat	53. New York
14. a black bird	34. a straw hat	54. Long Beach
15. a greenhouse	35. a chairperson	55. Central Park
16. a green house	36. Ph.D.	56. a raw deal
17. a green thumb	37. IBM	57. a deal breaker
18. a parking ticket	38. MIT	58. the bottom line
19. a one-way ticket	39. USA	59. a bottom feeder
20. an unpaid ticket	40. ASAP	60. a new low

Exercise 1-51: Description and Set Phrase Test Track 84

Let's check and see if the concepts are clear. Underline or highlight the stressed word. (Check Answer Key on page 216.) Repeat after me.

1. He's a **nice guy.**
2. He's an **American guy** from **San Francisco.**
3. The **cheerleader** needs a **rubber band** to hold her **ponytail.**
4. The **executive assistant** needs a **paper clip** for the **final report.**
5. The **law student** took an **English test** in a **foreign country.**
6. The **policeman** saw a **red car** on the **freeway** in **Los Angeles.**
7. My **old dog** has **long ears** and a **flea problem.**
8. The **new teacher** broke his **coffee cup** on the **first day.**
9. His **best friend** has a **broken cup** in his **other office.**
10. Let's play **football** on the **weekend** in **New York.**
11. "**Jingle Bells**" is a **nice song.**
12. Where are my **new shoes?**
13. Where are my **tennis shoes**?
14. I have a **headache** from the **heat wave** in **South Carolina.**
15. The **newlyweds** took a **long walk** in **Long Beach.**

16. The **little dog** was sitting on the **sidewalk.**
17. The **famous athlete** changed clothes in the **locker room.**
18. The **art exhibit** was held in an **empty room.**
19. There was a **class reunion** at the **high school.**
20. The **headlines** indicated a **new policy.**
21. We got **online** and went to AmericanAccent **dot com.**
22. The **stock options** were listed in the **company directory.**
23. All the **second-graders** were out on the **playground.**

> Hey, aren't you that rope?

> No, I'm a frayed knot!

Exercise 1-52: Descriptions and Set Phrases—Goldilocks   **Track 85**

Read the story and stress the indicated words. Notice if they are a description, *a* set phrase, *or* contrast. *Repeat after me. (For the next level of this topic, go to page 128.)*

There is a *little girl.* Her name is *Goldilocks.* She is in a *sunny forest.* She sees a *small house.* She *knocks on* the door, but *no one* answers. She *goes inside.* In the *large room,* there are *three chairs. Goldilocks* sits on the *biggest chair,* but it is *too high.* She sits on the *middle-sized* one, but it is *too low.* She sits on the *small chair* and it *is just right.* On the table, there are *three bowls.* There is *hot porridge* in the bowls. She tries *the first one,* but it is *too hot;* the *second one* is *too cold,* and the *third one* is *just right,* so she eats it all. *After that,* she *goes upstairs.* She *looks around.* There are *three beds,* so she *sits down.* The *biggest bed* is *too hard.* The *middle-sized* bed is *too soft.* The *little one is just right,* so she *lies down.* Soon, she *falls asleep.* In the *meantime,* the family of *three bears* comes home—the *Papa bear,* the *Mama bear,* and the *Baby bear.* They *look around.*

They say, "Who's been sitting in our chairs and eating our porridge?" Then they *run upstairs.* They say, "Who's been sleeping in our beds?" *Goldilocks wakes up.* She is *very scared.* She *runs away. Goldilocks* never *comes back.*

Track 86

Sound/Pronunciation

This is an opportune moment, then, to go into the quality of your voice. In my observation, when people speak a foreign language, they tense up their throat, so their whole communication style sounds forced, pinched, strained, artificial, or nasal. The foreign speaker's voice is also generally higher pitched than would be considered desirable. To practice the difference between high pitch and lower pitch, work on **uh-oh.** In addition to pitch, this exercise will let you discover the difference between a tinny, nasal tone and a deep, rich, mellifluous, basso profundo tone. The tilde (~) is used to indicate a nasal sound. If you try to deepen your voice by expanding your throat, you'll end up with an odd, hollow sound.

Phrasal Verbs

When you have a *verb* and a *preposition*, it's called a *phrasal verb*. These are idiomatic expressions that can't be translated literally. They tend to be stressed on the second word, such as sit **down**, fall **off**, get **up**, put **away**, come **back**, etc. If you have a phrasal verb, such as pick **up**, and you put the stress on the first word, it turns into a noun meaning *truck*, as in, "He was driving a **pick**up truck."

Don't come **back**!	He's planning his big **come**-back.
Let's back **up** and start again.	Do you have a **back**up plan?
The children have run **off**.	The sewer **run**off polluted the stream.
Could you print this **out**?	Could you make a **print**out?
They broke **up** last week.	It was a terrible **break**up.
Could you call me **back**?	I'm still waiting for a **call** back.
We're going to have to cut **back**.	The **cut**backs are ruining the program.
Sure, go **ahead**.	We got the **go**-ahead.
We need to work **around** the problem.	He came up with a good **work**-around.
The heirlooms were handed **down**.	I won't wear **hand**-me-downs!
How much was left **over**?	What? **Left**overs again!
It didn't work **out**.	It was a great **work** out.
The dogs ran **away**.	It was a **run**away bestseller.
He knocked me **down** and dragged me **out**.	It was a **knock**-down **drag**-out fight.

Mark the proper syllables. Check Answer Key on page 216.

1. The plane **took off**. The **takeoff** was worse than the landing.
2. **Cleanup** on aisle five! Please **clean up** the mess on aisle five.
3. Why is he **showing off**? He's such a **show-off**!
4. We need to **check in**! What time is **check-in**?
5. We missed the **cut-off** time by five minutes! Why did they have to **cut** it **off** so early?!!
6. The kids were playing **dress up**. The adults had to **dress up** for the dinner party.
7. The teachers **handed out** the tests, but missed giving us one of the most important **handouts**.
8. The workers wanted jobs, not **handouts**.
9. **Wake up**! We missed the **wake-up** call!
10. We had such a nice **get-together**. We should **get together** again soon!
11. He gave him the **go-ahead** to get started. He said, "**Go ahead**! It's fine!"
12. It was such a **letdown** to lose in the finals. We felt that we'd **let down** the whole school.
13. B **goes between** A and C.
14. He was a reluctant **go-between** for the warring factions.
15. They wanted to **try out** for the team, but they missed the **tryouts**.
16. Could you **pick me up** at 5:00, please? And bring me a coffee, as I'll need a **pick-me-up**!
17. It's freezing, we need to **warm up**! Let's do some **warm-up** exercises before we start yoga.
18. **Back up**, you're standing too close to the edge. If you fall off, we'll need a **back up** plan!
19. I **took out** cash from the ATM, so let's order **takeout**.
20. Darn, I **mixed up** millions and billions on the math test. What a **mix-up**!

Pinch your nose closed and say **æ**. *You should feel a high vibration in your nasal passages, as well as in your fingers. Now, continue holding your nose and completely relax your throat—allow an* **ah** *sound to flow from deep in your chest. There should be no vibration in your nose at all. Go back and forth several times. Next, we practice flowing from one position to the other, so you can feel exactly when it changes from a nasal sound to a deep, rich schwa. Remember how it was imitating a man's voice when you were little? Do that, pinch your nose, and repeat after me.*

Nose				Throat				Chest		
ãæ	▶	ãæ	▶	ãä	▶	ä	▶	ə	▶	ə

Here, we will practice the same progression, but we will stick with the same sound, **æ**.

Nose				Throat				Chest		
ãæ	▶	ãæ	▶	æ	▶	æ	▶	æ	▶	æ

There are three nasal consonants, **m**, **n**, *and* **ng**. *These have non-nasal counterparts,* **m/b**, **n/d**, **ng/g**. *We're going to practice totally denasalizing your voice for a moment, which means turning the nasals into the other consonants. We'll read the same sentence three times. The first will be quite nasal. The second will sound like you have a cold. The third will have appropriate nasal consonants, but denasalized vowels. Repeat after me.*

Nasal	Hollow	Normal
Mãry might need money.	Berry bite deed buddy.	Mary might need money.

The Underlying Hum

Track 90

The underlying hum is quite important and it, too, has to do with your throat. You want to keep the vibration going from one word to the next, gluing the whole phrase together. If words are the train, the hum is the tracks. After applying this technique, a Lebanese doctor was told by his own wife, "Your accent has changed! You're adding extra sounds as if you are filling in the blanks between the words. There's like this background music going on." Exactly! There are no blanks between the words and there is a continuous hum.

I Closed My Eyes and Listened Carefully

Track 91

The secret to finally getting the American accent you want is just to *listen*. The most successful speakers say, "I closed my eyes and listened carefully." So while the sentence, **Bob and Sam brought a good book**, may be hard to pronounce at first as **Bäb an Sæm brädə güd bük**, if you close your eyes and listen to the individual sounds, you will hear the way it actually *is*, and not the way it's *spelled*.

Go-To Phrase

Here's a quick trick. When I put on a German accent, I pick out a few sounds that are particular to that language, and a phrase that contains them, such as **Germans will have to work on the V & W**. I then tighten my lips and from the front of my mouth say, **Cheumans vill haff too veuk ohn zee Fee ent Doppel yu**. It may not be perfect, but it certainly gets me in the ballpark.

American English is generated in the back of the mouth and the throat. A couple of go-to phrases in English, to get you in the zone, are *Bob got a water bottle, Sam sat back and laughed,* or *Rory ran around.*

Exercise 1-55: Mr. Thingamajig	Track 92a

Sometimes, Americans have little mental pauses, where something's right on the tip of our tongue, but we can't think of the exact word—or when we want to euphemize unseemly speech. Fortunately, there's a way around this. We use substitution words that can mean anything and everything.

I was rooting willy-nilly through a buncha stuff, looking every whichway for the dinky little whatchamacallit to fix the goldong thingamajig, but good ol' whatsizname had put it in the hooziwhatsit, as usual! Boy oh boy, what a load of hooey. Always the same old rigamarole with that cockamamie bozo. He's such a pipsqueak! If I found it, ka-ching, I'd be rich, which would be just jim dandy! I'd be totally discombobulated. You-know-who had done you-know-what with the goofy little gadget again, so whaddyaknow . . . there was something-or-other wrong with it. What a snafu!

I had a heck of a time getting ahold of whatsername to come over and take care of it with her special little doohickey that she keeps there in the thingamabob. For the gazillionth time, the flightly little flibbertigibbit said alrighty, she wouldn't shilly shally, she'd schlep over with her widget fixer and whatnot to do a bodaciously whizbang job on the whole shebang. That's right, the whole kit 'n caboodle, no ifs, ands, or buts about it . . . no malarkey.

Okee dokey, but she was a skosh busy right then, yada, yada, yada. Yessirreebob, we usually have gadgets galore, but what with the this-and-that, and all the hooplah, it's all topsy turvy today, 'cuz that humungous nincompoop is still in the whatsit acting like everything's just hunky dory.

That's just a bunch gobbledeegook. Pure gibberish. He's such an old rapscallion. Jeeminy Christmas, the shenanigans of that old fogey. Yackety schmackety, blah, blah, blah! Shucks, I wanted to find it on my own, and not be penalized for it—I'm just so darned tired of gimme's and gotcha's by a lotta has-been nosybones out hobnobbing with hoity toity wannabes.

The real nitty gritty is that, young and old, they're just a buncha happy-go-lucky whippersnappers and cantankerous old fuddyduddies who don't know diddly. I poked among the gewgaws, tchotchkes, gimcracks, and knickknacks, there in the doodad, but I found zilch, zero, zippo, nil, nada, and null. So-and-so told me such-and-such about the deeleebob, but I just don't know where that little gizmo is. Sheesh! It's a big whoopdedoo when you can't even remember where the gosh diddly darned whaddyacallit is!

Translation

I was looking randomly through my belongings for the little unnamed object to fix the darned other little thing, but some guy had put it in the unnamed place, as usual! How annoying. Always the same nonsense with that guy. He's such a small, insignificant person! If I found it (sound of cash register), I'd be rich, which would be just great. I'd be totally confused! That unnamed person had misplaced the unnamed thing again, so surprise, surprise! There was something wrong with it. What a confused situation!

I had a hard time getting in touch with some girl to come over and take care of it with her special little contraption that she keeps in the unspecified location. For the hundredth time, the silly girl said OK, she wouldn't waste time—she'd come over with her mechanical device fixer and everything to do a great job on the whole project. That's right, the whole repair project, no excuses and no nonsense.

Yes, but she was a little busy right then, etc. Yes, we usually do have many devices, but with all the activity and excitement, it's all out of control because that big fool is still in the unnamed location, acting like everything's fine.

That's a lot of nonsense! He's such an old-fashioned person. The antics of that guy! Well, I wanted to find it on my own, and not be penalized for it—I'm so tired of requests and catches by curious people who are past their prime, and out associating with snobbish people who used to be famous.

The truth is that young and old, they're just a group of cheerful lightweights and crabby old people who don't know anything. I looked through the trinkets, decorative objects, cheap and showy ornaments, and small worthless objects, there in the back of the unspecified place, but I couldn't find anything at all. Some guy gave me information about the unnamed thing, but I don't know where it is. It's a big problem when you can't even remember where the darned thing is!

2

Word Linking & Phrasing

Run your words together.

Track 93

As mentioned in the previous chapter, in American English words are not pronounced one by one. Usually, the end of one word attaches to the beginning of the next word. This is also true for initials, numbers, and spelling. Part of the glue that connects sentences is an underlying hum or drone that only breaks when you come to a period, and sometimes not even then. You have this underlying hum in your own language, and it helps a great deal toward making you sound like a native speaker.

Once you have a strong intonation, you need to connect all those stairsteps together so that each sentence sounds like one long word. This chapter is going to introduce you to the idea of liaisons, the connections between words, which allow us to speak in sound groups rather than in individual words. Just as we went over where to put intonation, here you're going to learn how to connect words. Once you understand and learn to use this technique, you can make the important leap from this practice book to other materials and your own conversation.

To make it easier for you to read, liaisons are written like this: **They tell me the dai measier.** (You will also encounter some liaisons in Exercises 3-7, 7-2, and 7-6.) It could also be written **theytellmethedaimeasier**, but it would be too hard to read.

Exercise 2-1: Spelling and Pronunciation   **Track 94**

---

*Read the following sentences. The last two sentences should be pronounced exactly the same, no matter how they are written. It is the **sound** that is important, not the spelling.*

The dime.
The dime easier.
They tell me the dime easier.
They tell me **the dime** easier to understand.
They tell me **that I'm** easier to understand.

WORDS ARE CONNECTED IN FOUR MAIN SITUATIONS

1. Consonant / Vowel
2. Consonant / Consonant
3. Vowel / Vowel
4. T, D, S, or Z + Y

Liaison Rule 1: Consonant / Vowel

Track 95

Words are connected when a word ends in a consonant sound and the next word starts with a vowel sound, including the semivowels **W**, **Y**, and **R**.

Exercise 2-2: Word Connections	Track 96

Read from the right-hand column and really push the consonant to the next sound.

My name is . . .	my nay•miz
because I've	b'k'zäiv
pick up on the American intonation	pi•kə pän the[(y)]əmer'kə ninətənashən

In the preceding example, the word *name* ends in a consonant sound *m* (the *e* is silent and doesn't count), and *is* starts with a vowel sound *i*, so *naymiz* just naturally flows together. In *because I've,* the *z* sound at the end of *because* and the *äi* sound of *I* blend together smoothly. When you say the last line, *pickəpän the[(y)] əmer'kəninətənashən*, you can feel each sound pushing into the next.

Exercise 2-3: Spelling and Number Connections	Track 97

You also use liaisons in spelling and numbers (see also Chapter 1):

LA (Los Angeles)	eh•lay
902-5050	nai•no•too fai•vo•fai•vo

What's the Difference Between a Vowel and a Consonant?

In pronunciation, a consonant touches at some point in the mouth. Try saying **p** with your mouth open—you can't do it because your lips must come together to make the **p** sound. A vowel, on the other hand, doesn't touch anywhere. You can easily say **e** without any part of the mouth, tongue, or lips coming into contact with any other part. This is why we are calling **W**, **Y**, and **R** semivowels, or glides.

Exercise 2-4: Consonant / Vowel Liaison Practice	Track 98

Reconnect the following words. On personal pronouns, it is common to drop the H. (Check Answer Key on page 217.) Repeat.

hold on	hol don
turn over	tur nover
tell her I miss her	tellerl misser

1.	read only
2.	fall off
3.	follow up on
4.	come in
5.	call him
6.	sell it
7.	take out
8.	fade away
9.	6-0
10.	MA

Liaison Rule 2: Consonant / Consonant

Words are connected when a word ends in a consonant sound and the next one starts with a consonant that is in a similar position. What is a similar position? Let's find out.

Exercise 2-5: Consonant / Consonant Liaisons Track 100

---

*Say the sound of each group of letters out loud (the sound of the letter, not the name: b is **buh** not **bee**). There are three general locations—the lips, behind the teeth, or in the throat. If a word ends with a sound created in the throat and the next word starts with a sound from that same general location, these words are going to be linked together. The same with the other two locations. Repeat after me.*

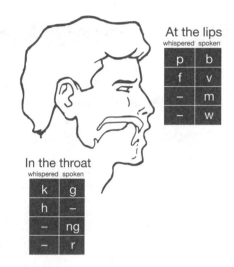

Behind the teeth

whispered	spoken
t	d
ch	j
–	l
–	n
s	z
sh	zh
–	y

At the lips

whispered	spoken
p	b
f	v
–	m
–	w

In the throat

whispered	spoken
k	g
h	–
–	ng
–	r

Exercise 2-6: Consonant / Consonant Liaisons Track 101

I just didn't get the chance.	I•jusdidn't•ge⁽ᵗ⁾the•chance.
I've been late twice.	I'vbinla⁽ᵗ⁾twice.

In the preceding examples, you can see that because the ending **st** of *just* and the beginning **d** of *didn't* are so near each other in the mouth, it's not worth the effort to start the sound all over again, so they just flow into each other. You don't say *I justə didn'tə getə the chance,* but do say *Ijusdidn't ge⁽ᵗ⁾the chance.* In the same way, it's too much work to say *I'və beenə lateə twice,* so you say it almost as if it were a single word: *I'vbinla⁽ᵗ⁾twice.*

The sound of **TH** is a special case. It is a floater between areas. The sound is sometimes created by the tongue popping out from between the teeth and other times on the back of the top teeth, combining with various letters to form a new composite sound. For instance, **s** moves forward and the **th** moves back to meet at the mid-point between the two.

Note *Each of the categories in the drawing contains two labels—voiced and unvoiced. What does that mean? Put your thumb and index fingers on your throat and say **z**; you should feel a vibration from your throat in your fingers. If you whisper that same sound, you end up with **s** and you feel that your fingers don't vibrate. So, **z** is a voiced sound, **s**, unvoiced. The consonants in the two left columns are paired like that. (See also Chapters 9, 11, 13, 16, and 17.)*

Consonants

Voiced	Unvoiced		Voiced	Unvoiced
b	p		—	h
d	t		l	—
v	f		r	—
g	k		m	—
j	ch		n	—
z	s		ng	—
<u>th</u>	th		y	—
zh	sh		w	—

Exercise 2-7: Liaisons with TH Combination Track 102

When the TH combination connects with certain sounds, the two sounds blend together to form a composite sound. In the following examples, see how the TH moves back and the L moves forward to meet in a new middle position. Repeat after me. (See also Chapter 8.)

th	+	l	with lemon	th	+	ch	both charges
th	+	n	with nachos	th	+	j	with juice
th	+	t	both times				
th	+	d	with delivery	n	+	th	in the
th	+	s	both sizes	z	+	th	was that
th	+	z	with zeal	d	+	th	hid those

Exercise 2-8: Consonant / Consonant Liaison Practice Track 103

Reconnect the following words as shown in the models. (Check Answer Key on page 217.) Repeat.

hard times	hardtimes
with luck	withluck

1. business deal
2. credit check
3. the top file
4. sell nine new cars
5. sit down
6. some plans need luck
7. check cashing
8. let them make conditions
9. had the
10. both days

Liaison Rule 3: Vowel / Vowel

Track 104

When a word ending in a *vowel* sound is next to one beginning with a *vowel* sound, they are connected with a glide between the two vowels. A glide is either a slight *y* sound or a slight *w* sound. How do you know which one to use? This will take care of itself—the position your lips are in will dictate either *y* or *w*.

Go away.	Go^(w)away.
I also need the other one.	I^(y)also need thee^(y)other one.

For example, if a word ends in **o** your lips are going to be in the forward position, so a *w* sound quite naturally leads into the next vowel sound—Go^(w)away. You don't want to say: Go . . . away and break the undercurrent of your voice. Run it all together: Go^(w)away.

After a long **ē** sound, your lips will be pulled back far enough to create a *y* glide or liaison: I^(y)also need thee^(y) other one. Don't force this sound too much, though. It's not a strong pushing sound. I(Y)also need thee(Y)other one would sound really weird.

Exercise 2-9: Vowel / Vowel Liaison Practice 🔊 **Track 105**

*Reconnect the following words as shown in the models. Add a (y) glide after an *e* sound, and a (w) glide after an *u* sound. Don't forget that the sound of the American O is really *ou*. (Check Answer Key on page 217.)*

she isn't	she^(y)isn't
who is	who^(w)iz

1. go anywhere
2. so honest
3. through our
4. you are
5. he is
6. do I?
7. I asked
8. to open
9. she always
10. too often

Liaison Rule 4: T, D, S, or Z + Y

Track 106

When the letter or sound of **T**, **D**, **S**, or **Z** is followed by a word that starts with **Y**, or its sound, both sounds are connected. These letters and sounds connect not only with **y**, but they do so as well with the initial unwritten **y**. (See also Chapter 13, "The Ridge.")

Exercise 2-10: T, D, S, or Z + Y Liaisons Track 107

Repeat the following.

T + Y = CH	What's your **name**?	wəcher **name**
	Can't you **do** it?	kænt chew **do**⁽ʷ⁾it
	Actually	**æk**·chully
	Don't you **like** it?	dont chew **lye** kit
	Wouldn't you?	**wood**en chew
	Haven't you? No, not **yet**.	**hæv**en chew? nou, nä **chet**
	I'll let you **know**.	I'll letcha **know**
	Can I get you a **drink**?	k'näi getchewə **drink**
	We thought you weren't **coming**.	we thä chew wrnt **kə**ming
	I'll bet you **ten** bucks he for**got**.	æl betcha **ten** buxee frg**ät**
	Is **that** your final **answer**?	is **thæ**chr fin'**læn** sr
	natural	**næch**rəl
	per**pe**tual	per**pe**chə⁽ʷ⁾əl
	virtual	**vr**chə⁽ʷ⁾əl
D + Y = J	Did you **see** it?	didjə **see**⁽ʸ⁾it
	How did you **like** it?	hæo•jə **lye** kit
	Could you **tell**?	küjə **tell**
	Where did you send your **check**?	wɛrjə senjer **check**
	What did your **fam**ily think?	wəjer **fæm**lee think
	Did you find your **keys**?	didjə fine jer **keez**
	We followed your in**struc**tions.	we fallow jerin **strəc**shunz
	Congratu**la**tions!	k'ngræj'**la**shunz
	edu**ca**tion	edjə·**ca**shun
	indi**vid**ual	ində**vij**ə⁽ʷ⁾əl
	gradu**a**tion	græjə⁽ʷ⁾**a**shun
	gradual	**græ**jə⁽ʷ⁾əl
S + Y = SH	**Yes**, you are.	**yesh**u are
	In**sur**ance	in**shur**ance
	Bless you!	**bless**hue
	Press your **hands** together.	**pressure hanz** d'gethr
	Can you **dress** yourself?	c 'new **dresh**ier self
	You can pass your **exams** this year.	yuk'n **pæsher egzæmz** thisheer
	I'll try to guess your **age**.	æl trydə **geshie**rage
	Let him gas your **car** for you.	leddim **gæshier cär** fr you
Z + Y = ZH	How's your **fam**ily?	**hæozhier fæm**lee
	How was your **trip**?	hæo•wəzhier **trip**
	Who's your **friend**?	hoozhier **frend**
	Where's your **mom**?	wɛrzh'r **mäm**

Exercise 2-10: T, D, S, or Z + Y Liaisons *continued*	Track 107

When's your **birth**day?	wɛnzh'r **brth**day
She says you're O**K**.	she sɛzhierou **kay**
Who does your **hair**?	hoo dəzhier **hɛr**
casual	**kæ**•zhyə(w)əl
visual	**vi**•zhyə(w)əl
usual	**yu**•zhyə(w)əl
version	**vr**zh'n
vision	**vi**zh'n

Exercise 2-11: T, D, S, or Z + Y Liaison Practice	Track 108

Reconnect or rewrite the following words. Remember that there may be a y sound that is not written. (Check Answer Key on page 217.) Repeat.

put your	pücher
gradual	gradjyə(w)l

1. did you		6. tissue
2. who's your		7. got your
3. just your		8. where's your
4. gesture		9. congratulations
5. miss you		10. had your

This word exchange really happened.

Now that you have the idea of how to link words, let's do some liaison work.

Exercise 2-12: Finding Liaisons and Glides	Track 109

In the following paragraph, connect as many of the words as possible. Mark your liaisons as we have done in the first two sentences. Add the (y) and (w) glides between the words. (Check Answer Key on page 217.)

Hello, my name is_____. I'm taking American **Accent** Training. There's a **lot** to **learn**, but I **hope** to make it as **enjoyable** as possible. I should pick **up** on the American **intonation** pattern pretty **easily**, although the(y)**only** way to **get** it is to **practice** all of the time. I use the **up** and down, or **peaks**

and valleys, **intonation** more than I **used** to. I've been paying attention to **pitch, too**. It's like **walking** down a **stair**case. I've been **talking** to^(w)a lot of **Americans** lately, and they tell me that I'm **easier** to understand. **Any**way, I could go **on** and on, but the **important** thing is to **listen** well and sound **good**. **Well**, what do you **think**? **Do** I?

▶ Practice reading the paragraph three times, focusing on running your words together.
◀ Repeat after me as I read. I'm going to exaggerate the linking of the words, drawing it out much longer than would be natural.

Exercise 2-13: Practicing Liaisons   Track 110

Back up to the last paragraph just read and repeat again. This time, however, read from the paragraph below. The intonation is marked for you in boldface. Use your rubber band on every stressed word.

Hello, **my nay** miz_____. **I'm** takingə merica **næccent**(t)raining. There zə **lättə** learn, bə däi **hope** t́ ma ki desen **joy**ablez pässible. I shüd pi **kə**pän the^(y)əmerica nintə**na**sh'n pæddern pridy^(y)**ezily**, although thee^(y)**ounly** waydə **ge**ddidiz t́ **præk**ti sälləv th' time. I^(y)use thee^(y)**up**'n down, or **peak** s'n valley zintə**na**shən more thə näi **used** to. Ivbn payingə tenshən t́ **pitch, too**. Itsläi **kwäl**king dow nə **stair**case. Ivbn **täl**king to^(w)ə läddəvə **mer**ican zla^(t)ely, 'n they tell me the däi**mee**zier to^(w)under**stænd**. **Any**way, I could go^(w)**ä** nə nän, bu^(t)thee^(y)im**port**ant thingiz t́ **lis**ənwellən soun^(d) **good**. Well, whəddyü **think**? **Do**^(w)I?

Exercise 2-14: Additional Liaison Practice   Track 111

▶ Use these techniques on texts of your own and in conversation.

  1. Take some written material and mark the *intonation,* then the *word groups,* and finally the *liaisons.*
  2. Practice saying it out loud.
  3. Record yourself and listen back.

▶ In conversation, think which word you want to make stand out, and change your pitch on that word. Then, run the in-between words together in the valleys. Listen carefully to how Americans do it and copy the sound.

Exercise 2-15: Colloquial Reductions and Liaisons   Track 112

In order for you to recognize these sounds when used by native speakers, they are presented here, but I don't recommend that you go out of your way to use them yourself. If, at some point, they come quite naturally of their own accord in casual conversation, you don't need to resist, but please don't force yourself to talk this way. Repeat. (See also Chapter 1.)

I have got to **go.**	I've gotta **go.**
I have got a **book.**	I've gotta **book.**
Do you want to **dance?**	Wanna **dance?**
Do you want a **banana?**	Wanna **banana?**
Let me **in.**	Lemme **in.**
Let me **go.**	Lemme **go.**
I'll let you **know.**	I'll letcha **know.**
Did you **do** it?	Dija **do** it?

Exercise 2-15: Colloquial Reductions and Liaisons *continued* 🔊 **Track 112**

Not **yet.**	Nä **chet.**
I'll meet you **later.**	I'll meechu **lay**der.
What do you **think?**	Whaddyu **think?**
What did you **do** with it?	Whajoo **do** with it?
How did you **like** it?	Howja **like** it?
When did you **get** it?	When ju **ge**ddit?
Why did you **take** it?	Whyju **tay** kit?
Why don't you **try** it?	Why don chu **try** it?
What are you **waiting** for?	Whaddya **wait**in' for?
What are you **doing?**	Whatcha **do**in'?
How is it **go**ing?	Howzit **go**ing?
Where's the **what**-you-may-call-it?	Where's the **what**chamacallit?
Where's **what**-is-his-name?	Where's **what**sizname?
How **about** it?	How **'bout** it?
He has got to **hurry** because he is **late.**	He's gotta **hurry** 'cuz he's **late.**
I could've been a **contender.**	I coulda bina con**ten**der.
Could you speed it **up**, please?	Couldjoo spee di **dup**, pleez?
Would you mind if I **tried** it?	Would joo mindifai **try** dit?
Aren't you Bob **Barker?**	Arnchoo Bab **Bar**ker?
Can't you see it **my** way for a change?	Kænchoo see it **my** way for a change?
Don't you **get** it?	Doancha **ge**ddit?
I should have **told** you.	I shoulda **tol**joo.
Tell her (that) I **miss** her.	Teller I **mi**sser.
Tell him (that) I **miss** him.	Tellim I **mi**ssim.

Extremely extreme reductions

Did you **eat?**	Jeet?
No, did **you?**	No, **joo?**
Why don't you **get a job?**	Whyncha **getta job?**
I don't know, **it's** too **hard.**	**I** dunno, stoo **härd.**
Could **we go?**	Kwee **gou?**
Let's **go!**	**Sko**!
I'm **go**ing to	**äi**mana

When a clock is hungry ...   It goes back four seconds.

SPOON OR SBOON?

An interesting thing about liaisons is that so much of it has to do with whether a consonant is voiced or not. The key thing to remember is that the vocal cords don't like switching around at the midpoint. If the first consonant is voiced, the next one will be as well. If the first one is unvoiced, the second one will sound unvoiced, no matter what you do. For example, say the word *spoon*. Now, say the word *sboon*. Hear how they sound the same? This is why I'd like you to always convert the preposition *to* to **də** when you're speaking English, no matter what comes before it. In the beginning, to get you used to the concept, we made a distinction between **tə** and **də**, but now that your schwa is in place, use a single **d'** sound everywhere, except at the very beginning of a sentence.

After a voiced sound:	He had to do it.	he hæ^(d)d' **du**^(w)'t
After an unvoiced sound:	He got to do it.	he gä^(t)d' **du**^(w)'t
At the beginning of a sentence:	To **be** or **not** to be.	t' **bee**^(y)r **nä**^(t)d'bee

To have your liaisons tested, call (800) 457-4255.

WORD GROUPS AND PHRASING

Use punctuation for phrasing. Commas sound different from periods.

Pauses for Related Thoughts, Ideas, or Breathing

By now you've begun developing a strong intonation, with clear peaks and reduced valleys, so you're ready for the next step. You may find yourself reading the paragraph (in Exercise 1-24) like this:

*Hellomynameis So-and-SoI'mtakingAmerican**Accent**Training.*
*There'sa**lot**tolearnbutI**hope**tomakeitasen**joy**ableaspossible.*

If so, your audience won't completely comprehend or enjoy your presentation.

In addition to intonation, there is another aspect of speech that indicates meaning. This can be called *phrasing* or *tone.* Have you ever caught just a snippet of a conversation in your own language and somehow known how to piece together what came before or after the part you heard? This has to do with phrasing.

In a sentence, phrasing tells the listener where the speaker is at the moment, where the speaker is going, and if the speaker is finished or not. Notice that the intonation stays on the nouns. (See also Chapter 1.)

Repeat after me.

Statement	**Dogs** eat **bones**.
Clauses	**Dogs** eat **bones**, but **cats** eat **fish**, *or* As we all **know**, **dogs** eat **bones**.
Listing	**Dogs** eat **bones**, **kibbles**, and **meat**.
Question	Do **dogs** eat **bones**?
Repeated Question	Do **dogs** eat **bones**?!!
Tag Question	**Dogs** eat bones, **don't** they?
Tag Statement	**Dogs** eat **bones**, **DON'T** they!
Indirect Speech	He asked if **dogs** ate **bones**.
Direct Speech	"Do **dogs** eat **bones**?" he **asked**.

For clarity, break your sentences with pauses between natural word groups of related thought or ideas. Of course, you will have to break at every comma and every period, but besides those breaks, add other little pauses to let your listeners catch up with you or think over the last burst of information and to allow you time to take a breath. Let's work on this technique. In doing the following exercise, you should think of using *breath groups* and *idea groups*.

Break the paragraph into natural word groups. Mark every place where you think a pause is needed with a slash.

Hello, **my** name is_____. I'm taking American **Accent** Training. There's a **lot** to **learn**, but I **hope** to make it as **enjoyable** as possible. I should pick **up** on the American **intonation** pattern pretty **easily**, although the **only** way to **get** it is to **practice** all of the time. I use the **up** and down, or **peaks** and valleys, **intonation** more than I **used** to. I've been paying attention to **pitch**, **too**. It's like **walking** down a **stair**case. I've been **talking** to a lot of **Americans** lately, and they tell me that I'm **easier** to under**stand**. **Any**way, I could go on and on, but the **important** thing is to **listen** well and sound **good**. **Well**, what do you **think**? **Do** I?

Note *In the beginning, your word groups should be very short. It'll be a sign of your growing sophistication when they get longer.*

When I read the paragraph this time, I will exaggerate the pauses. Although we're working on word groups here, remember, I don't want you to lose your intonation. Repeat each sentence group after me.

Hello, | my name is _____ . | I'm taking American Accent Training. | There's a lot to learn, | but I hope to make it | as enjoyable as possible. | I should pick up on the American intonation pattern | pretty easily, | although the only way to get it is to practice all of the time. | I use the up and down, | or peaks and valleys, | intonation | more than I used to. | I've been paying attention to pitch, | too. | It's like walking down a staircase. | I've been talking | to a lot of Americans | lately, | and they tell me | that I'm easier | to understand. | Anyway, | I could go on and on, | but the important thing is to listen well | and sound good. | Well. | What do you think? | Do I?

✗ Next, practice the word groups three times using strong intonation. When reading, your pauses should be neither long nor dramatic—just enough to give your listener time to digest what you're saying. Be sure to take a breath for each phrase, not for each word or indeed the entire paragraph.

Take this quick quiz to make sure you can hear the punctuation-based phrasing. (Check Answer Key on page 217.)

1. I did it
   A. ☐ . B. ☐ , C. ☐ ? D. ☐ !
2. I did it
   A. ☐ . B. ☐ , C. ☐ ? D. ☐ !
3. I did it
   A. ☐ . B. ☐ , C. ☐ ? D. ☐ !
4. I did it
   A. ☐ . B. ☐ , C. ☐ ? D. ☐ !

Exercise 2-20: Tag Endings Track 119

Complete each sentence with a tag ending. Use the same verb, but with the opposite polarity—positive becomes negative, and negative becomes positive. (Check Answer Key on page 217.)

Intonation

With a query, the intonation rises. With confirmation, the intonation drops.

1. The new **clerk** is very **slow**, <u>isn't he</u>!	15. We'd better close the **office**, _____ !
2. But he can **improve**, _____ ?	16. We'd rather close the **office**, _____ ?
3. She doesn't **type** very well, _____ !	17. The office has **closed**, _____ ?
4. They lost their **way**, _____ ?	18. You couldn't **tell**, _____ !
5. You don't **think** so, _____ !	19. You'll be working **late** tonight, _____ ?
6. I don't think it's **easy**, _____ ?	20. He should have **been** here by now, ____ !
7. I'm your **friend**, _____ ?	21. He should be **promoted**, _____ !
8. You won't be **coming**, _____ !	22. I didn't send the **fax**, _____ ?
9. He keeps the **books**, _____ !	23. I won't get a **raise** this year, _____ ?
10. We have to close the **office**, _____ ?	24. You use the **computer**, _____ ?
11. We have closed the **office**, _____ ?	25. You're used to the **computer**, _____ !
12. We had to close the **office**, _____ !	26. You used to use the **computer**, _____ ?
13. We had the **office** closed, _____ ?	27. You never used to work **Saturdays**, ____ ?
14. We had already closed the **office**, _____ ?	28. That's **better**, _____ !

Pronunciation

Did he?	**Di**dee?	Wouldn't you?	**Wood**en chew?	Doesn't it?	**Duz**za nit?
Does he?	**Duz**zy?	Shouldn't I?	**Shüd**n näi?	Aren't I?	**Are** näi?
Was he?	**Wu**zzy?	Won't he?	**Woe** knee?	Won't you?	**Wone** chew?
Has he?	**Ha**zzy?	Didn't he?	**Did**n knee?	Don't you?	**Done** chew?
Is he?	**Iz**zy?	Hasn't he?	**Has** a knee?	Can't you?	**Can** chew?
Will he?	**Will**y?	Wouldn't he?	**Wood**en knee?	Could you?	**Cü**joo?
Would he?	**Wood**y?	Isn't he?	**Is** a knee?	Would you?	**Wü**joo?
Can he?	**Can**ny?	Isn't it?	**Is** a nit?		

The basic techniques introduced so far are *pitch, stress,* the *staircase* and *musical notes, reduced sounds,* and *word groups and phrasing.* In Chapters 3 through 17, we refine and expand this knowledge to cover every sound of the American accent.

Vowel and Consonant Mouth Positions

Track 120

The vowels are in a continuous stream from **e** to **ooh**, and the consonants are in three categories based on the point of contact.

Al A. Gator

Vowels

eeh | eh | æ | ah | uh / ih / ü | oh | ooh

Consonants
Lips

m | p / b | f / v | y

Tongue Tip

t / d | l | n | s / z | sh / zh / ch / j | th

Throat

k / g / h / x / ng | r | w / q

For the **R**, do **not** touch the ridge at the top of your mouth.

For the **Th**, do **not** stick your tongue out. Press it against your top teeth and **pop** the air out.

The first step is to re-program you away from **spelling** to the actual **sounds** of English. Start by mastering these sounds, combining initial consonants and vowels. This will give you a strong leg up on pronunciation.

3
Cat? Caught? Cut?

A = æ   O = ä   U = ə

After laying our foundation with intonation and liaisons, here we finally begin to refine your pronunciation! We are now going to work on the differences between æ, ä, and ə, as well as ō, ā, and ɛ. Let's start out with the æ sound. (See also pages vi–vii, Chapters 1, 10, and 12, and the Nationality Guides.)

THE æ SOUND

Although not a common sound, æ is very distinctive to the ear and is typically American. In the practice paragraph this sound occurs five times. As its phonetic symbol indicates, æ is a combination of ä + ɛ. To pronounce it, drop your jaw down as if you were going to say ä; then from that position, try to say ɛ. The final sound is not two separate vowels, but rather the end result of the combination. It is very close to the sound that a goat makes: *ma-a-a-a*!

▶ Try it a few times now: ä ▶ æ

If you find yourself getting too nasal with æ, pinch your nose as you say it. If **kæt** turns into **kɛæt**, you need to pull the sound out of your nose and down into your throat.

Note *As you look for the œ sound you might think that words like **down** or **sound** have an æ in them. For this diphthong, try æ + oh, or æo. This way, **down** would be written dœon. Because it is a combined sound, however, it's not included in the Cat? category. (See Pronunciation Points on page vii.)*

THE ä SOUND

The ä sound occurs a little more frequently; you will find ten such sounds in the exercise. To pronounce ä, relax your tongue and drop your jaw as far down as it will go. As a matter of fact, put your hand under your chin and say **mä, pä, tä, sä**. Your hand should be pushed down by your jaw as it opens. Remember, it's the sound that you make when the doctor wants to see your throat, so open it up and *dräp your jäw.*

THE SCHWA ə SOUND

Last is the schwa **ə**, the *most common* sound in American English. When you work on the practice paragraph, depending on how fast you speak, how smoothly you make liaisons, how strong your intonation is, and how much you relax your sounds, you will find from 50 to 75 schwas. Spelling doesn't help identify it, because it can appear as any one of the vowels, or a combination of them. It is a neutral vowel sound, *uh*. It is usually in an unstressed syllable, though it can be stressed as well. Whenever you find a vowel that can be crossed out and its absence wouldn't change the pronunciation of the word, you have probably found a schwa: *photography* **ph'togr'phy** (the two apostrophes show the location of the neutral vowel sounds).

Because it is so common, however, the wrong pronunciation of this one little sound can leave your speech strongly accented, even if you Americanized everything else.

Note *Some dictionaries use two different written characters, ə and ʌ, but for simplicity we are only going to use the first one.*

Silent or Neutral?

A schwa is neutral, but it is not silent. By comparison, the silent **e** at the end of a word is a signal for pronunciation, but it is not pronounced itself: *code* is **kōd**. The **e** tells you to say an **o**. If you leave the **e** off, you have *cod,* **käd**. The schwa, on the other hand, is neutral, but it is an actual sound—*uh.* For example, you could also write *photography* as **phuh•tah•gruh•fee.**

Because it's a neutral sound, the schwa doesn't have any distinctive characteristics, yet it is *the most common sound in the English language.*

To make the **ə** sound, put your hand on your diaphragm and push until a grunt escapes. Don't move your jaw, tongue, or lips; just allow the sound to flow past your vocal cords. It should sound like *uh.*

Once you master this sound, you will have an even easier time with pronouncing *can* and *can't.* In a sentence, *can't* sounds like *kæn(t)*, but *can* becomes *kən*, unless it is stressed, when it is *kæn* (as we saw in Exercise 1-23 on page 16). Repeat.

I can **do** it.	I kən **do** it
I **can't do** it.	I **kæn't do** it

VOWEL CHART

In the vowel chart that follows, the four corners represent the four most extreme positions of the mouth. The center box represents the least extreme position—the neutral schwa. For these four positions, only move your lips and jaw. Your tongue should stay in the same place—with the tip resting behind the bottom teeth.

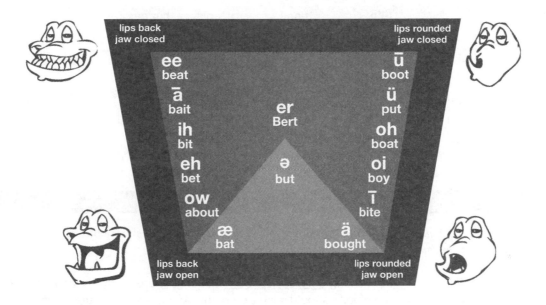

1. To pronounce *beat,* your lips should be drawn back, but your teeth should be close together. Your mouth should form the shape of a *banana.*

2. To pronounce *boot,* your lips should be fully rounded, and your teeth should be close together. Your mouth should form the shape of a *Cheerio.*

3. To pronounce *bought,* drop your jaw straight down from the *boot* position. Your mouth should form the shape of an *egg.*

4. To pronounce *bat,* keep your jaw down, pull your lips back, and try to simultaneously say **ä** and **ɛ**. Your mouth should form the shape of a *box.*

Note *Word-by-word pronunciation will be different than individual sounds within a sentence.* **That, than, as, at, and, have, had, can,** *and so on, contain æ sounds when they stand alone, but are weak words that reduce quickly in speech.*

Exercise 3-1: Word-by-Word and In a Sentence				Track 122

Read from the last column.

Stressed		Unstressed		
that	thæt	th't	thət	He said th't it's OK.
than	thæn	th'n	thən	It's bigger th'n before.
as	æz	'z	əz	'z soon 'z he gets here
at	æt	't	ət	Look 't the time!
and	ænd	'n	ən	ham 'n eggs
have	hæv	h'v	həv	Where h'v you been?
had	hæd	h'd	həd	He h'd been at home.
can	cæn	c'n	cən	C'n you do it?

Exercise 3-2: Finding æ, ä, and ə Sounds	Track 123

There are five æ, ten ä, and 50 to 75 ə sounds in the following paragraph. Underscore them in pen or pencil. (The first one of each sound is marked for you.)

Hello, **my** name is_____. I'm taking <u>ə</u>mer<u>ə</u>c<u>ə</u>n <u>ǣ</u>cs<u>ə</u>nt Training. There's a l<u>ä</u>t to **learn**, but I **hope** to make it as **enjoyable** as possible. I should pick **up** on the American **intonation** pattern pretty **easily**, although the **only** way to **get** it is to **practice** all of the time. I use the **up** and down, or **peaks** and valleys, **intonation** more than I **used** to. I've been paying attention to **pitch**, **too**. It's like **walking** down a **stair**case. I've been **talking** to a lot of **Americans** lately, and they tell me that I'm **easier** to under**stand**. **Any**way, I could go **on** and on, but the **important** thing is to **listen** well and sound **good**. **Well**, what do you **think**? **Do** I?

▶ Next, check your answers with the Answer Key on page 217. Finally, take your markers and give a color to each sound. For example, mark **æ** green, **ä** blue, and **ə** yellow.

✗ Read the paragraph three times on your own.

Note *It sounds regional to end a sentence with* **ustə**. *In the middle of a sentence, however, it is more standard: I* **ustə** *live there.*

Exercise 3-3: Vowel-Sound Differentiation Track 124

*Here we will read down from 1 to 24, then we will read each row across. Give the ā sound a clear double sound ε + ee. Also, the o is a longer sound than you might be expecting. Add the full **ooh** sound after each "o."*

Tracks 124a–f

	æ	ä	ə	ou	ā	ε
1.	Ann	on	un–	own	ain't	end
2.	ban	bond	bun	bone	bane	Ben
3.	can	con	come	cone	cane	Ken
4.	cat	caught/cot	cut	coat	Kate	ketch
5.	Dan	Don/dawn	done	don't	Dane	den
6.	fan	fawn	fun	phone	feign	fend
7.	gap	gone	gun	goat	gain	again
8.	hat	hot	hut	hotel	hate	het up
9.	Jan	John	jump	Joan	Jane	Jenny
10.	lamp	lawn	lump	loan	lane	Len
11.	man	monster	Monday	moan	main	men
12.	matter	motto	mutter	motor	made her	met her
13.	Nan	non–	none/nun	known	name	nemesis
14.	gnat	not/knot	nut	note	Nate	net
15.	pan	pawn	pun	pony	pain/pane	pen
16.	ran	Ron	run	roan	rain/reign	wren
17.	sand	sawn	sun	sewn/sown	sane	send
18.	shall	Sean	shut	show	Shane	Shen
19.	chance	chalk	chuck	choke	change	check
20.	tack	talk	tuck	token	take	tech
21.	van	Von	vug	vogue	vague	vent
22.	wax	want	won/one	won't	wane	when
23.	yam	yawn	young	yo!	yea!	yen
24.	zap	czar	result	zone	zany	zen

	single	double
ä	dock	dog
ə	duck	dug

To have your pronunciation tested, call (800) 457-4255.

Exercise 3-4: Reading the æ Sound   Track 125

Listen to the audio and then read the following aloud.

▶ **The Tæn Mæn**

A fashionably tan man sat casually at the bat stand, lashing a handful of practice bats. The manager, a crabby old bag of bones, passed by and laughed, "You're about average, Jack. Can't you lash faster than that?" Jack had had enough, so he clambered to his feet and lashed bats faster than any man had ever lashed bats. As a matter of fact, he lashed bats so fast that he seemed to dance. The manager was aghast. "Jack, you're a master bat lasher!" he gasped. Satisfied at last, Jack sat back and never lashed another bat.

✗ Read *The Tæn Mæn* aloud.

Exercise 3-5: Reading the ä Sound   Track 126

Listen to the audio and then read the following aloud.

A Lät of Läng, Hät Wälks in the Gärden

John was not sorry when the boss called off the walks in the garden. Obviously, to him, it was awfully hot, and the walks were far too long. He had not thought that walking would have caught on the way it did, and he fought the policy from the onset. At first, he thought he could talk it over at the law office and have it quashed, but a small obstacle* halted that thought. The top lawyers always bought coffee at the shop across the lawn and they didn't want to stop on John's account. John's problem was not office politics, but office policy. He resolved the problem by bombing the garden.

* lobster • a small lobster • lobstacle • a small obstacle

✗ Read *A Lät of Läng, Hät Wälks in the Gärden* aloud.

Exercise 3-6: Reading the ə Sound   Track 127

When you read the following schwa paragraph, try clenching your teeth the first time. It won't sound completely natural, but it will get rid of all of the excess lip and jaw movement and force your tongue to work harder than usual. Remember that in speaking American English we don't move our lips much, and we talk though our teeth from far back in our throats. I'm going to read with my teeth clenched together and you follow along, holding your teeth together.

What Must the Sun Above Wonder About?

Some pundits proposed that the sun wonders unnecessarily about sundry and assorted conundrums. One cannot but speculate what can come of their proposal. It wasn't enough to trouble us,* but it was done so underhandedly that hundreds of sun lovers rushed to the defense of their beloved sun. None of this was relevant on Monday, however, when the sun burned up the entire country.

*ət wəzənənəf tə trəbələs

✗ Read *What Must the Sun Above Wonder About?* twice. Try it with your teeth clenched the first time and normally the second time.

THE MIRACLE TECHNIQUE

Listen for the actual sounds . . . not what you *think* they are! As you saw in Chapter 1 with **Bobby bought a bike (bäbee bädə bäik)**, there is a difference between pure sound and spelling.

Regaining Long-Lost Listening Skills

The trouble with starting accent training after you know a great deal of English is that you know a great deal *about* English. You have a lot of preconceptions and, unfortunately, misconceptions about the sound of English.

A Child Can Learn Any Language

Every sound of every language is within every child. So, what happens with adults? People learn their native language and stop listening for the sounds that they never hear; then they lose the ability to hear those sounds. Later, when you study a foreign language, you learn a lot of spelling rules that take you still further away from the real sound of that language—in this case, English.

What we are going to do here is teach you to *hear* again. So many times, you've heard what a native speaker said, translated it into your own accent, and repeated it with your accent. Why? Because you "knew" how to say it.

Exercise 3-7: Tell Me Wədai Say   **Track 129**

*The first thing you're going to do is write down exactly what I say. It will be nonsense to you for two reasons: First, because I will be saying **sound units**, not **word units**. Second, because I will be starting at the **end** of the sentence instead of the **beginning**. Listen carefully and write down exactly what you hear, regardless of meaning. The first sound is given to you—**kit**.*

_____ _____ ´ kit

▶ *Once you have written it down, check with the version below.*

äi **lie** kit

▶ *Read it out loud to yourself and try to hear what the regular English is. Don't look ahead until you've figured out the sense of it.*

I **like** it.

Exercise 3-8: Listening for Pure Sounds   **Track 130**

Again, listen carefully and write the sounds you hear. Start at the end and fill in the blanks right to left, then read them back left to right. Write whichever symbols are easiest for you to read back. The answers are on page 66.

1. _____ _____ dəp´.

2. _____ _____ dæout´.

3. _____ _____ _____ ´.

4. _____ _____ _____ _____ ´.

Exercise 3-9: Extended Listening Practice   Track 131

Let's do a few more pure-sound exercises to fine-tune your ear. Remember, start at the end and fill in the blanks right to left, then read them back left to right. You will only need five non-alphabet symbols: æ, ä, ə, ü, and ɛ. There are clues sprinkled around for you (and all the answers are in the Answer Key on page 217).

1. _____´ _____!

2. thæng´ _____.

3. _____ _____´ _____´ _____ _____ _____´ _____!

4. wə _____ _____ _____´ ?

5. kwee _____ _____ _____ _____?

6. _____ _____ _____ _____ _____´ _____ _____ _____ _____?

7. _____ _____ _____ _____´ _____ _____ bæou _____.

8. _____ _____, _____ _____ _____´ _____ _____!

9. _____ _____ _____ _____´ _____ wən.

10. wyn _____ _____ _____ _____´ ?

11. _____ _____ _____´ _____ _____ frə _____?

Answers for Exercise 3-8

1.	Yoo zih **dəp**.	2.	Weh rih **dæout**.	3.	May kit **doo**.	4.	Orr doo with **æout**.
	Use it up.		Wear it out.		Make it do.		Or do without.

4

The American T

Middle T sounds like D.

The American **T** is influenced very strongly by intonation and its position in a word or phrase. At the *top* of a staircase, **T** is pronounced T, as in *Ted* or *Italian;* a **T** in the *middle* of a staircase is pronounced **D**, as in *Beddy* or *Idaly*, whereas a **T** at the *bottom* of a staircase isn't pronounced at all, *ho⁽ᵗ⁾*. Look at *Italian* and *Italy* in the examples below. The **tæl** of *Italian* is at the top of the staircase and is strong: *Italian*. The **də** of *Italy* is in the middle and is weak: *Italy*. (See also Chapter 13.)

Exercise 4-1: Stressed and Unstressed T	Track 133

Repeat after me.

Italian	Italy
attack	attic
atomic	atom
photography	photograph

Exercise 4-2: Betty Bought a Bit of Better Butter	Track 134

In the sentence **Betty bought a bit of better butter**, *all of the Ts are in weak positions, so they all sound like soft Ds. Repeat the sentence slowly, word by word:* Beddy . . . badə . . . bidə . . . bedder . . . budder. *Feel the tip of your tongue flick across that area behind your top teeth. Think of the music of a cello again when you say,* **Betty bought a bit of better butter**.

Betty Bought a Bit of Better Butter	
Betty bought a bit of better butter,	Beddy bä də bihda bedder budder.
But, said she,	Bu(t), said she,
This butter's bitter.	This budder'z bidder.
If I put it in my batter,	If I püdi din my bædder,
It'll make my batter bitter.	Id'll make my bædder bidder.

If you speak any language—such as Spanish, Japanese, Hindi, Italian, or Dutch, among others—where your **R** touches behind the teeth, you are in luck with the American **T**. Just fix the association in your mind so that when you see a middle position **T**, you automatically give it your native **R** sound. Say, *Beri bara bira . . .* with your native accent. (*Not* if you are French, German, or Chinese!) Along with liaisons, the American **T** contributes a great deal to the smooth, relaxed sound of English. When you say a word like *atom,* imagine that you've been to the dentist and you're a little numb, or that you've had a couple of drinks, or maybe that you're very sleepy. You won't be wanting to use a lot of energy saying **æ•tom**, so just relax everything and say **adəm**, like the masculine name, **Adam**. It's a very smooth, fluid sound. Rather than saying, *BeTTy boughT a biT of beTTer buTTer,* which is physically more demanding, try, *Beddy bada bidda bedder budder.* It's easy because you really don't need much muscle tension to say it this way.

The staircase concept will help clarify the various **T** sounds. The American **T** can be a little tricky if you base your pronunciation on spelling. Here are six rules to guide you.

1. **T is T** at the beginning of a word or in a stressed syllable.
2. **T is D** in the middle of a word.
3. **T is Held** at the end of a word.
4. **T is Held before N** in *-tain* and *-ten* endings.
5. **T is Silent after N** with lax vowels.
6. **T is Held** before glottal consonants **w, r, k, g,** and **y.**

Exercise 4-3: Rule 1—Top of the Staircase   Track 135

When a T or a D is at the top of a staircase, in a stressed position, it should be a clear, popped sound.

1. In the beginning of a word, **T** is **t.**
   Ted took ten tomatoes.

2. With a stressed **T** and **ST, TS, TR, CT,** and **LT,** and sometimes **NT** combinations, **T** is **t.**
   *He was con**tent** with the **con**tract.*

T replaces **D** in the past tense, after an unvoiced consonant sound—**f, k, p, s, ch, sh, th**—(except T).

T: *laughed* **lœft,** *picked* **pikt,** *hoped* **houpt,** *raced* **rast,** *watched* **wächt,** *washed* **wäsht,** *unearthed* **uneartht**

D: *halved* **hœvd,** *rigged* **rigd,** *nabbed* **næbd,** *raised* **razd,** *judged* **j'jd,** *garaged* **garazhd,** *smoothed* **smoothd**
Exceptions: *wicked/***wikəd,** *naked/***nakəd,** *crooked/***krükəd,** etc.

Exercise 4-4: Rule 1—Top of the Staircase Practice   Track 136

Read the following sentences out loud. Make sure that the blue (stressed) Ts are sharp and clear.

1. It took Tim ten times to try the telephone.
2. Stop touching Ted's toes.
3. Turn toward Stella and study her contract together.
4. Control your tears.
5. It's Tommy's turn to tell the teacher the truth.

Exercise 4-5: Rule 2—Middle of the Staircase   Track 137

An unstressed T in the middle of a staircase between two vowel sounds should be pronounced as a soft D.

Betty bought a bit of better butter.	Beddy bädə bida bedder budder
Pat ought to sit on a lap.	pædädə sidänə læp

Read the following sentences out loud. Make sure that the blue (unstressed) Ts sound like a soft D.

1.	What a good **idea**.	wədə gudai **dee**yə
2.	Put it in a **bottle**.	püdidinə **bä**ddl

3.	Write it in a **letter**.	räididinə **led**dr
4.	Set it on the metal **gutter**.	sedidän thə medl **gə**ddr
5.	Put all the **data** in the **computer**.	püdäl the **dei**də in the c'm**pyu**dr
6.	Insert a quarter in the **meter**.	inserdə **kwor**der in the **mee**dr
7.	Get a better **water** heater.	gedə beddr **wä**dr heedr
8.	Let her put a **sweater** on.	ledr püdə **swe**der än
9.	**Betty**'s at a **meeting**.	**bed**dy's ædə **mee**ding
10.	It's getting hotter and **hotter**.	its gedding häddr•rən **hä**ddr
11.	**Patty** ought to write a better **letter**.	**pæ**ddy⁽ʸ⁾ädə ride a beddr **led**dr
12.	**Freida** had a **little** metal **bottle**.	**free**də hædə **lid**dl medl **bä**ddl

---

Exercise 4-6: Rule 3—Bottom of the Staircase 🔊 Track 138

T at the bottom of a staircase is in the held position. By held, I mean that the tongue is in the T position, but the air isn't released. To compare, when you say T as in Tom, there's a sharp burst of air over the tip of the tongue, and when you say Betty, there's a soft puff of air over the tip of the tongue. When you hold a T, as in hot, your tongue is in the position for T, but you keep the air in.

1. She hit the hot hut with her hat.
2. We went to that 'Net site to get what we needed.
3. Pat was quite right, wasn't she?
4. What? Put my hat back!
5. hot, late, fat, goat, hit, put, not, hurt, what, set, paint, wait, sit, dirt, note, fit, lot, light, suit, point, incident, tight

---

Exercise 4-7: Rule 4—"Held T" Before N 🔊 Track 139

*The "held T" is, strictly speaking, not really a T at all. Remember t and n are very close in the mouth (see Liaisons, Exercise 2-5). If you have an N immediately after a T, you don't pop the T—the tongue is in the T position—but you release the air with the N, **not** the T. There is no t and no ə. Make a special point of not letting your tongue release from the top of your mouth before you drop into the n; otherwise, bu(tt)on would sound like two words: but-ton. An unstressed T or TT followed by N is held. Read the following words and sentences out loud. Make sure that the blue Ts are held. Remember, there is no uh sound before the n.*

Note *Another point to remember is that you need a sharp upward sliding intonation up to the "held T," then a quick drop for the **N**. Just go to the T position and hum: writt•nnnn.*

	written	**t**		
written	ri⁽ᵗ⁾n			
			written	kitten
			sentence	patent
			forgotten	mutant
sentence	sen⁽ᵗ⁾ns		certain	latent
			curtain	mountain
		n	mitten	recently
lately	la⁽ᵗ⁾lee		Martin	lately
			bitten	partly
			button	frequently

1. He's **forgotten** the **carton** of satin **mittens**.
2. She'**s certain** that he has **written** it.
3. The cotton **curtain** is not in the **fountain**.
4. The **hikers** went in the **mountains**.
5. **Martin** has gotten a **kitten**.
6. **Students** study **Latin** in **Britain**.
7. **Whitney** has **a patent** on those **sentences**.
8. He has not **forgotten** what was **written** about the **mutant** on the **mountain**.
9. It's not **certain** that it was gotten from the **fountain**.
10. You need to put an **orange** cotton **curtain** on that **window**.
11. We like that certain **satin** better than the **carton** of cotton **curtains**.
12. The intercontinental **hotel** is in **Seattle**.
13. The frightened **witness** had forgotten the **important** written **message**.
14. The child wasn't **beaten** because he had **bitten** the **button**.

Exercise 4-8: Rule 5—The Silent T Track 140

T and N are so close in the mouth that the t can simply disappear. Repeat.

1.	**int**erview	**inn**erview
2.	**int**erface	**inn**erface
3.	**Int**ernet	**inn**ernet
4.	**int**erstate	**inn**erstate
5.	inter**rupt**	inner**rupt**
6.	inter**fere**	inner**fere**
7.	inter**active**	inner**active**
8.	inter**nati**onal	inner**nati**onal
9.	ad**van**tage	əd**væn**'j
10.	per**cen**tage	per**cen**'j
11.	**twen**ty	**twen**ny
12.	**print**out	**prin**nout or **prin**^dout
13.	**print**er	**prin**ner or **prin**^der
14.	**win**ter	**win**ner or **win**^der
15.	**ent**er	**enn**er or **en**^der
16.	**pen**tagon	**pen**nagon

Exercise 4-9: Rule 5—The Silent T Track 141

Read the following sentences out loud. Make sure that the blue highlighted Ts are silent.

1.	He had a great **int**erview.	he hædə gray ᵈ**inn**erview
2.	Try to en**t**er the infor**ma**tion.	trydə enner the infrmation
3.	Turn the **print**er on.	trn thə **prinn**erän
4.	Finish the **print**ing.	f 'n'sh thə **prin**ning
5.	She's at the in**t**erna**t**ional cen**t**er.	sheez' ⁽ᵗ⁾the⁽ʸ⁾inner**na**tional senner
6.	It's twen**t**y de**gree**s in Toron**t**o.	'ts twenny d'**gree**zin **trä**nno
7.	I don't under**stand** it.	I doe nənder **stæn** d't
8.	She in**vent**ed it in San**t**a **Mo**nica.	she⁽ʸ⁾in**ven**əd'din sænə **mä**nəkə
9.	He can't even **do** it.	he kæneevən **du**⁽ʷ⁾'t
10.	They don't even **want** it.	they doe neevən **wä**n't
11.	They won't ever **try**.	they woe never **try**
12.	What's the **point** of it?	w'ts the **poi** n'v't
13.	She's the in**t**ercon**t**i**nent**al represen**t**ative.	shez thee⁽ʸ⁾innercän⁽ᵗ⁾n•**nen**l repr'**zen**'d'v
14.	**Has**n't he?	**hæ**zə nee
15.	**Is**n't he?	**i**zə nee
16.	**Are**n't I?	**är** näi
17.	**Won**'t he?	**woe** nee
18.	**Does**n't he?	**də**zənee
19.	**Would**n't it?	**wü**dənit
20.	**Did**n't I?	**did**n•näi

Exercise 4-10: Rule 6—"Held T" Before Glottal Consonants Track 142

*Before a throat consonant, **T** is held by the back of the tongue. Repeat the following phrases.*

1. bright white	11. it can
2. white car	12. it runs
3. rent control	13. that we
4. quit claim	14. what we
5. get one	15. that one
6. what was	16. heat wave
7. that when	17. net worth
8. it will	18. but, yeah
9. not really	19. what could
10. not good	20. what would

Sometimes Americans will hear the expression **quit claim** as **quick claim**.

Here are some extremely common middle T combinations. Repeat after me:

	What	But	That
a	wədə	bədə	thədə
I	wədäi	bədäi	thədäi
I'm	wədäim	bədäim	thədäim
I've	wədäiv	bədäiv	thədäiv
if	wədif	bədif	thədif
it	wədit	bədit	thədit
it's	wədits	bədits	thədits
is	wədiz	bədiz	thədiz
isn't	wədiznᵗ	bədiznᵗ	thədiznᵗ
are	wədr	bədr	thədr
aren't	wədärnᵗ	bədärnᵗ	thədärnᵗ
he	wədee	bədee	thədee
he's	wədeez	bədeez	thədeez
her	wədr	bədr	thədr
you	wəchew	bəchew	thəchew
you'll	wəchül	bəchül	thəchül
you've	wəchoov	bəchoov	thəchoov
you're	wəchr	bəchr	thəchr

Repeat the following sentences.

1.	I don't know what it **means**.	I don⁽ᵗ⁾know wədit **meenz**
2.	But it **look**s like what I **need**.	bədi⁽ᵗ⁾**lük** sly kwədäi **need**
3.	But you **said** that you **wouldn't**.	bəchew **sed** thəchew **wüdnt**
4.	I **know** what you **think**.	I **know** wəchew **think**
5.	But I don't **think** that he **will**.	bədäi don⁽ᵗ⁾**think** thədee **will**
6.	He said that if **we can do** it, he'll **help**.	he sed the diff we k'n **do**⁽ʷ⁾it, hill **help**
7.	But isn't it **easier** this **way**?	bədizni **dee**zier thi sway?
8.	We **want** something that isn't **here**.	we **wänt** something thədiznᵗ **here**
9.	You'll **like** it, **but** you'll **regret** it **later**.	yül **lye** kit, bəchül r'**gre** dit **laydr**
10.	But he's not **right** for what I **want**.	bədeez nät **right** fr wədäi **wänt**
11.	It's **amazing** what you've **accomplished**.	its amazing wəchoovə**ccäm**plisht
12.	What if he **forgets**?	wədifee fr**gets**
13.	**OK**, but aren't you **missing** something?	**OK**, bədärnᵗ chew **miss**ing səmthing
14.	I think that he's **OK** now.	I think thədeez **OK** næo
15.	She **wanted** to, but her **car** broke down.	She **wän**əd to, bədr **cär** broke dæon
16.	We **think** that you're taking a **chance**.	We **think** thəchr taking a **chænce**
17.	They don't know what it's **about**.	They doe noe wədit sə**bæot**

This exercise is for the practice of the difference between words that end in either a vowel or a voiced consonant, which means that the vowel is lengthened or doubled. Therefore, these words are on a much larger, longer stairstep. Words that end in an unvoiced consonant are on a smaller, shorter stairstep. This occurs whether the vowel in question is tense or lax.

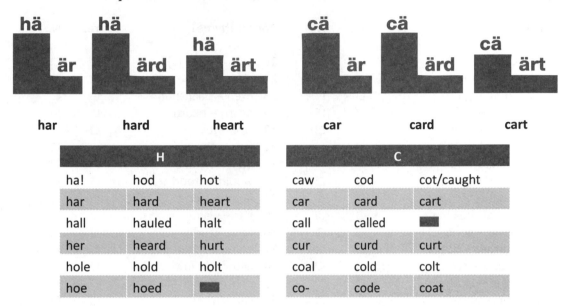

	H				C	
ha!	hod	hot		caw	cod	cot/caught
har	hard	heart		car	card	cart
hall	hauled	halt		call	called	▉
her	heard	hurt		cur	curd	curt
hole	hold	holt		coal	cold	colt
hoe	hoed	▉		co-	code	coat

Once again, go over the following familiar paragraph. First, find all the **T***s that are pronounced* **D** *(there are nine to thirteen here). Second, find all the held* **T***s (there are seven). The first one of each is marked for you in blue. (Check Answer Key on page 217.)*

Hello, **my** name is_____. I'm taking American **Accen(t)** Training. There's a **lo(t)** to **learn**, but[d] I **hope** to make it as **enjoyable** as possible. I should pick **up** on the American **intonation** pattern pretty **easily**, although the **only** way to **get** it is to **practice** all of the time. I use the **up** and down, or **peaks** and valleys, **intonation** more than I **used** to. I've been paying attention to **pitch**, **too**. It's like **walking** down a **stair**case. I've been **talking** to a lot of **Americans** lately, and they tell me that I'm **easier** to understand. **Any**way, I could go **on** and on, but the **important** thing is to **listen** well and sound **good**. **Well**, what do you **think**? **Do** I?

Exercise 4-15: Rhyme Time   Track 147

*Let's check your understanding of the differences between the **appearance** of English and the **pronunciation** of spoken American English. Say each pair of words out loud to yourself. If the two words rhyme, check the first box. If they don't rhyme, check the second box. (Check Answer Key, page 217. Unless you score 100% on your first try, spend at least an hour on the vowel and consonant overviews on pages ix–x).*

Does it rhyme?	Yes	No	Does it rhyme?	Yes	No
1. give – hive	☐	☐	26. goes – does (v)	☐	☐
2. have – save	☐	☐	27. glove – move	☐	☐
3. come – gum	☐	☐	28. oxen – dachshund	☐	☐
4. been – tin	☐	☐	29. beard – heard	☐	☐
5. know – now	☐	☐	30. sew – few	☐	☐
6. use (v) – choose	☐	☐	31. flew – through	☐	☐
7. monkey – donkey	☐	☐	32. little – middle	☐	☐
8. been* – seen	☐	☐	33. would – stood	☐	☐
9. great – heat	☐	☐	34. flood – stood	☐	☐
10. eight – height	☐	☐	35. has – was	☐	☐
11. done – gone	☐	☐	36. food – rude	☐	☐
12. mother – bother	☐	☐	37. enough – though	☐	☐
13. bruise – stews	☐	☐	38. allow – below	☐	☐
14. froze – clothes	☐	☐	39. debt – let	☐	☐
15. her – sure†	☐	☐	40. says – pays	☐	☐
16. where – were	☐	☐	41. dance – pants	☐	☐
17. hour – flower	☐	☐	42. eagle – legal	☐	☐
18. good – food	☐	☐	43. know – though	☐	☐
19. come – dome	☐	☐	44. thought – taught	☐	☐
20. turn – earn	☐	☐	45. laugh – half	☐	☐
21. beard – weird	☐	☐	46. first – worst	☐	☐
22. comb – tomb	☐	☐	47. full – wool	☐	☐
23. taste – waist	☐	☐	48. fool – wool	☐	☐
24. anger – danger	☐	☐	49. drawer – floor	☐	☐
25. cupboard – blubbered	☐	☐	50. maître d' – undersea	☐	☐

*been (typically pronounced *bin*) is also pronounced *ben* or *been* in various locales.

†sure (typically pronounced *shrr*) is also heard in some places as *shore, shoo-er,* or *shoo-wah.*

5

The American R

The tongue doesn't touch anywhere. Growl out the R in the throat.

American English, today—although continually changing—is made up of the sounds of the various people who have come to settle here from many countries. All of them have put in their linguistic two cents, the end result being that the easiest way to pronounce things has almost always been adopted as the most American. **R** is an exception, along with **L** and the sounds of **æ** and **th**, and is one of the most troublesome sounds for people to acquire. Not only is it difficult for adults learning the language, but also for American children, who pronounce it like a **W** or skip over it altogether and only pick it up after they've learned all the other sounds. (See also Chapter 1 and the Nationality Guides.)

THE INVISIBLE R

The trouble is that you can't see an **R** from the outside. With a **P**, for instance, you can see when people put their lips together and pop out a little puff. With **R**, however, everything takes place behind almost closed lips—back down in the throat—and who can tell what the tongue is doing? It is really hard to tell what's going on if, when someone speaks, you can only hear the *err* sound, especially if you're used to making an **R** by touching your tongue to the ridge behind your teeth. So, what should your tongue be doing? This technique can help you visualize the correct tongue movements in pronouncing the **R**.

1. Hold your hand out flat, with the palm up, slightly dropping the back end of it. That's basically the position your tongue is in when you say *ah ä*, so your flat hand will represent this sound.
2. Now, to go from *ah* to the *er*, take your fingers and curl them into a tight fist. Again, your tongue should follow that action. The sides of your tongue should come up a bit, too. When the air passes over that hollow in the middle of your tongue, that's what creates the *er* sound.

Try it using both your hand and tongue simultaneously. Say *ah,* with your throat open (and your hand flat), then curl your tongue up (and your fingers) and say *errr.* The tip of the tongue should be aimed at a middle position in the mouth, but never touching, and your throat should relax and expand. **R**, like **L**, has a slight schwa in it. This is what pulls the *er* down so far back in your throat.

Another way to get to *er* is to put a spoon on your tongue and go from the *ee* sound and slide your tongue straight back like a collapsing accordion, letting the two sides of your tongue touch the insides of your molars; the tip of the tongue, however, again, should not touch anything. Now from *ee,* pull your tongue back toward the center of your throat and pull the sound down into your throat:

> ee ▶ ee ▶ eeeer

Since the **R** is produced in the throat, let's link it with other throat sounds.

Exercise 5-1: R Location Practice Track 149

Repeat after me.

g, gr, greek, green, grass, grow, crow, core, cork, coral, cur, curl, girl, gorilla, her, erg, error, mirror, were, war, gore, wrong, wringer, church, pearl

While you're perfecting your **R**, you might want to rush to it, and in doing so, neglect the preceding vowel. There are certain vowels that you can neglect, but there are others that demand their full sound. We're going to practice the ones that require you to keep that clear sound before you add an **R**.

Exercise 5-2: Double Vowel with R Track 150

Refer to the subsequent lists of sounds and words as you work through each of the directions that follow them. Repeat each sound, first the vowel and then the ər, and each word in columns 1 to 3. We will read all the way across.

1	2	3
ä + ər	hä•ərd	hard
e + ər	he•ər	here
ɛ + ər	shɛ•ər	share
o + ər	mo•ər	more
ər + ər	wər•ər	were

hä

ə rd

We will next read column 3 only; try to keep that doubled sound, but let the vowel flow smoothly into the **ər**; imagine a double stairstep that cannot be avoided. Don't make them two staccato sounds, though, like **ha•rd**. Instead, flow them smoothly over the double stairstep: *Hääärrrd.*

Of course, they're not *that* long; this is an exaggeration, and you're going to shorten them up once you get better at the sound. When you say the first one, *hard,* to get your jaw open for the **hä**, imagine that you are getting ready to bite into an apple: **hä**. Then, for the *er* sound, you would bite into it: **hä•erd**, *hard.*

▶ Practice five times on your own.

From a spelling standpoint, the American **R** can be a little difficult to figure out. With words like *where* **wɛər** and *were* **wər**, it's confusing to know which one has two different vowel sounds *(where)* and which one has just the **ər** *(were)*. When there is a full vowel, you must make sure to give it its complete sound and not chop it short, **wɛ + ər**.

For words with only the schwa + R **ər**, don't try to introduce another vowel sound before the **ər**, *regardless of spelling.* The following words, for example, do not have any other vowel sounds in them.

Looks like	Sounds like
word	wərd
hurt	hərt
girl	gərl
pearl	pərl

The following exercise will further clarify this for you.

Exercise 5-3: How to Pronounce Troublesome Rs	Track 151

*The following seven **R** sounds, which are represented by the ten words, give people a lot of trouble, so we're going to work with them and make them easy for you. Repeat.*

1.	were	wər•ər
2.	word/whirred	wər•ərd
3.	whirl	wərrul
4.	world/whirled	were rolled
5.	wore/war	woər
6.	whorl	worul
7.	where/wear	wɛər

1. *Were* is pronounced with a doubled **ər**: **wər•ər**

2. *Word* is also doubled, but after the second **ər** you're going to put your tongue in place for the **D** and hold it there, keeping all the air in your mouth, opening your throat to give it that full-voiced quality (imagine yourself puffing your throat out like a bullfrog): **wərərd**, *word*. Not **wərd**, which is too short. Not **wordə**, which is too strong at the end. But **wər•ər**[d] *word*.

3. In *whirl* the **R** is followed by **L**. The **R** is in the throat and the back of the tongue stays down because, as we've practiced, **L** starts with the schwa, but the tip of the tongue comes up for the **L**: **wər•rə•lə**, *whirl*.

4. *World/whirled,* like 5 and 7, has two spellings (and two different meanings, of course). You're going to do the same thing as for *whirl,* but you're going to add that voiced **D** at the end, holding the air in: **wər•rəl**[d], *world/ whirled.* It should sound almost like two words: *wére rolled.*

5. Here, you have an **o** sound in either spelling before the **ər**: **wo•ər,** *wore/war.*

6. For *whorl,* you're going to do the same thing as in 5, but you're going to add a schwa + **L** at the end: **wo•ərəl,** *whorl.*

7. This sound is similar to 5, but you have **ɛ** before the **ər**: **wɛ•ər,** *where/wear.*

Track 152

The following words are typical in that they are spelled one way and pronounced in another way. The *ar* combination frequently sounds like **ɛr**, as in *embarrass* **embɛrəs**. This sound is particularly clear on the West Coast. On the East Coast, you may hear **embærəs**.

Repeat after me.

			Common Combinations
embarrass	stationary	Larry	
vocabulary	care	Sarah	
parent	carry	narrate	ar
parallel	carriage	guarantee	par
paragraph	marriage	larynx	bar
para–	maritime	laryngitis	mar
parrot	barrier	necessary	lar
apparent	baritone	itinerary	kar
parish	Barron's	said	war
Paris	library	says	har
area	character	transparency	sar
aware	Karen	dictionary	nar
compare	Harry	many	gar
imaginary	Mary	any	rar

Don't think about spelling here. Just pronounce each column of words as the heading indicates.

	ər	är	ɛr	or	eer	æwr
1.	earn	art	air	or	ear	hour
2.	hurt	heart	hair	horse	here	how're
3.	heard	hard	haired	horde	here's	■
4.	pert	part	pair	pour	peer	power
5.	word	■	where	war	we're	■
6.	a word	■	aware	award	a weird	■
7.	work	■	wear	warm	weird	■
8.	first	far	fair	four	fear	flower
9.	firm	farm	fairy	form	fierce	■
10.	rather	cathartic	there	Thor	theory	11th hour
11.	murky	mar	mare	more	mere	■
12.	spur	spar	spare	sport	spear	■
13.	sure	sharp	share	shore	shear	shower
14.	churn	char	chair	chore	cheer	chowder
15.	gird	guard	scared	gored	geared	Gower
16.	cur	car	care	core	kir	cower
17.	turtle	tar	tear	tore	tear	tower
18.	dirt	dark	dare	door	dear	dour
19.	stir	star	stair	store	steer	■
20.	sir	sorry	Sarah	sore	seer	sour
21.	burn	barn	bear	born	beer	bower

Repeat after me.

The Hurly Burly Mirror Store at Vermont and Beverly featured hundreds of first-rate mirrors. There were several mirrors on the chest of drawers,* and the largest one was turned toward the door in order to make the room look bigger. One of the girls who worked there was concerned that a bird might get hurt by hurtling into its own reflection. She learned by trial and error** how to preserve both the mirrors and the birds. Her earnings were proportionately increased at the mirror store to reflect her contribution to the greater good.
*chesta drorz
**tryla nerr'r

✗ Practice reading out loud three times on your own.

Go through our familiar paragraph and find all the **R** *sounds. The first one is marked for you in blue.*

Hello, my name is _____. I'm taking American **Accent** Training. There's a **lot** to **learn**, but **I hope** to make it as **enjoyable** as possible. I should pick **up** on the American **intonation** pattern pretty **easily**, although the **only** way to **get** it is to **practice** all of the time. I use the **up** and down, or **peaks** and valleys, **intonation** more than I **used** to. I've been paying attention to **pitch, too**. It's like **walking** down a **stair**case. I've been **talking** to a lot of **Americans** lately, and they tell me that I'm **easier** to understand. **Any**way, I could go **on** and on, but the **important** thing is to **listen** well and sound **good. Well,** what do you **think**? **Do** I?

▶ Answer Key on page 217.

> One of the best ways to get the **R** is to literally growl.
> Say **grrrr** as if you were a wild animal growling in the woods.

VOICED CONSONANTS AND REDUCED VOWELS

Track 157

The strong intonation in American English creates certain tendencies in your spoken language. Here are four consistent conditions that are a result of intonation's tense peaks and relaxed valleys:

1. Reduced vowels
You were introduced to reduced vowels in Chapter 1. They appear in the valleys that are formed by the strong peaks of intonation. The more you reduce the words in the valleys, the smoother and more natural your speech will sound. A characteristic of reduced vowels is that your throat muscles should be very relaxed. This will allow the unstressed vowels to reduce toward the schwa. Neutral vowels take less energy and muscularity to produce than tense vowels. For example, the word *unbelievable* should only have one hard vowel: **ənbəlēvəbəl**.

2. Voiced consonants

The mouth muscles are relaxed to create a voiced sound like **z** or **d**. For unvoiced consonants, such as **s** or **t**, they are sharp and tense. Relaxing your muscles will simultaneously reduce your vowels and voice your consonants. Think of *voiced consonants* as *reduced consonants.* Both reduced consonants and reduced vowels are unconsciously preferred by a native speaker of American English. This explains why **T** so frequently becomes **D** and **S** becomes **Z**: *Get it is to . . .* **gedidizdə.**

3. Like sound with like sound

It's not easy to change horses midstream, so when you have a voiced consonant let the consonant that follows it be voiced as well. In the verb *used* **yuzd**, for example, the **S** is really a **Z**, so it is followed by **D**. The phrase *used to* **yus tu**, on the other hand, has a real **S**, so it is followed by **T**. Vowels are, by definition, voiced. So when one is followed by a common, reducible word, it will change that word's first sound—like the preposition *to,* which will change to **də.**

> The only way to get it is to practice all of the time.
> They only wei•də•geddidiz•də•practice all of the time.

Again, this will take time. In the beginning, work on recognizing these patterns when you hear them. When you are confident that you understand the structure beneath these sounds and you can intuit where they belong, you can start to try them out. It's not advisable to memorize one reduced word and stick it into an otherwise overpronounced sentence. It would sound strange.

4. R'læææææææææx

You've probably noticed that the preceding three conditions, as well as other areas that we've covered, such as liaisons and the schwa, have one thing in common—the idea that *it's physically easier this way.* This is one of the most remarkable characteristics of American English. You need to relax your mouth and throat muscles (except for **æ**, **ä**, and other tense vowels) and let the sounds flow smoothly out. If you find yourself tensing up, pursing your lips, or tightening your throat, you are going to strangle and lose the sound you are pursuing. Relax, relax, relax.

6
The El

The tongue tip touches the ridge, even at the end of a word.

This chapter discusses the sound of **L** (not to be confused with that of the American **R**, which was covered in the last chapter). We'll approach this sound first by touching on the difficulties it presents to foreign speakers of English, and next by comparing **L** to the related sounds of **T**, **D**, and **N**. (See also Chapter 13, and for related sounds see Chapters 4 and 16.)

L AND FOREIGN SPEAKERS OF ENGLISH

The English **L** is usually no problem at the beginning or in the middle of a word. The native language of some people, however, causes them to make their English **L** much too short. At the end of a word, the **L** is especially noticeable if it is either missing (Chinese) or too short (Spanish). In addition, most people consider the **L** as a simple consonant. This can also cause a lot of trouble. Thus, two things are at work here: location of language sounds in the mouth and the complexity of the **L** sound.

Location of Language in the Mouth

The sounds of many Romance languages are generally located far forward in the mouth. My French teacher told me that if I couldn't see my lips when I spoke French—it wasn't French! Spanish is sometimes even called the smiling language. Chinese, on the other hand, is similar to American English in that it is mostly produced far back in the mouth. The principal difference is that English also requires clear use of the tongue's tip, a large component of the sound of **L**.

The Compound Sound of L

The **L** is not a simple consonant; it is a compound made up of a vowel and a consonant. Like the æ sound (discussed in Chapter 3), the sound of **L** is a combination of ə and *L*. The ə, being a reduced vowel sound, is created in the throat, but the *L* part requires a clear movement of the tongue. First, the tip must touch behind the teeth. (This part is simple enough.) But then, the back of the tongue must drop down and back for the continuing schwa sound. Especially at the end of a word, Spanish-speaking people tend to leave out the schwa and shorten the **L**, and Chinese speakers usually leave it off entirely.

One way to avoid the pronunciation difficulty of a final **L**, as in *call*, is to make a liaison when the next word begins with a vowel. For example, if you want to say *I have to call on my friend,* let the liaison do your work for you; say *I have to kälän my friend.*

L Compared with T, D, and N

When you learn to pronounce the **L** correctly, you will feel its similarity with **T**, **D**, and **N**. Actually, the tongue is positioned in the same place in the mouth for all four sounds—behind the teeth. The difference is in how and where the air comes out. (See the drawings in Exercise 6-1.)

T AND D

The sound of both **T** and **D** is produced by allowing a puff of air to come out over the tip of the tongue.

N

The sound of **N** is nasal. The tongue completely blocks all air from leaving through the mouth, allowing it to come out only through the nose. You should be able to feel the edges of your tongue touching your teeth when you say *nnn*.

L

With **L**, the tip of the tongue is securely touching the roof of the mouth behind the teeth, but the sides of the tongue are dropped down and tensed. This is where **L** is different from **N**. With **N**, the tongue is relaxed and covers the entire area around the back of the teeth so that no air can come out. With **L**, the tongue is very tense, and the air comes out around its sides.

At the beginning, it's helpful to exaggerate the position of the tongue. Look at yourself in the mirror as you stick out the tip of your tongue between your front teeth. With your tongue in this position, say *el* several times. Then, try saying it with your tongue behind your teeth. This sounds complicated, but it is easier to do than to describe. (You can practice this again later with Exercise 6-3.) Our first exercise, however, must focus on differentiating the sounds.

Exercise 6-1: Sounds Comparing L with T, D, and N   Track 160

For this exercise, concentrate on the different ways in which the air comes out of the mouth when producing each sound of L, T, D, and N. Look at the drawings included here to see the correct position of the tongue. Instructions for reading the groups of words listed in Exercise 6-2 are given after the words.

T/D Plosive
A puff of air comes out over the tip of the tongue. The tongue is somewhat tense.

N
Nasal
Air comes out through the nose.
The tongue is completely relaxed.

L
Lateral
Air flows around the sides of the tongue.
The tongue is very tense.

The lips are *not* rounded!

Repeat after me, first down and then across.

1.	At the beginning of a word			
	law	gnaw	taw	daw
	low	know	toe	dough
	lee	knee	tea	D
2.	In the middle of a word			
	belly	Benny		Betty
	caller	Conner		cotter
	alley	Annie's		at ease
3.	At the end of a word			
A	hole	hold	hone	hoed
	call	called	con	cod
B	fill	full	fool	fail
	fell	feel	fuel	furl

▶ Look at group 3, B. This exercise has three functions:

1. Practice final *els.*
2. Review vowel sounds.
3. Review the same words with the staircase.

Note *Notice that each word has a tiny schwa after the* **el.** *This is to encourage your tongue to be in the right position to give your words a "finished" sound. Exaggerate the final* **el** *and its otherwise inaudible schwa.*

▶ Repeat the last group of words.

 Once you are comfortable with your tongue in this position, let it just languish there while you continue vocalizing, which is what a native speaker does.

▶ Repeat again: fillll, fullll, foollll, faillll, feellll, fuellll, furllll

WHAT ARE ALL THOSE EXTRA SOUNDS I'M HEARING?

Track 162

I hope that you're asking a question like this about now. Putting all of those short little words on a staircase will reveal exactly how many extra sounds you have to put in to make it "sound right." For example, if you were to pronounce *fail* as **fāl**, the sound is too abbreviated for the American ear—we need to hear the full **fāyəlᵊ**.

Repeat after me.

1 fill fih
2 full fü
3 fool foo
4 fail fay
5 fell feh
6 feel fee
7 fuel fyoo
8 furl fr

Exercise 6-4: Many Final Els   🔊 Track 164

This time, simply hold the L sound extra long. Repeat after me.

1 fill fih
2 full fü
3 fool foo
4 fail fay
5 fell feh
6 feel fee
7 fuel fyoo
8 furl fr

Exercise 6-5: Liaise the Ls   🔊 Track 165

As you work with the following exercise, here are two points you should keep in mind. When a word ends with an L sound, either (a) connect it to the next word if you can or (b) add a slight schwa for an exaggerated lə sound. For example:

(a) enjoyable as	enjoyəbələz
(b) possible	pasəbələ

Note *Although (a) is really the way you want to say it, (b) is an interim measure to help you put your tongue in the right place. It would sound strange if you were to always add the slight schwa. Once you can feel where you want your tongue to be, hold it there while you continue to make the L sound. Here are three examples:*

Call		
caw	kä	(incorrect)
call	cälə	(understandable)
call	källl	(correct)

*You can do the same thing to stop an **N** from becoming an **NG**.*

Con		
cong	käng	(incorrect)
con	känə	(understandable)
con	kännn	(correct)

Exercise 6-6: Finding L Sounds　　　　　　　 Track 166

Find and mark all the L sounds in the familiar paragraph below; the first one is marked for you. There are seventeen of them; five are silent. (Answer Key on page 218.)

Hello, **my** name is _____. I'm taking American **Accent** Training. There's a **lot** to **learn**, but I **hope** to make it as **enjoyable** as possible. I should pick **up** on the American **intonation** pattern pretty **easily**, although the **only** way to **get** it is to **practice** all of the time. **I use** the **up** and down, or **peaks** and valleys, **intonation** more than I **used** to. I've been paying attention to **pitch, too**. It's like **walking** down a **stair**case. I've been **talking** to **a** lot of **Americans** lately, and they tell me that I'm **easier** to understand. **Any**way, I could go **on** and on, but the **important** thing is to **listen** well and sound **good**. **Well**, what do you **think**? **Do** I?

Exercise 6-7: Silent Ls　　　　　　　 Track 167

Once you've found all the L sounds, the good news is that very often you don't even have to pronounce them. Read the following list of words after me.

1.	would	could	should
2.	chalk	talk	walk
3.	calm	palm	psalm
4.	already	alright	almond
5.	although	almost	always
6.	salmon	alms	Albany
7.	folk	caulk	polka
8.	half	calf	behalf
9.	yolk	colonel	Lincoln

Track 168

Before reading about **Little Lola** in the next exercise, I'm going to get off the specific subject of **L** for the moment to talk about learning in general. Frequently, when you have some difficult task to do, you either avoid it or do it with dread. I'd like you to take the opposite point of view. For this exercise, you're going to completely focus on the thing that's most difficult: leaving your tongue attached to the top of your mouth. And rather than saying, "Oh, here comes an **L**, I'd better do something with my tongue," just leave your tongue attached *all through the entire paragraph!*

Remember our clenched-teeth reading of **What Must the Sun Above Wonder About?** (in Chapter 3)? Well, it's time for us to make weird sounds again.

Exercise 6-8: Hold Your Tongue **Track 169**

You and I are going to read with our tongues firmly held at the roofs of our mouths. If you want, hold a clean dime there with the tongue's tip; the dime will let you know when you have dropped your tongue because it will fall out. (Do not use candy; it will hold itself there since wet candy is sticky.) If you prefer, you can read with your tongue between your teeth instead of the standard behind-the-teeth position, and use a small mirror. Remember that with this technique you can actually see your tongue disappear as you hear your ʟ sounds drop off.

It's going to sound ridiculous, of course, and nobody would ever intentionally sound like this, but no one will hear you practice. You don't want to sound like this: llllllllll. Force your tongue to make all the various vowels in spite of its position. Let's go.

Leave a little for Lola!

Exercise 6-9: Little Lola **Track 170**

Now that we've done this, instead of ʟ being a hard letter to pronounce, it's the easiest one because the tongue is stuck in that position. Practice the reading on your own, again, with your tongue stuck to the top of your mouth. Read the following paragraph after me with your tongue in the normal position. Use good, strong intonation. Follow my lead as I start dropping ʜ's here.

Little Lola felt left out in life. She told herself that luck controlled her and she truly believed that only by loyally following an exalted leader could she be delivered from her solitude. Unfortunately, she learned a little late that her life was her own to deal with. When she realized it, she was already eligible for Social Security and she had lent her lifelong earnings to a lowlife in Long Beach. She lay on her linoleum and slid along the floor in anguish. A little later, she leapt up and laughed. She no longer longed for a leader to tell her how to live her life. Little Lola was finally all well.

Track 171

In our next paragraph about **Thirty Little Turtles,** we deal with another aspect of **L**, namely consonant clusters. When you have a *dl* combination, you need to apply what you learned about liaisons and the American **T** as well as the **L**.

Since the two sounds are located in a similar position in the mouth, you know that they are going to be connected, right? You also know that all of these middle **T**s are going to be pronounced **D**, and that you're going to leave the tongue stuck to the top of your mouth. That may leave you wondering: Where is the air to escape? The **L** sound is what determines that. For the **D**, you hold the air in, the same as for a final **D**; then for the **L**, you release it around the sides of the tongue. Let's go through the steps before proceeding to our next exercise.

Exercise 6-10: Dull versus –dle **Track 172**

Repeat after me.

laid   Don't pop the final **D** sound.

ladle   Segue gently from the **D** to the **L**, with a small schwa in-between. Leave your tongue touching behind the teeth and just drop the sides to let the air pass out.

lay dull   Here, your tongue can drop between the **D** and the **L**.

To hear the difference between dəl and dəᵊl, contrast the sentences, *Don't lay dull tiles* and *Don't ladle tiles*.

lay dull

lay **də**

ladle

lay

Exercise 6-11: Final L Practice 🔊 **Track 173**

Repeat the following lists.

	üll	äll	æwl	ell	ale	oll	eel	dl
1.	bull	ball	bowel	bell	bale	bowl	Beal	bottle
2.	▬	hall	howl	hell	hail	hole	heel	huddle
3.	▬	hauled	howled	held	hailed	hold	healed	hurtle
4.	pull	pall	Powell	pell	pail	pole	peel	poodle
5.	wool	wall	▬	well	whale	whole	wheel	wheedle
6.	full	fall	foul	fell	fail	foal	feel	fetal
7.	Schultz	shawl	▬	shell	shale	shoal	she'll	shuttle
8.	tulle	tall	towel	tell	tale	toll	teal	turtle
9.	▬	vault	vowel	veldt	veil	vole	veal	vital
10.	you'll	yawl	yowl	yell	Yale	▬	yield	yodel
11.	▬	call	cowl	Kelly	kale	cold	keel	coddle

Exercise 6-12: Thirty Little Turtles in a Bottle of Bottled Water 🔊 **Track 174**

Repeat the following paragraph, focusing on the consonant + ᵊl combinations. (This paragraph was quoted in the New York Times *by Pulitzer Prize–winning journalist, Thomas Friedman.)*

Thrdee Liddəl Terdəl Zinə Bäddələ Bäddəl Dwäder

A bottle of bottled water held 30 little turtles. It didn't matter that each turtle had to rattle a metal ladle in order to get a little bit of noodles, a total turtle delicacy. The problem was that there were many turtle battles for the less than oodles of noodles. The littlest turtles always lost, because every time they thought about grappling with the haggler turtles, their little turtle minds boggled and they only caught a little bit of noodles.

Exercise 6-13: Speed-reading Track 175

We've already practiced strong intonation, so now we'll just pick up the speed. First, I'm going to read our familiar paragraph as fast as I can. Subsequently, you'll practice on your own, and then we'll go over it together, sentence by sentence, to let you practice reading very fast, right after me. By then you will have more or less mastered the idea, so record yourself reading really fast and with very strong intonation. Listen back to see if you sound more fluent. Listen as I read.

Hello, my name is _____. I'm taking American **Accent** Training. There's a **lot** to **learn**, but I **hope** to make it as **enjoyable** as possible. I should pick **up** on the American **intonation** pattern pretty **easily**, although the **only** way to **get** it is to **practice** all of the time. I use the **up** and down, or **peaks** and valleys, **intonation** more than I **used** to. I've been paying attention to **pitch, too**. It's like **walking** down **a stair**case. I've been **talking** to a lot of **Americans** lately, and they tell me that I'm **easier** to under**stand. Any**way, I could go **on** and on, but the **important** thing is to **listen** well and sound **good. Well**, what do you **think**? **Do** I?

▶ Practice speed-reading on your own five times.
▶ Repeat each sentence after me.
▶ Record yourself speed-reading with strong intonation.

Exercise 6-14: Tandem Reading Track 176

The last reading that I'd like you to do is one along with me. Up to now, I have read first and you have repeated in the pause that followed. Now, however, I would like you to read along at exactly the same time that I read so that we sound like one person reading. Read along with me.

There's a self-help group for people who talk too much.

On and On Anon

7

Reduced Sounds

Unstressed words have reduced vowels.

THE DOWN SIDE OF INTONATION

Track 177

Reduced sounds are all those extra sounds created by an absence of lip, tongue, jaw, and throat movement. They are a principal function of intonation and are truly indicative of the American sound. (See also Chapter 1.)

Reduced Sounds Are "Valleys"

American intonation is made up of peaks and valleys—tops of staircases and bottoms of staircases. To have strong *peaks,* you will have to develop deep *valleys.* These deep valleys should be filled with all kinds of reduced vowels, one in particular—the completely neutral *schwa.* Ignore spelling. Since you probably first became acquainted with English through the printed word, this is going to be quite a challenge. The position of a syllable is more important than spelling as an indication of correct pronunciation. For example, the words *photograph* and *photography* each have two **O**'s and an **A**. The first word is stressed on the first syllable, so **pho**tograph sounds like *fod'græf.* The second word is stressed on the second syllable, *photography,* so the word comes out *f'tahgr'fee.* You can see here that their spelling doesn't tell you how they sound. Word stress or intonation will determine the pronunciation. Work on listening to words. Concentrate on hearing the pure sounds, not on trying to make the word fit a familiar spelling. Otherwise, you will be taking the long way around and giving yourself both a lot of extra work and an accent!

Syllables that are perched atop a peak or a staircase are strong sounds; that is, they maintain their original pronunciation. On the other hand, syllables that fall in the valleys or on a lower stairstep are weak sounds; thus, they are reduced. Some vowels are reduced completely to schwas, a very relaxed sound, while others are only toned down. In the following exercises, we will be dealing with these "toned down" sounds.

In the introduction ("Read This First," page iv) I talked about *overpronouncing.* This section will handle that overpronunciation. You're going to skim over words; you're going to dash through certain sounds. Your peaks are going to be quite strong, but your valleys, blurry—a very intuitive aspect of intonation that this practice will help you develop.

Articles (such as *the, a*) are usually very reduced sounds. Before a consonant, *the* and *a* are both schwa sounds, which are reduced. Before a vowel, however, you'll notice a change—the schwa of *the* turns into a long *e* plus a connecting ⁽ʸ⁾—**Th'** *book* changes to *thee*⁽ʸ⁾*only book; A hat* becomes *a nugly hat.* The article *a* becomes *an.* Think of **ə•nornj** rather than *an orange;* **ə•nopening, ə•neye, ə•nimaginary animal.**

Listen and repeat.

Consonants			Vowels	
the man	a girl	thee⁽ʸ⁾apple	an orange	ə•nornj
the best	a banana	thee⁽ʸ⁾egg	an opening	ə•nop'ning
the last one	a computer	thee⁽ʸ⁾easy way	an interview	ə•ninerview

Track 179

When you used the rubber band with *Däg zeet bounz* and when you built your own sentence, you saw that intonation reduces the unstressed words. Intonation is the peak and reduced sounds are the valleys. In the beginning, you should make extra-high peaks and long, deep valleys. When you are not sure, reduce. In the following exercise, work with this idea. Small words such as articles, prepositions, pronouns, conjunctions, relative pronouns, and auxiliary verbs are lightly skimmed over and almost not pronounced.

You have seen how intonation changes the meaning in words and sentences. Inside a one-syllable word, it distinguishes between a final voiced or unvoiced consonant *be-ed* and *bet.* Inside a longer word, *éunuch* versus *unique,* the pronunciation and meaning change in terms of vocabulary. In a sentence (He seems **nice**; He **seems** nice.), the meaning changes in terms of intent.

In a sentence, intonation can also make a clear vowel sound disappear. When a vowel is *stressed,* it has a certain sound; when it is *not stressed,* it usually sounds like *uh,* pronounced ə. Small words like **to**, **at**, or **as** are usually not stressed, so the vowel disappears.

Read aloud from the right-hand column. The intonation is marked for you.

To	Looks Like . . .	Sounds Like . . .
The preposition **to** usually reduces so much that it's like dropping the vowel.	today	t'**day**
	tonight	t'**night**
	tomorrow	t'**mä**rou
	to work	t'**wrk**
	to school	t' **school**
	to the store	t' th' **store**
Use a **t'** or **tə** sound to replace **to**.	We have to go now.	we hæftə **go** næo
	He went to work.	he wentə **work**
	They hope to find it.	they houptə **fine** dit
	I can't wait to find out.	äi **cæn**⁽ᵗ⁾wai⁽ᵗ⁾tə fine **dæot**
	We don't know what to do.	we dont know w'⁽ᵗ⁾t' **do**
	Don't jump to conclusions.	dont j'm t' c'n**cloo**zh'nz
	To be or not to be . . .	t'**bee**⁽ʸ⁾r **nät** t' bee
	He didn't get to go.	he din ge⁽ᵗ⁾tə **gou**

Exercise 7-2: Reduced Sounds *continued*　　　🔊 **Track 180**

To (continued)	Looks Like . . .	Sounds Like . . .
If that same **to** follows a vowel sound, it will become **d'** or **də**.	He told me to help.	he told meedə **help**
	She told you to get it.	she tol joodə **geddit**
	I go to work	ai goudə **wrk**
	at a quarter to two	ædə kworder də **two**
	The only way to get it is . . .	thee[(y)]**only** waydə **ge**ddidiz
	You've got to pay to get it.	yoov gäddə paydə **geddit**
	We plan to do it.	we plæn də **do** it
	Let's go to lunch.	lets goudə **lunch**
	The score was 4–6.	th' score w'z for də **six**
	It's the only way to do it.	its thee[(y)]**ounly** weidə **do**[(w)]'t
	So to speak . . .	soda **speak**
	I don't know how to say it.	äi don[(t)]know hæwdə **say**[(y)]it
	Go to page 8.	goudə pay **jate**
	Show me how to get it.	show me hæodə **ge**ddit
	You need to know when to do it.	you nee[(d)]də nou wendə **do**[(w)]it
	Who's to blame?	hooz də **blame**

At		
At is just the opposite of **to**. It's a small grunt followed by a reduced **t**.	We're at home.	wir[ə]t **home**
	I'll see you at lunch.	äiyəl see you[(w)]ət **lunch**
	Dinner's at five.	d'nnerz[ə(t)] **five**
	Leave them at the door.	leev[ə]m[ə(t)]th[ə] **door**
	The meeting's at one.	th' meeding z't **w'n**
	He's at the post office.	heez[ə(t)]the **pouss**däff[ə]s
	They're at the bank.	thɛr[ə(t)]th' **bænk**
	I'm at school.	äim[ə(t)]**school**
If **at** is followed by a vowel sound, it will become **'d** or **əd**.	I'll see you at eleven.	äiyəl see you[(w)]ədə **lɛv'n**
	He's at a meeting.	heez' də **meeding**
	She laughed at his idea.	she **læf** dədi zy **deey**ə
	One at a time	wənədə **time**
	We got it at an auction.	we gädidədə **näk**sh'n
	The show started at eight.	th' **show** stardədə **date**
	The dog jumped out at us.	th' däg jump **dæo** dədəs
	I was at a friend's house.	äi w'z'd' **frenz** hæos

	Looks Like . . .	Sounds Like . . .
It	Can you do it?	k'niu **do**^{(w)'}t
It and at sound the same in context—**'t**	Give it to me.	g'v'^(t)t' me
	Buy it tomorrow.	bäi^{(y)ə(t)}t' **märrow**
	It can wait.	't c'n **wait**
	Read it twice.	ree d'^(t)**twice**
	Forget about it!	frgedd' bæodit
. . . and they both turn to **'d** or **əd** between vowels or voiced consonants.	Give it a try.	gividə **try**
	Let it alone.	ledidə **lone**
	Take it away.	tay kida **way**
	I got it in London.	äi gädidin **l'nd**'n
	What is it about?	w'd'z'd'**bæot**
	Let's try it again.	lets try'd' **gen**
	Look! There it is!	**lük** there'd'**z**
For	This is for you.	th's'z fr **you**
	It's for my friend.	ts fr my **friend**
	A table for four, please.	ə table fr **four**, pleeze
	We planned it for later.	we **plan** dit fr **layd'r**
	For example, for instance	fregg **zæmple frin** st'nss
	What is this for?	w'd'z **this** for *(for is not reduced at*
	What did you do it for?	w'j' **do**^(w)it for *the end of a sentence)*
	Who did you get it for?	hoojya **ged**dit for
From	It's from the IRS.	ts frm thee^(y)äi^(y)ä **ress**
	I'm from Arkansas.	äim fr'm **ärk'** nsä
	There's a call from Bob.	therzə **cäll** fr'm **Bäb**
	This letter's from Alaska!	this **ledderz** frəmə **læskə**
	Who's it from?	hoozit **frəm**
	Where are you from?	wher'r you **frəm**
In	It's in the bag.	tsin thə **bæg**
	What's in it?	w'**ts**'n't
	I'll be back in a minute.	äiyəl be **bæk**'nə **m'n't**
	This movie? Who's in it?	this **movie** . . . hooz'n't
	Come in.	c '**min**
	He's in America.	heez'nə **mɛrəkə**

	Looks Like . . .	Sounds Like . . .
An	He's an American.	heez'nə **mɛrəkən**
	I got an A in English.	äi gäddə **nay** ih **nin**glish
	He got an F in Algebra.	hee gäddə **neffinæl** jəbrə
	He had an accident.	he hædə **næk**səd'nt
	We want an orange.	we want'n **nornj**
	He didn't have an excuse.	he didnt hævə neks **kyooss**
	I'll be there in an instant.	äi⁽ʸ⁾'l be there inə **nin**stnt
	It's an easy mistake to make.	itsə **nee**zee m' stake t' **make**
And	ham and eggs	hæmə **neggz**
	bread and butter	bredn **buddr**
	Coffee? With cream and sugar?	**käffee** . . . with creem'n **sh'g'r**
	No, lemon and sugar.	**nou** . . . **lem**'n'n sh'g'r
	. . . And some more cookies?	'n smore **cükeez**
	They kept going back and forth.	they kep going bækn **forth**
	We watched it again and again.	we **wäch** didə **gen'n' gen**
	He did it over and over.	he di di **dov**erə **no**ver
	We learned by trial and error.	we lrnd by tryələ**ner**ər
Or	Soup or salad?	super **salad**
	now or later	næ⁽ʷ⁾r **lay**dr
	more or less	**mor**'r less
	left or right	**left**er **right**
	For here or to go?	f'r **hir**'r d'**go**
	Are you going up or down?	are you going **úp**per **dówn**
	*This is an **either / or** question: **Up? Down?***	
	*Notice how the intonation is different from "Cream and **sugar?**", which is a **yes / no** question.*	
Are	What are you doing?	w'dr you **do**ing
	Where are you going?	wer'r you **go**ing
	What're you planning on doing?	w'dr yü planning än **do**ing
	How are you?	hæwr **you**
	Those are no good.	thozer no **good**
	How are you doing?	hæwer you **do**ing
	The kids are still asleep.	the **kid**zer stillə **sleep**

	Looks Like . . .	Sounds Like . . .
Your	How's your family?	hæozhier **fæm**lee
	Where're your keys?	wher'r y'r **keez**
	You're American, aren't you?	yerə **mer**'k'n, arn choo
	Tell me when you're ready.	tell me wen yr **red**dy
	Is this your car?	izzis y'r **cär**
	You're late again, Bob.	yer lay də **gen**, Bäb
One	Which one is yours?	which w'n'z **y'rz**
	Which one is better?	which w'n'z **bed**der
	One of them is broken.	w'n'v'm'z **brok**'n
	I'll use the other one.	æl yuz thee⁽ʸ⁾**əther** w'n
	I like the red one, Edwin.	äi like the **red**w'n, edw'n
	That's the last one.	thæts th' lass **dw'n**
	The next one'll be better.	the **necks** dw'n'll be **bedd'r**
	Here's one for you.	**hir** zw'n f'r **you**
	Let them go one by one.	led'm gou w'n by **w'n**
The	It's the best.	ts th' **best**
	What's the matter?	w'ts th' **mad**der
	What's the problem?	w'tsə **präb**l'm
	I have to go to the bathroom.	äi hæf t' go d' th' **bæth**room
	Who's the boss around here?	hoozə **bäss** səræond hir
	Give it to the dog.	g'v'⁽ᵗ⁾tə th' **däg**
	Put it in the drawer.	püdidin th' **dror**
A	It's a present.	tsə **pre**znt
	You need a break.	you needə **bray-eek**
	Give him a chance.	g'v'mə **chæns**
	Let's get a new pair of shoes.	lets geddə new perə **shooz**
	Can I have a Coke, please?	c'nai hævə **kouk**, pleez
	Is that a computer?	izzædə k'm**pyoo**dr
	Where's a public telephone?	wherzə pəblic **tel**əfoun

	Looks Like . . .	Sounds Like . . .
Of	It's the top of the line.	tsə täp'v th' **line**
	It's a state of the art printer.	tsə **stay** də thee[(v)]ärt **prin**ner
	As a matter of fact, . . .	z'mæddərə **fækt** . . .
	Get out of here.	ged**dæow** də hir
	Practice all of the time.	**præk**t'säll'v th' time
	Today's the first of May.	t'**dayz** th' frss d'v **May**
	What's the name of that movie?	w'ts th' **nay** m'v thæt **movie**
	That's the best of all!	**thæts** th' bess d'**väll**
	some of them	**sə**məvəm
	all of them	**äll**əvəm
	most of them	**mos**dəvəm
	none of them	**nə**nəvəm
	any of them	**enn**yəvəm
	the rest of them	th' **res**dəvəm
Can	Can you speak English?	k'new spee **king**lish
	I can only do it on Wednesday.	äi k'**noun**ly du[(w)]idän **wen**zday
	A can opener can open cans.	ə **kæn**op'ner k'nopen **kænz**
	Can I help you?	k'näi **hel** piu
	Can you do it?	k'niu **do**[(w)]'t
	We can try it later.	we k'n **try** it **layder**
	I hope you can sell it.	äi **hou** piu k'n **sell**'t
	No one can fix it.	nou w'n k'n **fick** sit
	Let me know if you can find it.	lemme no[(w)]'few k'n **fine** dit
Had	Jack had had enough.	jæk'd hæd' **n'f**
	Bill had forgotten again.	bil'd frga[(t)]n nə **gen**
	What had he done to deserve it?	w'd'dee d'nd'd' **zr** vit
	We'd already seen it.	weedäl reddy **see** nit
	He'd never been there.	heed never **bin** there
	Had you ever had one?	h'jou[(w)]ever **hæd**w'n
	Where had he hidden it?	wer dee **hid**n•nit
	Bob said he'd looked into it.	bäb sedeed lük**din** tu[(w)]it
Would	He would have helped, if . . .	he wüda **help** dif . . .
	Would he like one?	woody **lye** kw'n
	Do you think he'd do it?	dyiu thing keed **du**[(w)]'t
	Why would I tell her?	why wüdäi **teller**
	We'd see it again, if . . .	weed see[(v)]idəgen, if . . .
	He'd never be there on time.	heed never **be** therän time
	Would you ever have one?	w'jou[(w)]ever **hæv**w'n

95

Exercise 7-2: Reduced Sounds *continued*　　　　　🔊 Track 180

	Looks Like . . .	Sounds Like . . .
Was	He was only trying to help.	he w'zounly trying də help
	Mark was American.	**mär** kw'z'**mer**'k'n
	Where was it?	wer **w'z**'t
	How was it?	hæo**w'z**'t
	That was great!	thæt w'z **great**
	Who was with you?	hoow'z **with** you
	She was very clear.	she w'z very **clear**
	When was the war of 1812?	wen w'z th' **wor'v** ei⁽ᵗ⁾teen **twelv**
What	What time is it?	w't **tye** m'z't
	What's up?	w'ts'**p**
	What's on your agenda?	w'tsänyrə **jen**də
	What do you mean?	w'd'y' **mean**
	What did you mean?	w'j'**mean**
	What did you do about it?	w'j' **du**⁽ʷ⁾əbæodit
	What took so long?	w't **tük** so läng
	What do you think of this?	w'ddyə thing k'v **this**
	What did you do then?	w'jiu do **then**
	I don't know what he wants.	I dont know wədee **wänts**
Some	Some are better than others.	s'**mr** beddr thənəth**erz**
	There are some leftovers.	ther'r s'm **lef** doverz
	Let's buy some ice cream.	let spy s' **mice** creem
	Could we get some other ones?	kwee get s'**mother** w'nz
	Take some of mine.	**take** səməv **mine**
	Would you like some more?	w' joo like s'**more**
	(or, very casually)	jlike **smore**
	Do you have some ice?	dyü hæv sə**mice**
	Do you have some mice?	dyü hæv sə**mice**

"You can fool some of the people some of the time,
but you can't fool all of the people all of the time."

yuk'n **fool səmə** thə peepᵊl **səmə** thə time, b'choo **kænt fool ällə**thə peepᵊl **ällə**thə time

| | Exercise 7-3: Intonation and Pronunciation of "That" | Track 181 |

That is a special case because it serves three different grammatical functions. The relative pronoun and the conjunction are reducible. The demonstrative pronoun cannot be reduced to a schwa sound. It must stay æ.

Relative Pronoun	The car that she ordered is red.	the **car** th't she order diz **red**
Conjunction	He said that he liked it.	he sed the dee **läik**dit.
Demonstrative	Why did you do that?	why dijoo **do** thæt?
Combination	I know that he'll read that book that I told you about.	äi **know** the dill read thæt **bük** the dai **tol**joo^{(w)'} bæot

| Exercise 7-4: Crossing Out Reduced Sounds | Track 182 |

Cross out any sound that is not clearly pronounced, including to, for, and, that, than, the, a, the soft i, and unstressed syllables that do not have strong vowel sounds.

Hello, **my** name is _____. I'm taking American **Acc**ent Training. There's a **lot** to **learn**, but I **hope** to make it as en**joy**able as possible. I should pick **up** on the American into**na**tion pattern pretty **eas**ily, although the **only** way to **get** it is to **prac**tice all of the time. I use the **up** and down, or **peaks** and valleys, intonation more than I **used** to. I've been paying attention to **pitch**, **too**. It's like **walk**ing down a **stair**case. I've been **talk**ing to a lot of **Americans** lately, and they tell me that I'm **ea**sier to under**stand**. **Any**way, I could go **on** and on, but the im**port**ant thing is to **listen** well and sound **good**. **Well**, what do you **think**? **Do** I?

| Exercise 7-5: Reading Reduced Sounds | Track 183 |

Repeat the paragraph after me. Although you're getting rid of the vowel sounds, you want to maintain a strong intonation and let the sounds flow together. For the first reading of this paragraph, it is helpful to keep your teeth clenched together to reduce excess jaw and lip movement. Let's begin.

Hello, **my** name'z _____. I'm taking 'mer'k'n **Acc**'nt Train'ng. Therez' **lott**' **learn**, b't I **hope** t' make 't'z 'n**joy**'bl'z poss'bl. I sh'd p'ck '**p** on the 'mer'k'n 'nt'**na**sh'n pattern pretty **eas**'ly, although the **on**ly way t' **get** 't z t' **prac**t's all 'v th' time. I use the '**p**'n down, or **peaks** 'n valleys, 'nt'nash'n more th'n I **used** to. Ive b'n pay'ng 'ttensh'n t' **p'ch**, **too**. 'Ts like **walk**'ng down' **stair**case. Ive b'n **talk**'ng to' lot 'v**mer**'k'ns lately, 'n they tell me th't Im **ea**sier to 'nder**stand**. **Any**way, I k'd go **on** 'n on, b't the '**mport**'nt th'ng 'z t' **l's**'n wel'n sound **g'd**. **W'll**, wh' d'y' **th'nk**? **Do** I?

GRAMMAR IN A NUTSHELL

Even in complex sentences, stress the noun (unless there is contrast).

Everything You Ever Wanted to Know About Grammar But Were Afraid to Use

English is a chronological language. We just love to know when something happened, and this is indicated by the range and depth of our verb tenses.

*I **had** already seen it by the time she **brought** it in.*

The confusing part is that in English the verb tenses are very important, but instead of putting them up on the *peaks* of a sentence, we throw them all deep down in the *valleys*! Therefore, two sentences with strong intonation—such as, "***Dogs** eat **bones***" and "*The **dogs'll've** eaten the **bones***"— sound amazingly similar. Why? Because it takes the same amount of time to say both sentences since they have the same number of stresses. The three original words and the rhythm stay the same in these sentences, but the meaning changes as you add more stressed words. Articles and verb tense changes are usually not stressed.

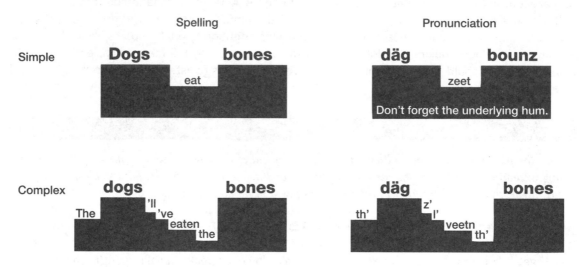

Now, let's see how this works in the exercises that follow.

Exercise 7-6: Consistent Noun Stress in Changing Verb Tenses Track 185

This is a condensed exercise for you to practice simple intonation with a wide range of verb tenses. When you do the exercise the first time, go through stressing only the nouns: **Dogs eat bones.** *Practice this until you are quite comfortable with the intonation. The pronunciation and word connections are on the right, and the full verb tenses are on the far left.*

eat	1.	The **dogs** eat the **bones.**	the **däg** zeet the **bounz**
ate	2.	The **dogs** ate the **bones.**	the **däg** zɛit the **bounz**
are eating	3.	The **dogs**'re eating the **bones.**	the **däg** zr reeding the **bounz**
will eat	4.	The **dogs**'ll eat the **bones** (if)	the **däg** zə leet the **bounz** (if)
would eat	5.	The **dogs**'d eat the **bones** (if)	the **däg** zə deet the **bounz** (if)
would have eaten	6.	The **dogs**'d've eaten the **bones** (if)	the **däg** zədə veetn the **bounz** (if)
that have eaten	7.	The **dogs** that've eaten the **bones** (are)	the **däg** zədə veetn the **bounz** (are)
have eaten	8.	The **dogs**'ve eaten the **bones.**	the **däg** zə veetn the **bounz**
had eaten	9.	The **dogs**'d eaten the **bones.**	the **däg** zə deetn the **bounz**
will have eaten	10.	The **dogs**'ll've eaten the **bones.**	the **däg** zələ veetn the **bounz**
ought to eat	11.	The **dogs** ought to eat the **bones.**	the **däg** zädə eat the **bounz**
should eat	12.	The **dogs** should eat the **bones.**	the **dägz** sh'deet the **bounz**
should not eat	13.	The **dogs** shouldn't eat the **bones.**	the **dägz** sh'dn•neet the **bounz**
should have eaten	14.	The **dogs** should've eaten the **bones.**	the **dägz** sh'də veetn the **bounz**
should not have	15.	The **dogs** shouldn't've eaten the **bones.**	the **dägz** sh'dn•nə veetn the **bounz**
could eat	16.	The **dogs** could eat the **bones.**	the **dägz** c'deet the **bounz**
could not eat	17.	The **dogs** couldn't eat the **bones.**	the **dägz** c'dn•neet the **bounz**
could have eaten	18.	The **dogs** could've eaten the **bones.**	the **dägz** c'də veetn the **bounz**
could not have	19.	The **dogs** couldn't've eaten the **bones.**	the **dägz** c'dn•nə veetn the **bounz**
might eat	20.	The **dogs** might eat the **bones.**	the **dägz** mydeet the **bounz**
might have eaten	21.	The **dogs** might've eaten the **bones.**	the **dägz** mydəveetn the **bounz**
must eat	22.	The **dogs** must eat the **bones.**	the **dägz** məss deet the **bounz**
must have eaten	23.	The **dogs** must've eaten the **bones.**	the **dägz** məsdəveetn the **bounz**
can eat	24.	The **dogs** can eat the **bones.**	the **dägz** c'neet the **bounz**
can't eat	25.	The **dogs can't eat** the **bones.**	the **dägz** cæn(d)eet the **bounz**

Exercise 7-7: Consistent Pronoun Stress in Changing Verb Tenses Track 186

*This is the same as the previous exercise, except you now stress the verbs: They **eat** them. Practice this until you are quite comfortable with the intonation. Notice that in fluent speech, the **th** of **them** is frequently dropped (as is the **h** in the other object pronouns, **him, her**). The pronunciation and word connections are on the right, and the tense name is on the far left.*

present	1.	They **eat** them.	they**eed**'m
past	2.	They **ate** them.	they**ɛid**'m
continuous	3.	They're **eating** them.	the**ree**ding'm
future	4.	They'll **eat** them (if . . .)	the**lee**d'm (if . . .)
present conditional	5.	They'd **eat** them (if . . .)	they **dee**d'm (if . . .)
past conditional	6.	They'd've **eaten** them (if . . .)	they də**vee**tn'm (if . . .)
relative pronoun	7.	The ones that've **eaten** them (are . . .)	the wənzədə**vee**tn'm (are . . .)
present perfect	8.	They've **eaten** them (many times).	they **vee**tn'm (many times)
past perfect	9.	They'd **eaten** them (before . . .)	they **dee**tn'm (before . . .)
future perfect	10.	They'll have **eaten** them (by . . .)	they lə**vee**tn'm (by . . .)
obligation	11.	They ought to **eat** them.	they ädə**eed**'m
obligation	12.	They should **eat** them.	they sh'**dee**d'm
obligation	13.	They shouldn't **eat** them.	they sh'dn•**nee**d'm
obligation	14.	They should have **eaten** them.	they sh'də**vee**tn'm
obligation	15.	They shouldn't've **eaten** them.	they sh'dn•nə**vee**tn'm
possibility/ability	16.	They could **eat** them.	they c'**dee**d'm
possibility/ability	17.	They couldn't **eat** them.	they c'dn•**nee**d'm
possibility/ability	18.	They could have **eaten** them.	they c'də **vee**tn'm
possibility/ability	19.	They couldn't have **eaten** them.	they c'dn•nə **vee**tn'm
possibility	20.	They might **eat** them.	they my**dee**d'm
possibility	21.	They might have **eaten** them.	they my də **vee**tn'm
probability	22.	They must **eat** them.	they məss **dee**d'm
probability	23.	They must have eaten them.	they məsdə**vee**tn'm
ability	24.	They can **eat** them.	they c'**nee**d'm
ability	25.	They **can't eat** them.	they **cæn**(d)**eed**'m

In the blanks below, fill in the phonetic pronunciation (using the guidelines from Exercise 7-6). Remember, don't rely on spelling, and use the contracted forms wherever possible. (Check Answer Key on page 218.)

1.	Bob	writes	a letter.	
	bä	• bry	• tsə ledder	
2.	Bob	wrote	a letter.	
	bä	• bro	• də ledder	
3.	Bob	is writing	a letter.	
	bä	• _____	• _____	ledder
4.	Bob	will write	a letter.	
	bä	• _____	• _____	ledder
5.	Bob	would write	a letter, if . . .	
	bä	• bədry	• də ledderif	
6.	Bob	would have written	a letter.	
	bä	• _____	• _____	ledder
7.	The guy	that has written	a letter . . .	
	thə gäi	• _____	• _____	ledder
8.	Bob	has written	a letter.	
	bä	• _____	• _____	ledder
9.	Bob	had written	a letter.	
	bä	• _____	• _____	ledder
10.	Bob	will have written	a letter.	
	bä	• _____	• _____	ledder
11.	Bob	ought to write	a letter.	
	bä	• bädə ry	• də ledder	
12.	Bob	should write	a letter.	
	bäb	• _____	• _____	ledder
13.	Bob	shouldn't write	a letter.	
	bäb	• _____	• _____	ledder
14.	Bob	should've written	a letter.	
	bäb	• _____	• _____	ledder
15.	Bob	shouldn't've written	a letter.	
	bäb	• shüdnə vri(t)n	• nə ledder	
16.	Bob	could write	a letter.	
	bäb	• _____	• _____	ledder
17.	Bob	couldn't write	a letter.	
	bäb	• _____	• _____	ledder
18.	Bob	could've written	a letter.	
	bäb	• _____	• _____	ledder
19.	Bob	couldn't've written	a letter.	
	bäb	• _____	• _____	ledder

Exercise 7-8: Writing Your Own Phonetics *continued*   Track 187

20.	Bob	might write	a letter.	
	bäb	• _____	• _____	ledder
21.	Bob	might've written	a letter.	
	bäb	• _____	• _____	ledder
22.	Bob	must write	a letter.	
	bäb	• _____	• _____	ledder
23.	Bob	must've written	a letter.	
	bäb	• _____	_____	ledder
24.	Bob	can write	a letter.	
	bäb	• _____	_____	ledder
25.	Bob	can't write	a letter.	
	bäb	• _____	_____	ledder

Exercise 7-9: Supporting Words   Track 188

For this next part of the intonation of grammatical elements, each sentence has a few extra words to help you get the meaning. Keep the same strong intonation that you used before and add the new stress where you see the bold face. Use your rubber band.

The **dogs** eat the **bones** every **day**.	th' **däg** zeet th' **bounz**evree **day**
The **dogs** ate the **bones** last **week**.	th' **däg** zɛit th' **bounz**læss **dweek**
The **dogs**'re eating the **bones** right now.	th' **däg** zr reeding th' **bounz** räit næo
The **dogs**'ll eat the **bones** if they're **here**.	th' **däg** zə leet th' **bounz**if thɛr hir
The **dogs**'d eat the **bones** if they were **here**.	th' **däg** zə deet th' **bounz**if they wr **hir**
The **dogs**'d've eaten the **bones** if they'd **been** here.	th' **däg** zədə veetn th' **bounz**if theyd bin hir
The **dogs** that've eaten the **bones** are **sick**.	th' **däg** zədə veetn th' **bounz**r sick
The **dogs**'ve eaten the **bones** every **day**.	th' **däg** zə veetn th' **bounz**ɛvry day
The **dogs**'d eaten the **bones** by the time we **got** there.	th' **däg** zə deetn th' **bounz** by th' time we **gät** thɛr
The **dogs**'ll have eaten the **bones** by the time we **get** there.	th' **däg** zələ veetn th' **bounz** by th' time we **get** thɛr

English has a fixed word order that does not change with additional words.

	auxiliary	negative	perfect auxiliary	adverb	passive	continuous	main verb
Draw!							
							Draw!
He draws.							
He							draws.
He does draw.							
He	does						draw.
He is drawing.							
He	is						drawing.
He is not drawing.							
He	is	not					drawing.
He is not always drawing.							
He	is	not		always			drawing.
He is not always being drawn.							
He	is	not		always		being	drawn.
He has not always been drawn.							
He	has	not		always	been		drawn.
He has not always been being drawn.							
He	has	not		always	been	being	drawn.
He will not have always been being drawn.							
He	will	not	have	always	been	being	drawn.

Now, let's work with contrast. For example, The dogs'd eat the bones *and* The dogs'd eaten the bones *are so close in sound, yet so far apart in meaning, that you need to make a special point of recognizing the difference by listening for content. Repeat each group of sentences, originally from Exercise 7-6, as noted by the numbers in the second column, using sound and intonation for contrast.*

would eat	#5	The **dogs'**d eat the **bones**.	the **däg** zə deet the **bounz**
had eaten	#9	The **dogs'**d eaten the **bones**.	the **däg** zə deetn the **bounz**

would have eaten	#6	The **dogs'**d've eaten the **bones**.	the **däg** zədə veetn the **bounz**
that have eaten	#7	The **dogs** that've eaten the **bones**.	the **däg** zədə veetn the **bounz**

will eat	#4	The **dogs'**ll eat the **bones**.	the **däg** zə leet the **bounz**
would eat	#5	The **dogs'**d eat the **bones**.	the **däg** zə deet the **bounz**
would have eaten	#6	The **dogs'**d've eaten the **bones**.	the **däg** zədə veetn the **bounz**

have eaten	#8	The **dogs'**ve eaten the **bones**.	the **däg** zə veetn the **bounz**
had eaten	#9	The **dogs'**d eaten the **bones**.	the **däg** zə deetn the **bounz**
will have eaten	#10	The **dogs'**ll have eaten the **bones**.	the **däg** zələ veetn the **bounz**

would eat	#5	The **dogs'**d eat the **bones**.	the **däg** zə deet the **bounz**
ought to eat	#11	The **dogs** ought to eat the **bones**.	the **däg** zädə eat the **bounz**

can eat	#24	The **dogs** can eat the **bones**.	the **dägz** c'neet the **bounz**
can't eat	#25	The dogs **can't eat** the bones.	the dägz **cæn**[(d)]**eet** the **bounz**

Exercise 7-11: Building an Intonation Sentence Track 191

Repeat after me.

1. I bought a **sand**wich.
2. I **said** I bought a **sand**wich.
3. I **said** I think I bought a **sand**wich.
4. I said I **really** think I bought a **sand**wich.
5. I said I **really** think I bought a chicken **sand**wich.
6. I said I **really** think I bought a **chicken** salad **sand**wich.
7. I said I **really** think I bought a **half** a chicken salad **sand**wich.
8. I said I **really** think I bought a **half** a chicken salad **sand**wich this after**noon**.
9. I **actually** said I **really** think I bought a **half** a chicken salad **sand**wich this after**noon**.
10. I **actually** said I **really** think I bought another **half** a chicken salad **sand**wich this after**noon**.
11. Can you **believe** I **actually** said I **really** think I bought another **half** a chicken salad **sand**wich this after**noon**?

1. I **did** it.
2. I did it **again**.
3. I already **did** it again.
4. I think I already **did** it again.
5. I **said** I think I already **did** it again.
6. I **said** I think I already did it again **yes**terday.
7. I **said** I think I already **did** it again the day before **yes**terday.

1. I want a **ball**.
2. I want a large **ball**.
3. I want a **large**, **red ball**.
4. I want a **large**, red, bouncy **ball**.
5. I want a **large**, red, bouncy rubber **ball**.
6. I want a **large**, red, bouncy rubber **basket**ball.

1. I want a **raise**.
2. I want a **big raise**.
3. I want a **big**, impressive **raise**.
4. I want a **big**, impressive, annual **raise**.
5. I want a **big**, impressive, annual cost of **living** raise.

Exercise 7-12: Building Your Own Intonation Sentences 🔊 Track 192

Build your own sentence using everyday words and phrases, such as think, hope, nice, really, actually, even, this afternoon, big, small, pretty, and so on.

1.
2.
3.
4.
5.
6.
7.
8.
9.
10.

BREATHING EXERCISES

Track 193

Different languages have different breathing patterns. Because Americans are a little louder than you may expect, in order to emulate this projection of the voice, you're going to have to take deeper breaths than you're accustomed to. Stand up straight, chest out, inhale deeply, and in a deep voice say, "Hi! How's it going?"

As you saw with *Phrasing*, your breathing should be in sync with the phrasing and punctuation. If you're saying something short, you can get away with a more shallow inhale, but short panting breaths are interpreted as nervous or impatient, whereas long, deep exhalations of sound are considered calm and confident. Take deeper breaths than usual and push the sound out from deep in your chest.

Pay particular attention that you do not push the air out through your nose, which would create a very unattractive nasal quality to your speech. (Practice with the long sentences on pages 99–105, 128, and 154.)

8
Tee Aitch

*Th is a **popped** sound.*
The tongue tip is pressed firmly behind the top teeth.

Track 194

I'd like you to consider words as rocks for a moment. When a rock first rolls into the ocean, it is sharp and well defined. After tumbling about for a few millennia, it becomes round and smooth. A word goes through a similar process. When it first rolls into English, it may have a lot of sharp, well-defined vowels or consonants in it, but after rolling off of a few million tongues, it becomes round and smooth. This smoothing process occurs when a tense vowel becomes reduced and when an unvoiced consonant becomes voiced. The most common words are the smoothest, the most reduced, the most often voiced. There are several very common words that are all voiced: *this, that, the, those, them, they, their, there, then, than, though.* The strong words such as *thank, think,* or *thing,* as well as long or unusual words such as *thermometer* or *theologian,* stay unvoiced.

The sound of the **TH** combination seems to exist only in English, Greek, and Castillian Spanish. Just as with most of the other consonants, there are two types—voiced and unvoiced. The voiced **TH** is like a **D**, but instead of being in back of the teeth, it's 1/4 inch lower and forward, between the teeth. The unvoiced **TH** is like an **S** between the teeth. Most people tend to replace the unvoiced **TH** with **S** or **T** and the voiced one with **Z** or **D**, so instead of *thing,* they say *sing* or *ting,* and instead of *that,* they say *zat* or *dat.*

To pronounce **TH** correctly, think of a snake's tongue. You don't want to take a big relaxed tongue, throw it out of your mouth for a long distance, and leave it out there for a long time. Make only a very quick, sharp little movement. Keep your tongue's tip very tense. It darts out between your teeth and snaps back very quickly—*thing, that, this.* The tongue's position for the unvoiced **TH** is similar to that of **S**, but for **TH** the tongue is extended through the teeth, instead of hissing behind the back of the teeth. The voiced **TH** is like a **D** except that the tongue is placed between the teeth, or even pressed behind the teeth. Now, we're ready for some practice.

Exercise 8-1: Targeting the TH Sound   **Track 195**

In order to target the TH sound, first, hold a mirror in front of you and read our familiar paragraph silently, moving only your tongue. It should be visible in the mirror each time you come to a TH. Second, find all of the THs, both voiced and unvoiced. Remember, a voiced sound makes your throat vibrate, and you can feel that vibration by placing your fingers on your throat. There are ten voiced and two unvoiced THs here. You can mark them by underscoring the former and drawing a circle around the latter. Or, if you prefer, use two of your color markers. Mark the TH sounds. (Don't forget to check your answers against the Answer Key on page 218. See also Chapter 1 and Chapters 4 and 9 for related sounds.)

Hello, my name is_____. I'm taking American **Accent** Training. There's a **lot** to **learn**, but I **hope** to make it as **enjoyable** as possible. I should pick **up** on the American **intonation** pattern pretty **easily**, although the **only way** to **get** it is to **practice all** of the time. I **use** the **up** and down, or **peaks** and valleys, **intonation** more than I **used** to. I've been paying attention to **pitch, too**. It's like **walking** down a staircase. I've been **talking** to a lot of **Americans** lately, and they tell me that I'm **easier** to under**stand**. Anyway, I could go **on** and on, but the **important** thing is to **listen** well and sound **good**. **Well**, what do you **think**? **Do** I?

Exercise 8-2: The Thuringian Thermometers   **Track 196**

I'm going to read the following paragraph once straight through so you can hear that no matter how fast I read it, all the THs are still there. It is a distinctive sound, but, when you repeat it, don't put too much effort into it. Listen to my reading.

The throng of thermometers from the Thuringian Thermometer Folks arrived on Thursday. There were a thousand thirty-three thick thermometers, though, instead of a thousand thirty-six thin thermometers, which was three thermometers fewer than the thousand thirty-six we were expecting, not to mention that they were thick ones rather than thin ones. We thoroughly thought that we had ordered a thousand thirty-six, not a thousand thirty-three, thermometers, and asked the Thuringian Thermometer Folks to reship the thermometers; thin, not thick. They apologized for sending only a thousand thirty-three thermometers rather than a thousand thirty-six and promised to replace the thick thermometers with thin thermometers.

th = voiced (17)
th = unvoiced (44)

Exercise 8-3: Tongue Twisters   **Track 197**

Feeling confident? Good! Try the following tongue twisters and have some fun.

1. The sixth sick Sheik's sixth thick sheep.
2. This is a zither. Is this a zither?
3. I thought a thought. But the thought I thought wasn't the thought I thought I thought. If the thought I thought I thought had been the thought I thought, I wouldn't have thought so much.

9

S or Z?

*S is hissed, **Z** is buzzed. Most **S**'s are pronounced as **Z**'s.*

Track 198

The sound of the letter **S** is *s* only if it follows an unvoiced consonant. Otherwise, it becomes a **Z** in disguise. When an **S** follows a vowel, a voiced consonant, or another **S**, it turns into a *z* sound. The following exercise will let you hear and practice **S** with its dual sound. There are many more *z* sounds in English than *s* sounds. (See also Chapters 8 and 13 for related sounds.)

Exercise 9-1: When S Becomes Z   Track 199

In the lists that follow, notice how the voiced word is drawn out, then repeat the word after the speaker. Both voiced and unvoiced diphthongs have the underlying structure of the tone shift, or the double stairstep, but the shift is much larger for the voiced ones.

Contrast

	S	Z
1.	price	prize
2.	peace	peas
3.	place	plays
4.	ice	eyes
5.	hiss	his
6.	close	to close
7.	use	to use
8.	rice	rise
9.	pace	pays
10.	lacey	lazy
11.	thirsty	Thursday
12.	bus	buzz
13.	dust	does
14.	face	phase
15.	Sue	zoo
16.	loose	lose

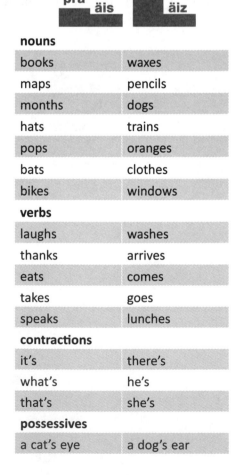

prä äis	prä äiz
nouns	
books	waxes
maps	pencils
months	dogs
hats	trains
pops	oranges
bats	clothes
bikes	windows
verbs	
laughs	washes
thanks	arrives
eats	comes
takes	goes
speaks	lunches
contractions	
it's	there's
what's	he's
that's	she's
possessives	
a cat's eye	a dog's ear

Exercise 9-2: A Surly Sergeant Socked an Insolent Sailor Track 200

Repeat the s sounds in the paragraph below.

Sam, a surly sergeant from Cisco, Texas, saw a sailor sit silently on a small seat reserved for youngsters. He stayed for several minutes, while tots swarmed around. Sam asked the sailor to cease and desist, but he sneered in his face. Sam was so incensed that he considered it sufficient incentive to sock the sailor. The sailor stood there for a second, astonished, and then strolled away. Sam was perplexed, but satisfied, and the tots scampered like ants over to the see-saw.

Exercise 9-3: Allz Well That Endz Well Track 201

Repeat the z sounds in the paragraph below.

A lazy Thursday at the zoo found the zebras grazing on zinnias, posing for pictures, and teasing the zookeeper, whose nose was bronzed by the sun. The biggest zebra's name was Zachary, but his friends called him Zack. Zack was a confusing zebra whose zeal for reason caused his cousins, who were naturally unreasoning, to pause in their conversations. While they browsed, he philosophized. As they grazed, he practiced zen. Because they were Zack's cousins, the zebras said nothing, but they wished he would muzzle himself at times.

Track 202

As mentioned (page 80), like sounds follow naturally. If one consonant is voiced, chances are, the following plural **S** will be voiced as well (**dogz**). If it's unvoiced, the following sound will be as well (**cats**). In the past tense, **S** can be both voiced *z* and unvoiced *s* in some cases.

Exercise 9-4: Voiced and Unvoiced Endings in the Past Tense Track 203

The following will explain the differences between four expressions that are similar in appearance but different in both meaning and pronunciation.

	Meaning	Example	Pronunciation
S	Past action	I used to eat rice.	yūst tu
	To be accustomed to	I am used to eating rice.	yūs tu
Z	Present passive verb	Chopsticks are used to eat rice.	yūzd tu
	Simple past	I used chopsticks to eat rice.	yūzd

Used to, depending on its position in a sentence, will take either a tense **ū** or a schwa. At the end of a sentence, you need to say, . . . *more than I used tooo;* in the middle of a sentence you can say, *He usta live there.*

I wanted to be sure and win the pun contest, so I submitted ten of them.

Unfortunately, no pun in ten did.

Exercise 9-5: Finding S and Z Sounds	Track 204

Go through the paragraph and underline all of the s sounds. The first, æksent is marked for you. Next, circle all of the z sounds, no matter how the word is written (is = iz, as = æz, and so on). (Check Answer Key on page 218.)

Hello, my name iz _____. I'm taking American **æksent** Training. There's a **lot** to **learn**, but I **hope** to make it as **enjoyable** as possible. I should pick **up** on the American **intonation** pattern pretty **easily**, although the **only** way to **get** it is to **practice** all of the time. I use the **up** and down, or **peaks** and valleys, **intonation** more than I **used** to. I've been paying attention to **pitch**, **too**. It's like **walking** down a **stair**case. I've been **talking** to a lot of **Americans** lately, and they tell me that I'm **easier** to understand. **Any**way, I could go **on** and on, but the **important** thing is to **listen** well and sound **good**. **Well**, what do you **think**? **Do** I?

▶ Practice reading the paragraph three times on your own, concentrating on strong **Z's**.

Exercise 9-6: Application Steps with S and Z	Track 205

Build up the following sentence, adding each aspect one at a time.

Always be a little kinder than necessary.

1. Intonation	**Always** be a little **kinder** than **necessary**.
2. Word Groups	Always be a little kinder(pause) than necessary.
3. Liaisons	Always be(y)a little kinder tha(n)necessary.
4. æ ä ə	äweez be ə littªl kinder thən nesəssary.
5. The American T	Always be a liddle kinder than necessary.
6. The American R	Always be a little kindər than necessɛry.
7. Combination of 1 through 6	äweez be(y)ə liddªl kindər(pause) thə(n)necəssɛry.

Exercise 9-7: Your Own Application Steps with S and Z	Track 206

Write your own sentence, and then build it up, adding each aspect one at a time.

1. Intonation	
2. Word Groups	
3. Liaisons	
4. æ ä ə	
5. The American T	
6. The American R	
7. Combination of 1 through 6	

Telephone Tutoring

Track 207

MID-POINT DIAGNOSTIC ANALYSIS

After three to six months, you're ready for the follow-up analysis. If you are studying on your own, contact toll-free (800) 457-4255 or go to *AmericanAccent.com* for a referral to a qualified telephone analyst. The diagnostic analysis is designed to evaluate your current speech patterns to let you know where your accent is standard and nonstandard.

> Think the United Auto Workers can beat Caterpillar Inc. in their bitter contract battle? Before placing your bets, talk to Paul Branan, who can't wait to cross the picket line at Caterpillar's factory in East Peoria. Branan, recently laid off by a rubber-parts plant where he earned base pay of $6.30 an hour, lives one block from a heavily picketed gate at the Cat complex. Now he's applying to replace one of the 12,600 workers who have been on strike for the past five months. "Seventeen dollars an hour and they don't want to work?" asks Branan. "I don't want to take another guy's job, but I'm hurting, too."

1. saw, lost, cough	5. shine, time, my	9. some, dull, possible	13. how, down, around
2. can, Dan, last	6. sit, silk, been	10. tooth, two, blue	14. appoint, avoid, boil
3. same, say, rail	7. seat, see, bean	11. look, bull, should	
4. yet, says, Paris	8. word, girl, first	12. don't, so, whole	

A	B	C	D	E	F
1. parry	1. bury	1. apple	1. able	1. mop	1. mob
2. ferry	2. very	2. afraid	2. avoid	2. off	2. of
3. stew	3. zoo	3. races	3. raises	3. face	3. phase
4. sheer	4. girl	4. pressure	4. pleasure	4. crush	4. garage
5. two	5. do	5. petal	5. pedal	5. not	5. nod
6. choke	6. joke	6. gaucho	6. gouger	6. rich	6. ridge
7. think	7. that	7. ether	7. either	7. tooth	7. smooth
8. come	8. gum	8. bicker	8. bigger	8. pick	8. pig
9. yes	9. rate	9. accent	9. exit	9. tax	9. tags
10. wool	10. grow	10. player	10. correct	10. day	10. tower
11. his	11. me	11. shower	11. carry	11. now	11. neater
12. late	12. next	12. ahead	12. swimmer	12. towel	12. same
13. bleed		13. collect	13. connect	13. needle	13. man
		14. Kelly	14. finger		14. ring

1. Who opened it?	1. Write a letter to Betty.
2. We opened it.	
3. Put it away.	2. Ride a ledder d' Beddy.
4. Bob ate an orange.	
5. Can it be done?	3. tatter tattoo
	4. platter platoon
1. Who⁽ʷ⁾oup'n did?	5. pattern perturb
2. We⁽ʸ⁾oup'n dit.	6. critic critique
3. Pü di də way.	
4. Bä bei d' nornj.	7. let led
5. C'n't be dən?	
	8. witten ridden

111

Chapters 1–9
Review and Expansion

How and what to do.

SO YOU'RE IN A TOUGH RELATIONSHIP WITH ENGLISH—LET'S TALK ABOUT THAT!

Track 208

Maybe you've tried to pick up an American accent before and it made you uncomfortable. Maybe your family thinks that you shouldn't change. Maybe you've tried and failed, and now you're frustrated. Whatever the reason, you've got an unsatisfying relationship with English. We're here to fix that.

Let's Get Your Head in the Right Place

Track 209

Learning a whole language is indeed a big deal, but you've already done all the heavy lifting, having learned the grammar and vocabulary. Right now, we're just doing the fine-tuning and working on your accent. Here's what you should expect after the first 1–6 weeks (depending on your diligence).

There are two ways to pick up the accent—All at once or step by step

Track 210

There's the do-it-now people and the people who like to change slowly, thinking that there is no validity to things that happen quickly to them. People don't think it's real if it's fast. But that's the Nike® slogan: "Just do it!" You know you can, and even if it is faster than you expect, it's still valid. It's all about behavior modeling. You don't have to believe it, you just have to do it.

All at Once
Just do it! Listen to the sounds and rhythms. Capture some essential elements and go!

Step by Step
Apply each technique one by one to develop your voice quality, pronunciation, intonation, phrasing, and linking. After you have mastered each of these elements, work on integrating them into speech.

Which method will work best for you? We'll try the all-at-once way first to see if we can jumpstart you with this shortcut. This isn't so much about the American accent as much as it's about your doing pure mimicry. Don't think. Don't overanalyze. Just imitate exactly what you hear in every aspect—voice quality, pronunciation, rhythm, phrasing, and wordflow.

Review Exercise 1: Pure Mimicry Track 211

Listen to this heavy Australian accent, record yourself, and compare the two.

Track 212

Please call Stella.

Track 213

When comparing your recording with our Aussie friend, see if you copied his nasality, used *plays* for the pronunciation of *please* and included the distinctive phrasing as he finishes up the sentence. If your recording matches closely and you were comfortable with the process, get started. If it wasn't entirely satisfying for you, or your recording didn't sound like him, let's take a moment to think about who you are and how you learn best.

Review Exercise 2: Are You Steadfast or Freewheeling? Track 214

Answer the following questions with a checkmark in the appropriate box.

1. Would you rather answer . . .
   - ☐ An essay question
   - ☐ A multiple-choice question

2. Do you . . .
   - ☐ Start from yes
   - ☐ Start from no

3. Do you prefer solutions that are . . .
   - ☐ Open-ended, abstract, and subject to interpretation
   - ☐ Clear-cut, precise, and objective

4. Are you . . .
   - ☐ Comfortable with a flexible time frame with constant updates
   - ☐ More deadline oriented

5. Do you prefer to . . .
   - ☐ Follow another person's lead
   - ☐ Do things your own way

If you selected the second option two or more times, try this experiment. Just for today, when someone says something to you, practice temporarily suspending judgment. Respond with, "Hmm, that's interesting," "Tell me more," or "You could be right." Not only will this help you listen better, but it will also make you a better conversationalist and open your mind to picking up and using this accent.

Review Exercise 3: Mimicry Track 215

Say the following sentence out loud:

Track 216

There was a time when people really had a way with words.

Track 217

Did you say it out loud (not to yourself, actually out loud)? If you did, go on to the next exercise. If not, let's talk about why you didn't. As we all know, *stubborn* is a negative word, and nobody wants to attribute a negative word to himself or herself. As the famous curmudgeon Bertrand Russell said, "I am firm. **You** are obstinate. **He** is a pig-headed fool." Interestingly, stubbornness has both *positive* (consistent, reliable, persistent) and *negative* (stubborn, inflexible, rigid) aspects.

Think back in your life to a time when persistence paid off. It may have been following through on an idea to successful fruition or overcoming apparently insurmountable odds on something important to you. Own that—it's yours. One of my favorite responses was when I asked a successful businessman if he'd had everything handed to him, if building his business had been easy, or if he'd had to fight to succeed. "Fight?!" he barked, "I've had to kill!"

Now, however, we're going to look at how stubbornness can get in your way. Stubbornness isn't necessarily something that just happens later in life, but is often an innate trait. Many of us have a deep-seated feeling of what is *right*, and it's hard to go against this. If you're a visual learner, chances are you did well on spelling tests, and so you have a sense of the *rightness* of spelling. It can be checked and validated. Speech, however, may seem very fluid and freeform to you. For this process, however, you need to embrace the *rightness* of phonetic spelling for speech as much as you embrace the *rightness* of spelling for written English and the *rightness* of mathematical notation for numbers.

Sometimes you're not being stubborn—you really *do* forget because you're focusing on **what** you're saying instead of **how** you're saying it. To illustrate this, a researcher had a problem with the door of the lab refrigeration unit, whose tall, upright handle had come loose. Not having time to fix it, he decided to open it by pulling on the side. Not five minutes later, he went back to grab some more vials and opened the fridge with the handle. It came completely loose and clonked him on the head! This time, he knew he had to remember, so he put a note right on the handle to remind himself. And again, a few minutes later, when he went back to get another vial, he grabbed the handle and hit himself on the head again. Clearly he needed a more dramatic solution. He took a whole page of newspaper and covered the entire handle of the fridge, so that the next time he mindlessly grabbed the handle, the newspaper crackled, and he realized what he was about to do. It's not like he *wanted* to get hit in the head, he just kept forgetting because he was focused on the **goal** and not the **process**. Sometimes people speaking English are so focused on the end product of using words in conversation, like he was in the end product of getting vials out of the fridge, that they forget to include the accent and pronunciation.

THINK, THEN ACT

🔊))
Track 218

When you have learned the techniques, but forget to apply them in speech, you are **acting** before **thinking**. In order to train yourself to think first, devise a strategy that works for you. For the researcher, it was putting a sheet of newspaper over the fridge handle. For you, it might be taking a deep breath before speaking, counting to three, pulling on a rubberband, or even the old school standby—a string around your finger. The point is, while you are internalizing these new sounds and rhythms, to create a stopgap measure to get you to focus on the process and not so much the goal.

THE FOUR STAGES OF LEARNING

Let's look at the transition you're going to be going through.

1. Unconscious incompetence (you don't even know you're making mistakes).
2. Conscious incompetence (you're aware, but you don't know how to fix them).
3. Conscious competence (when you focus really hard, you're actually pretty good).
4. Unconscious competence (you've internalized the concepts, and it's second nature).

You're most likely edging from 2 to 3. To get to 4, the key is consistent practice—a minimum of fifteen minutes per day, plus applying the techniques whenever you talk.

Review Exercise 4: Correlating Sounds & Phonetic Transcription Track 219

Listen to this sound and correlate it with this phonetic transcription:

Track 220

gäddit

Repeat this sound and notice the open *ah* sound of **gä**, the way the tip of your tongue flicks on the bumps on the top of your mouth, and the fact that the air doesn't pop out at the end of the word. Listen to the audio and say this out loud ten times.

Review Exercise 5: Correlating Phonetic Transcription & Regular Spelling Track 221

Listen to this sound and correlate it with this phonetic transcription:

gäddit   Got it!

Using the exact same sounds as before, observe how different the spelling is. Listen to the audio and say this out loud ten times.

SKIDIZ

Track 222

Let me tell you a little story about how I came to "get" word connections in French, or, as they like to call them, liaisons. I stumbled upon the word **skidiz** and was amazed that it could represent **ce qu'ils disent**. "Wow! That looks different!" I thought to myself. "They'll never understand me if I say it like that." Fortunately, my empirical side prevailed and I thought, "Okay, fine, I'll try it, even if it's just to prove that it doesn't work."

I was in Marseilles, so I combined it with the local pronunciation of **Je ne sais pas,** and managed to work **Sheh pah skidiz** in as a conversational response. Whoa! To my huge surprise, it worked, and the person started talking to me in real French and not baby language. That led me to part two of the epiphany: "Yikes, if I do this, it'll totally raise their expectations of how well I speak," and then, "Ahh, I'm talking the way I want *them* to talk to *me*, so I can understand them more easily!"

Once I realized how I'd been sabotaging myself, I started trusting the phonetics and stopped basing my pronunciation on spelling. My confidence went up because thought follows behavior, and my new behavior resulted in more sophisticated, intelligent conversations. People didn't have to talk down to my language level, but could actually talk with me at my conversational level. It's my goal that you have that same realization with **gäddit**. My job is to give the epiphany. Your job is to hold on and use it.

Review Exercise 6: Gathering That Empirical Evidence Track 223

Trusting in this method is an important component of how successful you will be, so we're going to do a short trust exercise. Take this phrase out into the world and use it exactly the way it's presented here. Try it out on coworkers and friends. Watch how they respond to you now that they can hear you playing with the language a little.

gäddit / Got it!

 We tend to think of language primarily as a *tool*, or as a *weapon*. Instead, start playing around in the English *toybox*.

Play with the sounds, rhythms, and patterns. Have fun! You'll find that some of the inhibitions fall away and your linguistic adaptibility kicks in.

PHONETIC TRANSCRIPTION = MATHEMATICAL NOTATION

Track 224

If you accept that **2 × 2** can also be written **2²**, you are comfortable with multiple labels for a single concept. This is the same principle as the word **cat** also being written as **kæt**.

Here is a simple two-part rule for the letter **O**:

> **1.** In a *one-syllable* word, **o** sounds like **ä** (unless the word ends in **e**):
> **hot, lost, Tom, Bob, dot com**
>
> **2.** In a *stressed* syllable, **o** also sounds like **ä**:
> **possible, Holland, philosophy**

Here is a two-part rule for the letter **A**:

> **1.** In a *one-syllable* word, **a** sounds like **æ** (unless the word ends in **e**):
> **cat, Sam, drab**
>
> **2.** In a *stressed* syllable, **a** sounds like **æ**:
> **rational, manager, catastrophe**

(For more on these two vowels, see Chapter 3.)

Once you have internalized the basic rules of phonetics, you need to diligently, persistently, and *stubbornly* apply them universally. In computing terms, think of doing a global **Search All** and **Replace**.

Some people have an initial aversion to reading phonetics because it's new and confusing. *It doesn't even look like English!* This is where we're going to have you practice some of that open-mindedness and trust. Accept that if you read the phonetics, you *will* have an American accent.

An accountant kept making the same pronunciation errors in English over and over again. Asked why, her response was consistently, "I forgot!" When asked if she forgot arithmetic, the answer was, "Of course not, that would make my life miserable."

Well, not applying the phonetics was making her life miserable!

OVERCONFIDENCE

Track 225

Counterintuitively, it's sometimes overconfidence that gets in a person's way. You're used to the positive rewards of doing things quickly and independently—an algebraic equation, a sales report with a high closing rate, a dissertation. Because you're good at what you do, you can skip over certain details. However, if you try to rush through speaking English, you'll end up skipping crucial details. Furthermore, if you only rely on your *own* judgment about your accent, particularly if it's spelling based, you're going to fall far short of the mark.

What to do about it? Start from scratch and make a conscious effort to get rid of your preconceptions. Put yourself in the position of knowing nothing about pronunciation, intonation, voice quality, word connections, etc. Then, lay the foundation with basic sounds and rhythms. Rebuild a new strong structure using the grammar and vocab you've worked so hard to acquire.

THE "WHAT" FACTOR

Track 226

Let's do a quick assessment of what other people think of your accent. How often during a day does someone ask you to repeat yourself? How long does it take to give your email address, and how many times do you have to spell your name? That's your "What?" factor. But the real question is, how does this affect you? How does it affect your working situation, your home life, your life as a whole? Does it make you feel discouraged, or does it encourage you to change? Or does it make you feel like everyone else needs to change around you? Let me tell you a story about someone who felt this way. We'll call her Mei Li.

A Chinese professor was studying English in the United States, and her instructor had suggested that, for convenience, she Americanize the pronunciation of her name, and she flew into a rage. She excoriated him in a long email about how disrespectful this was to 5,000 years of her Chinese ancestors. The American instructor was stunned and passed her on upstairs.

The senior instructor set about finding out what was going on. To say Dr. Li was linguistically rigid is a profound understatement. The instructor would ask, "But let's say you're at the DMV. The clerk doesn't know from Chinese ancestors. Don't you just want him to catch your name the first time and to process the transaction?" "No!" she would declare. "It's my *name!*"

The instructor finally told her that they simply had to make a breakthrough, so her entire homework would consist of leaving a voicemail with her name Americanized so it would be easier to understand by any random person. She left eight to ten identical Chinese-sounding attempts. Finally, she left one that started with a deep sigh and a deeper voice, "My name is Mei Li." It was a thing of beauty. Unfortunately, 30 seconds later, she left another *very* nasal one, "My name is Mei Liiiiiiiiiiiiii!"

Go On, Change Your Name

Track 227

No, not permanently or legally, but get comfortable with saying your own name differently than you have for your entire life. It may feel weird, unreal, surreal, or just plain dumb, but it's an invaluable mental exercise. Every time that I landed in a new country, my first order of business was to find out who I was, or at least how my name was pronounced. I went from Madrid (*Me llamo Anita*), to Paris (*Je m'áppelle Annie*), to Tokyo (私はアニーです。).

DROP THE BAGGAGE!

For a lot of people, the American accent comes with a lot of emotional baggage. *Americans are loud! Emotionally immature! Unsophisticated!* It may be conflicting for an educated sophisticate such as yourself to work toward actually sounding like this. But you need to fit in and be understood, so drop off the baggage. Just focus on the pure sounds.

Emotional Investment in Particular Sounds

A man with a distinctly Spanish accent had trouble distinguishing *iPod* from *iPad*. He learned the **æ** sound for iPad, but didn't extrapolate that sound to other words, such as **cat**, **laugh**, or **dance**. It would be natural to think that he simply didn't know where to use it. But surprisingly, when asked why he didn't use the **æ** sound, he laughingly responded, "Because I hate it."

Some people have a strong identification with their pronunciation, considering it part of their identity or personal brand. They may reject a single sound or the entire accent. Unless the change wells from within, the accent won't take root and become a true part of them.

Motivation

Track 228

Sofia Vergara, a Colombian actor in the American sitcom *Modern Family*, was doing an interview, explaining that her 21-year-old son had seen a video of her many years earlier and said, "Mom, you're the only person who's come to America and your accent got worse!" Her utterly charming response was, "It's the moh-nee, I don't have to do eet anymore!" In another interview, Oprah Winfrey asked why her accent seems to be getting heavier, even though she'd been living in America for some time. Sofia explained that she actually does it for comedic effect: "I realized that sometimes it was funnier to say **YOOOUHH** rather than **you**." She's very self-aware and has excellent reasons for maintaining her brand.

Over the years, however, we've heard pretty much every excuse from people who have demonstrated that they are able to *create* the sounds in isolation, but don't go on to the next step of universally *applying the rules.*

I feel uncomfortable.	It's not possible.	I tried and can't.
I don't understand the rules.	Why should I have to?	It's not "right."
I wasn't thinking about it.	It makes me sound arrogant.	I forgot.
I was focusing on what I was saying.	People will laugh at me.	I was rushing.

DOES PRONUNCIATION REALLY MATTER?

People say, *It's just a detail . . . does it really matter? Isn't "okay" good enough for what's needed and not worth the effort of going to the next level? We don't have that sound in my language, and we communicate just fine without it.* This may be true, but if you're, let's say, a doctor, don't you want your patients to know the difference between your saying, "He's in urology" and "He's in neurology" or "We did a below-knee amputation" and not "We did a baloney amputation"? So yes: Pronunciation matters!

Go to Extremes

Track 229

As an exercise, we have people put on a caricature of an American accent, and generally it's quite accurate. They are reluctant, however, to use it because of the inherent mockery involved. It's okay! I can assure you that Americans won't even notice when you're putting on a super heavy American accent . . . . They'll just think your English got better.

Your family and friends may react negatively and make fun of your nascent attempts to modify your speech. They like you the way you are. They may think your accent is cute. They may think that if you change how you talk you may change who you are. The bottom line is that you will sound different, and they may not like it.

We recommend practicing on strangers. They don't have a baseline and can accept you at face value. At this point, it may be hard for you to conceive how differently you will be treated. A lot of Americans, I regret to say, turn off when they hear a foreign accent, or are less than kind. Since we can't change all of them, we can make a small change in you.

Your Own True Voice

Track 230

There is not, of course, just one American voice, even for one person. People associate their voices with themselves, but have many different voices throughout their lives. You have a different voice as a child than as an adult, different in business than at a party, and so on.

Stephen Hawking, the British astrophysicist, had an English accent prior to the paralyzation of his vocal cords. After using a robotic voice with an American accent, he came to associate himself with that voice. Several years later, when production of the DECtalk DCT01 voice synthesizer was discontinued, he declined to switch to a model with a British accent. He identified with the American voice and associated it with himself. "I would not want to change, even if I were offered a British-sounding voice. I would feel I had become a different person," he said.

7 STEPS TO A PERFECT ACCENT

Track 231

1. Yep, I have an accent, I want to change it, and I'm sure this program will work for me.
2. I'm making a conscious effort to apply the techniques in an orderly, step-by-step manner.
3. I have taken an inventory of the sounds and rhythm patterns.

4. I am keeping a daily log of the **What Factor**.
5. I record myself once a week, compare it with my original recording, and take specific and detailed notes of changes.
6. When I talk to people, I consciously and conscientiously apply the techniques.
7. I read aloud for 15 minutes a day with a phonetic transcription or imitate an audio text.

The Pledge

"It's not the duration, it's the consistency. I'm training my mouth, lips, tongue, and mind."

REVIEW AND EXPANSION

Track 232

In the first nine chapters of the American Accent Training program, we covered the concepts that form the basis of American speech—intonation, word groups, the staircase, and liaisons, or word connections. We also discussed some key sounds, such as **æ**, **ä**, and **ə** (Cat? Caught? Cut?), the **El**, the American T, and the American R. Let's briefly review each item.

pitch (or saying a word louder or even streeetch-

an't

)pinion
t **feels** like mink, but I think it's **rabbit**.

:an't
He **can't do** it.

ting intonation without changing any of the actual

)b).
about for **years**!).

the stress usually goes on the preposition: *pick up,* ons are placed in the valleys of your intonation. *It's*
put down, *f'r you., They're fr'm LA.*

    When you have initials, the stress goes on the last letter: IB**M**, P**O** Box, ASA**P**, IO**U**, and so on. (See also Chapter 1.)

Liaisons and Glides

Through liaisons, you learned about *voiced* and *unvoiced consonants*—where they are located in the mouth and which sounds are likely to attach to a following one. You were also introduced to glides. (See also Chapter 2.)

1.	**Consonant and Vowel**	Put it **on**.	Pu•di•dan
2.	**Consonant and Consonant**	**race**track	ray•stræk
3.	**Vowel and Vowel**	No **other**	No(w)other
4.	T and Y	Put you **on**	Puchü(w)än
	D and Y	**Had** you?	Hæjoo
	S and Y	**Yes**, you do.	Yeshu do
	Z and Y	Is your **cat**?	Izher cat

Cat? Caught? Cut?

This lesson was an introduction to pronunciation, especially those highly characteristic sounds, æ, ä, and ə. (See also Chapter 3.)

æ   The jaw moves down and back while the back of the tongue pushes forward and the tip touches the back of the bottom teeth. Sometimes it almost sounds like there's a Y in there: *cat* **kyæt**.

ä   Relax the tongue; open the throat like you're letting the doctor see all the way to your toes: *aah*.

ə   This sound is the sound that would come out if you were pushed (lightly) in the stomach: *uh*. You don't need to put your mouth in any particular position at all. The sound is created when the air is forced out of the diaphragm and past the vocal cords.

The American T

T is **T**, a clear popped sound, when it is at the **top** of the staircase.

- at the the beginning of a word, *table*
- in a stressed syllable, *intend*
- in **ST**, **TS**, **TR**, **CT** clusters, *instruct*
- replaces **D** after unvoiced consonants, *hoped* **hopt**

T is **D**, a softer sound, when it is in the **middle** of the staircase.

- in an unstressed position between vowels, *cattle* **caddle**

T and D are held (*not* pronounced with a sharp burst of air) when they are at the **bottom** of the staircase.

- at the end of a word, *bought* **bä**(t)

T is held before **N**.

- unstressed and followed by -*ten* or -*tain*, written **wri(tt)en**

T is swallowed by **N**, *interview* **innerview**.
(See also Chapter 4.)

The El

The El is closely connected with the schwa. Your tongue drops down in back as if it were going to say *uh,* but the tip curls up and attaches to the top of the mouth, which requires a strong movement of the tip of the tongue. The air comes out around the sides of the tongue, and the sound is held for slightly longer than you'd think. (See also Chapter 6.)

The American R

The main difference between a consonant and a vowel is that with a consonant there is contact at some point in your mouth. It might be the lips, **P**; the tongue tip, **N**; or the throat, **G**. Like a vowel, however, the **R** doesn't touch anywhere. It is similar to a schwa, but your tongue curls back in a retroflex movement and produces a sound deep in the throat. *The tongue doesn't touch the top of the mouth.* Another way to approach it is to put your tongue in position for *ee* and then slide straight back to *eeer.* Some people are more comfortable collapsing their tongue back, like an accordion, instead of curling it. It doesn't make any difference in the sound, so do whichever you prefer. (See also Chapter 5.)

APPLICATION EXERCISES

Now, you need to use the exercises you've learned so far and to make the transference to your everyday speech. In the beginning, the process is very slow and analytical, but as you do it over and over again, it becomes natural and unconscious. The exercises presented here will show you how. For example, take any phrase that may catch your ear during a conversation—because it is unfamiliar or for whatever other reason—and work it though the practice sequence used in Review Exercise 1 (page 113).

Review Exercise 7: To Have a Friend, Be a Friend.	Track 233

Read the following phrase with no preparation and record yourself doing it.

To have a friend, be a friend.

Review Exercise 8: To Have a Friend, Be a Friend.	Track 234

Take the repeated phrase through the following application steps. Apply each concept indicated, one at a time and in the sequence given. Read the sentence out loud two or three times, concentrating only on the one concept. This means that when you are working on liaisons, for instance, you don't have to pay much attention to intonation, just for that short time.

1. Intonation
You want to figure out where the intonation belongs when you first encounter a phrase. In this example, *friend* is repeated, so a good reason for intonation would be the contrast that lies in the verbs *have* and *be:*

To **have** a friend, **be** a friend.

2. Word groups
The pause in this case is easy because it's a short sentence with a comma, so we put one there. With your own phrases, look for a logical break or other hints. For example, when you have the verb *to be,* you usually pause very slightly just before it, because it means that you're introducing a definition:

A (pause) is **B**.
Cows(pause) are **ruminants**.
To **have** a friend,(pause) **be** a friend.

121

3. Liaisons

Figure out which words you want to run together. Look for words that start with vowels and connect them to the previous word:

To hava friend, be^(y)a friend.

4. æ, ä, ə

Label these common sounds in the sentence:

Tə hævə friend, be ə friend.

5. The American T

Work with it, making it into a **D** or **CH**, holding it back or getting rid of it altogether, as appropriate. In this phrase, there are no **T**s, but the **D** is held:

To have a frien^(d), be a frien^(d).

6. The American R

Mark all the **R**s.

To have a friend, be a friend.

7. Combination of concepts 1–6

Tə hævə frɛn^{(d), (pause)} be^(y)ə frɛnd^(d).

▶ Practice the sequence of steps a couple of times and then record yourself again; place your second recording right after the first one on your tape. Play them both back and see if you hear a strong difference.

Review Exercise 9: Get a Better Water Heater! Track 235

Go through the same steps with "Get a better water heater!"

1.	Intonation	**Get** a better **water** heater!
2.	Word groups	Get a better water heater! ^(pause)
3.	Liaisons	Geta better water heater!
4.	æ, ä, ə	Getə better wäter heater!
5.	The American T	Gedda bedder wadder heeder!
6.	The American R	Get a betterrr waterrr heaterrr!
7.	Combination of Concepts 1–6	**Gɛ**də bɛddrrr **wä**drrr heedrrr!

Review Exercise 10: Your Own Sentence Track 236

Apply the steps to your own sentences.

1.	Intonation	
2.	Word groups	
3.	Liaisons	
4.	æ, ä, ə	
5.	The American T	
6.	The American R	
7.	Combination of Concepts 1–6	

Are you shy? Does doing this embarrass you? Are you thinking that people will notice your new accent and criticize you for it? In the beginning, you may feel a little strange with these new sounds that you are using, but don't worry, it's like a new pair of shoes—they take a while to break in and make comfortable. Nevertheless, I hope that you are enjoying this program. Adopting a new accent can become too personal and too emotional an issue, so don't take it too seriously. Relax. Have a good time. Play with the sounds that you are making. Whenever a word or phrase strikes your fancy, go somewhere private and comfortable and try out a couple of different approaches, styles, and attitudes with it—as you are going to do in the next exercise. If possible, record yourself on tape so you can decide which one suits you best.

Review Exercise 11: Varying Emotions **Track 238**

Repeat the following statement and response expressing the various feelings or tones indicated in parentheses.

anger	I told you it wouldn't work!!	I thought it would!
excitement	I told you it wouldn't work!!	I thought it would!
disbelief	I told you it wouldn't work?	And I thought it would?
smugness	I told you it wouldn't work.	I thought it would. *(I-told-you-so attitude)*
humor	I told you it wouldn't work.	I thought it would
sadness	I told you it wouldn't work.	I thought it would.
relief	I told you it wouldn't work.	Whew! I thought it would.
resignation	I told you it wouldn't work.	I thought it would.

▶ Repeat the statement using three other tones that you'd like to try.

Your choice	I told you it wouldn't work	I thought it would
Your choice	I told you it wouldn't work	I thought it would
Your choice	I told you it wouldn't work	I thought it would

Now that you've run through a couple of emotions and practiced speaking with both meaning and feeling, try having some two-word conversations. These are pretty common in day-to-day situations.

Review Exercise 12: Really? Maybe! **Track 239**

Repeat the following statements and responses expressing the various feelings.

1.	Really?	(general curiosity)	Maybe.	(general potential)
2.	Really?	(avid curiosity)	Maybe.	(suggestive possibility)
3.	Really?	(boredom)	Maybe	(equal boredom)
4.	Really?	(laughing with disbelief)	Maybe.	(slight possibility)
5.	Really?	(sarcasm)	Maybe.	(self-justification)
6.	Really?	(sadness)	Maybe.	(equal sadness)
7.	Really?	(relief)	Maybe.	(hope)
8.	Really?	(coy interrogation)	Maybe.	(coy confirmation)
9.	Really?	(seeking confirmation)	Rilly!	(confirmation)

✗ *Try three on your own.*

10.	Really?	(your choice)	Maybe.	(your choice)
11.	Really?	(your choice)	Maybe.	(your choice)
12.	Really?	(your choice)	Maybe.	(your choice)

Repeat the following statements and responses expressing the various feelings.

1.	Who did it? (curiosity)	I don't know. (ignorance)
2.	Who did it? (interrogation)	I don't know. (self-protection)
3.	Who did it? (anger)	I don't know. (insistence)
4.	Who did it? (repeating)	I don't know. (strong denial)
5.	Who did it? (sarcasm)	I don't know. (self-justification)
6.	Who did it? (sadness)	I don't know. (despair)
7.	Who did it? (relief)	I sure don't know. (blithe ignorance)
8.	Whooo did it? (coy interrogation)	I don't know. (singsong)
9.	Who did it? (annoyance)	I don't know. (equal annoyance)
10.	Who did it? (laughing with disbelief)	I don't know. (laughing ignorance)
11.	Who did it? (surprise)	I dunno. (sullenness)
12.	Who did it? (your choice)	I don't know. (your choice)

Rəshəz əfensəv əgɛnst rebəlz in thə brɛikəway reejənəv Chechnyə iz entering ə nyu fɛiz. än thə wən hænd, Rəshən forsəzr teiking fül kəntrol əv thə Rəshən kæpədəl, Gräzny, ənd Mäskæo sez thə wor seemz tə be trning in its feivr. än thee əthr hænd, thə rebəlz küd be reetreeding Gräzny jəst tə fight ənəthr day—enshring ə läng grrilə wor. Thə for-mənth känflikt täpt thee əjendə tədäy during Sɛkrətery əv State Mædəlin älbräit's täks with ækting Rəshən prezəd'nt Vlædəmir Putin, älbräit then left fr Kro-^(w)ɛishə, əbæot which we will hear more shortly. Bət frst, we trn tə thə Wrldz Nenet Shevek in Mäskæo.

olbräit ɛn Pu-tin met feu lɔnger thɛn plennd tədäy—feu nillee three äwɛz. äftə thɛə tɔks, olbrait kɔld thɛ meeting intens, bət plɛznt, ɛn ɔfeud this ɛsɛsmɛnt ɛf Rəshəz ɛkting prezidɛnt.

I fæond him ə very wellin formd persən. Heez äveeəslee ə Rəshən paytreeət ən älso səmwən who seeks a norməl pəzishən fr Rəshə within thə West—ən he strɛck me əzə präbləm sälvr

 – ✦ –

Russia's offensive against rebels in the breakaway region of Chechnya is entering a new phase. On the one hand, Russian forces are taking full control of the Russian capital, Grozny, and Moscow says the war seems to be turning in its favor. On the other hand, the rebels could be retreating Grozny just to fight another day—ensuring a long guerilla war. The four-month conflict topped the agenda today during Secretary of State Madeline Albright's talks with acting Russian president Vladimir Putin. Albright then left for Croatia, about which we'll hear more shortly. But first, we turn to the World's Nennet Shevek in Moscow.

"Albright and Putin met for longer than planned today—for nearly three hours. After the talks, Albright called the meeting intense, but pleasant, and offered this assessment of Russia's acting president."

"I found him a very well-informed person. He's obviously a Russian patriot and also someone who seeks a normal position for Russia within the West—and he struck me as a problem solver."

TWO-WORD PHRASES

Exercise A–M are a synopsis of all intonation patterns that have been studied so far.

Review Exercise A: Contrasting Descriptive and Set Phrases Track 242

*(Here we are reprising the exercise from Exercises 1-39 to 1-52.) To review, an adjective and a noun make a **descriptive phrase**, and the second word is stressed. Two nouns make a compound noun, or **set phrase**, and the first word is stressed. Repeat the following sentences. Copy your descriptive phrases and set phrases from Exercise 1-46. You will continue using these word combinations throughout this series of exercises. (See also Chapter 1.)*

	Descriptive Phrase	Set Phrase
1.	It's a short **nail**.	It's a **finger**nail.
2.	It's a chocolate **cake**.	It's a **pan**cake.
3.	It's a hot **bath**.	It's a **hot** tub.
4.	It's a long **drive**.	It's a **hard** drive.
5.	It's the back **door**.	It's the **back**bone.
6.	There are four **cards**.	It's a **card** trick.
7.	It's a small **spot**.	It's a **spot**light.
8.	It's a good **book**.	It's a **phone** book.
9.	It's a _____.	It's a _____.
10.	It's a _____.	It's a _____.
11.	It's a _____.	It's a _____.

Review Exercise B: Intonation Review Test Track 243

Put an accent mark over the word that should be stressed. (Answer Key on page 218.)

1.	They live in **Los Angeles**.	11.	We like **everything**.
2.	Give me a **paper bag**.	12.	It's a **moving van**.
3.	Is that your **lunch bag**?	13.	It's a **new paper**.
4.	7-11 is a **convenience store**.	14.	It's the **newspaper**.
5.	Lucky's is a **convenient store**.	15.	The doll has **glass eyes**.
6.	Do your **homework**!	16.	The doll has **eyeglasses**.
7.	He's a **good writer**.	17.	It's a **high chair**.
8.	It's an **apple pie**.	18.	It's a **highchair**. *(for babies)*
9.	It's a **pineapple**.	19.	It's a **baseball**.
10.	We like **all things**.	20.	It's a **blue ball**.

THREE-WORD PHRASES

When you modify a descriptive phrase by adding an adjective or adverb, you maintain the original intonation pattern and simply add an additional stress point.

	Descriptive Phrase	Modified Descriptive Phrase
1.	It's a short **nail**.	It's a **really** short **nail**.
2.	It's a chocolate **cake**.	It's a **tasty** chocolate **cake**.
3.	I took a hot **bath**.	I took a **long**, hot **bath**.
4.	It's a hard **drive**.	It's a **long,** hard **drive**.
5.	It's the **back door**.	It's the **only** back **door**.
6.	There are four **cards**.	There **are four** slick **cards**.
7.	It's a little **spot**.	It's a **little** black **spot**.
8.	It's a good **book**.	It's a **really** good **book**.
9.	It's a _____.	It's a _____.
10.	It's a _____.	It's a _____.
11.	It's a _____.	It's a _____.

When you modify a set phrase, you maintain the same pattern, leaving the new adjective unstressed.

	Set Phrase	Modified Set Phrase
1.	It's a **finger**nail.	It's a short **finger**nail.
2.	It's a **pan**cake.	It's a delicious **pan**cake.
3.	It's a **hot** tub.	It's a leaky **hot** tub.
4.	It's a **hard** drive.	It's an expensive **hard** drive.
5.	It's the **back**bone.	It's a long **back**bone.
6.	It's a **card** trick.	It's a clever **card** trick.
7.	It's a **spot**light.	It's a bright **spot**light.
8.	It's a **phone** book.	It's the new **phone** book.
9.	It's a _____.	It's a _____.
10.	It's a _____.	It's a _____.
11.	It's a _____.	It's a _____.

Review Exercise E: Two- and Three-Word Set Phrases **Track 246**

*You should be pretty familiar with the idea of a set phrase by now. The next step is when you have more components that link together to form a new thing—a three-word set phrase. Combine **three things**: finger + nail + clipper. Leave the stress on the first word: **finger**nail clipper. Although you are now using three words, they still mean **one new thing.** Write your own sentences, using the word combinations from the previous exercises.*

	Two-Word Set Phrase	Three-Word Set Phrase
1.	It's a **finger**nail.	It's a **finger**nail clipper.
2.	It's a **pan**cake.	It's a **pan**cake shop.
3.	It's a **hot** tub.	It's a **hot** tub maker.
4.	It's a **hard** drive.	It's a **hard** drive holder.
5.	It's the **back**bone.	It's a **back**bone massage.
6.	It's a **playing** card.	It's a **playing** card rack.
7.	It's a **spot**light.	It's a **spot**light stand.
8.	It's a **phone** book.	It's a **phone** book listing.
9.	It's a _____.	It's a _____.
10.	It's a _____.	It's a _____.
11.	It's a _____.	It's a _____.

Review Exercise F: Three-Word Phrase Summary **Track 247**

Repeat the following sentences. Write your own sentences at the bottom, carrying over the same examples you used in the previous exercise.

Modified Description	Modified Set Phrase	3-Word Set Phrase
1.	a **really** short nail	a long **finger**nail	a **finger**nail clipper
2.	a **big** chocolate **cake**	a thin **pan**cake	a **pan**cake shop
3.	a **long**, hot **bath**	a leaky **hot** tub	a **hot** tub maker
4.	a **long**, boring **drive**	a new **hard** drive	a **hard** drive holder
5.	a **broken** back **door**	a long **back**bone	a **back**bone massage
6.	**four** slick **cards**	a new **playing** card	a **playing** card rack
7.	a **small** black **spot**	a bright **spot**light	a **spot**light stand
8.	a **well**-written **book**	an open **phone** book	a **phone** book listing
9.	▬	a blind **sales**man	a **blind** salesman
		(He can't see.)	(He sells blinds.)
10.	▬	a light **house**keeper	a **light**house keeper
		(She cleans the house.)	(She lives in a lighthouse.)
11.	▬	a green **house**plant	a **green**house plant
		(It's a healthy **house**plant.)	(It's from a **green**house.)

12.	It's a _____ .	It's a _____ .	It's a _____ .
13.	It's a _____ .	It's a _____ .	It's a _____ .
14.	It's a _____ .	It's a _____ .	It's a _____ .

Review Exercise G: Three-Word Phrases—Three Little Pigs   🔊 Track 248

*Notice where there are patterns, where the words change but the rhythm stays the same (**straw-cutting tools**, **woodcutting tools**, **bricklaying tools**). Read the story aloud.*

Once upon a time, there were *three little pigs.* They lived with their *kind old mother* near a *large, dark forest.* One day, they decided to build *their own houses.* The *first little pig* used straw. He took his *straw-cutting tools* and his *new lawnmower* and built a *little straw house.* The *second little pig* used sticks. He took his *woodcutting tools* and some *old paintbrushes* and built a *small wooden house.* The *third little pig,* who was a *very hard worker,* used bricks. He took his *bricklaying tools,* an *expensive mortarboard,* and built a *large brick house.* In the forest lived a *big bad wolf.* He wanted to eat the *three little pigs,* so he went to the *flimsy straw abode* and tried to blow it down. "Not by the hair of my *chinny chin chin*!" cried the *three little porkers.* But the house was *not very strong,* and the *big bad beast* blew it down. The *three little pigs* ran to the *rickety wooden structure,* but the *big bad wolf* blew it down, too. Quickly, the *three little piggies* ran to the *sturdy brick dwelling* and hid inside. The *big bad wolf* huffed and he puffed, but he couldn't blow the *strong brick house* down. The *three little pigs* laughed and danced and sang.

Review Exercise H: Sentence Balance—Goldilocks   🔊 Track 249

*One of the most fascinating things about spoken English is how the intonation prepares the listener for what is coming. As you know, the main job of intonation is to announce new information. However, there is a secondary function, and that is to alert the listener of changes down the road. Certain shifts will be dictated for the sake of **sentence balance**. Set phrases and contrast don't change, but the intonation of a descriptive phrase will move from the second word to the first, **without changing the meaning**. The stress change indicates that it's not the end of the sentence, but rather, there is more to come. This is why it is particularly important to speak in phrases instead of word by word.*

*When we practiced **Goldilocks and the Three Bears** the first time (page 42), we had very short sentences, so we didn't need sentence balance. All of the blue descriptive phrases would otherwise be stressed on the second word if the shift weren't needed.*

There is a *little girl* called *Goldilocks.* She is *walking* through a *sunny forest* and sees a *small house.* She *knocks* on the door, but *no one* answers. She *goes inside* to see what's *there.* There are *three chairs* in the *large room. Goldilocks* sits on the *biggest chair.* It's *too high* for her to *sit on.* She sits on the *middle-sized* one, but it's *too low.* She sits on the *small chair,* and it is *just right.* On the table, there are *three bowls* of *porridge.* She tries the *first one,* but it is *too hot* to *swallow.* The *second one* is *too cold,* and the *third one* is *just right,* so she eats it all. *After that,* she *goes* upstairs to *look around.* There are *three beds* in the *bedroom.*

She *sits down* on the *biggest one.* It's *too hard* to *sleep on.* The *middle-sized* bed is *too soft.* The *little* one is *just right,* so she *lies down and falls asleep.*

In the *meantime,* the family of *three bears* comes home—the *Papa bear,* the *Mama bear,* and the *Baby bear.* They *look around* and *say,* "Who's been sitting in our chairs and eating our porridge?" Then they *run upstairs* and *say,* "Who's been sleeping in our beds?" *Goldilocks wakes up* when she hears all the *noise* and is *so scared* that she *runs out* of the house and never *comes back.*

FOUR-WORD PHRASES

| Review Exercise I: Multiple Modifiers with Set Phrases | Track 250 |

When you continue to modify a set phrase, you maintain the original intonation pattern and simply add an additional stress point.

	Modified Set Phrase	Remodified Set Phrase
1.	It's a short **finger**nail.	It's a **really** short **finger**nail.
2.	It's a banana **pan**cake.	It's a **tasty** banana **pan**cake.
3.	It's a leaky **hot** tub.	It's a **leaky** old **hot** tub.
4.	It's a new **hard** drive.	It's a **brand** new **hard** drive.
5.	It's a long **back**bone.	It's a **long**, hard **back**bone.
6.	It's a wrinkled **playing** card.	It's a **wrinkled**, old **playing** card.
7.	It's a bright **spot**light.	It's a **bright** white **spot**light.
8.	It's the new **phone** book.	It's a **new** age **phone** book.
9.	It's a _____.	It's a _____.
10.	It's a _____.	It's a _____.
11.	It's a _____.	It's a _____.

| Review Exercise J: Compound Intonation of Numbers | Track 251 |

In short phrases (#1 and #2), –teen can be thought of as a separate word in terms of intonation. In longer phrases, the number + –teen becomes one word. Repeat after me.

1.	How **old** is he?	2.	How long has it **been**?	3.	How **old** is he?
	He's four**teen**. (for**téen**)		**Four**teen **years**.		He's **fourteen** years **old**.
	He's **for**ty. (fórdy)		Forty **years**.		He's **forty** years **old**.

Review Exercise K: Modifying Three-Word Set Phrases

Track 252

When you continue to modify a set phrase, you maintain the original intonation pattern and simply add an unstressed modifier.

Three-Word Set Phrase	Modified Three-Word Set Phrase
1. It's a **finger**nail clipper.	It's a new **finger**nail clipper.
2. It's a **pan**cake shop.	It's a good **pan**cake shop.
3. He's a **hot** tub maker.	He's the best **hot** tub maker.
4. It's a **hard** drive holder.	It's a plastic **hard** drive holder.
5. It's a **back**bone massage.	It's a painful **back**bone massage.
6. It's a **playing** card rack.	It's my best **playing** card rack.
7. It's a **spot**light bulb.	It's a fragile **spot**light bulb.
8. It's a **phone** book listing.	It's an unusual **phone** book listing.
9. It's a _____.	It's a _____.
10. It's a _____.	It's a _____.
11. It's a _____.	It's a _____.

Review Exercise L: Four-Word Phrase Story—Little Red Riding Hood

Track 253

Repeat after me.

Once upon a time, there was a *cute little redhead* named *Little Red Riding Hood*. One day, she told her mother that she wanted to take a *well-stocked picnic basket* to her *dear old grandmother* on the other side of the *dark, scary Black Forest*. Her mother warned her not to talk to strangers—especially the *dangerous big bad wolf*. *Little Red Riding Hood* said she would be careful, and left. Halfway there, she saw a *mild- mannered hitchhiker*. She pulled over in her *bright red sports car* and offered him a ride. Just before they got to the *freeway turnoff* for her *old grandmother's house*, the *heavily bearded young man* jumped out and ran away. (Was he the wolf?) He hurried ahead to the *waiting grandmother's house*, let himself in, ate her, and jumped into her bed to wait for *Little Red Riding Hood*. When *Little Red Riding Hood* got to the house, she was surprised, "Grandmother, what big *eyes* you have!" The wolf replied, "The better to *see* you with, my dear . . ." "But Grandmother, what big *ears* you have!" "The better to *hear* you with, my dear . . ." "Oh, Grandmother, what big *teeth* you have!" "The better to *eat* you with!" And the wolf jumped out of the bed to eat *Little Red Riding Hood*. Fortunately for her, she was a *recently paid-up member* of the *infamous National Rifle Association* so she pulled out her *brand new shotgun* and shot the wolf dead.

Review Exercise M: Building Up to Five-Word Phrases Track 254

Repeat after me, then write your own phrases, using the same order and form.

1.	It's a **pot**.	*noun*
2.	It's **new**.	*adjective*
3.	It's a new **pot**.	*descriptive phrase (noun)*
4.	It's brand **new**.	*descriptive phrase (adjective)*
5.	It's a **brand** new **pot**.	*modified descriptive phrase*
6.	It's a **tea**pot.	*two-word set phrase*
7.	It's a new **tea**pot.	*modified set phrase*
8.	It's a **brand** new **tea**pot.	*modified set phrase*
9.	It's a **tea**pot lid.	*three-word set phrase*
10.	It's a new **tea**pot lid.	*modified three-word set phrase*
11.	It's a **brand** new **tea**pot lid.	*modified three-word set phrase*

1.	_____	*noun*
2.	_____	*adjective*
3.	_____	*descriptive phrase (noun)*
4.	_____	*descriptive phrase (adjective)*
5.	_____	*modified descriptive phrase*
6.	_____	*two-word set phrase*
7.	_____	*modified set phrase*
8.	_____	*modified set phrase*
9.	_____	*three-word set phrase*
10.	_____	*modified three-word set phrase*
11.	_____	*modified three-word set phrase*

Track 255

Since so many people are familiar with the binary system, let's do a quick review of how complex intonation can be viewed with zeroes and ones.

pot	1
new	1
new **pot**	01
brand **new**	01
brand new **pot**	101
teapot	10
new **tea**pot	010
brand new **tea**pot	1010
teapot lid	100
new **tea**pot lid	0100
brand new **tea**pot lid	10100

Do a global **Search All** and **Replace** for these patterns.

Review Exercise 15: Ignorance on Parade   Track 256

Now, let's dissect a standard paragraph, including its title, as we did in Review Exercise 1. First—in the **blue phrases** *in the first paragraph, decide which is a descriptive phrase, which is a set phrase, and where any additional stress might fall. Remember, descriptive phrases are stressed on the second word and set phrases on the first. Use one of your colored markers to indicate the stressed words. Second—go through the second paragraph and mark the remaining stressed words. Third—put slash marks where you think a short pause is appropriate in the third paragraph. In the last paragraph, change Ts to either a D or a held T, as needed. Listen as the speaker reads the paragraph. (See also Chapters 1 and 2.)*

✗ Do the written exercises, including intonation; word groups; liaisons; æ, ä, ə; and the American **T**.

1. Two-word phrases, intonation, and phrasing
Ignorance on Parade
You say you don't know a proton from a crouton? Well, you're not the only one. A recent nationwide survey funded by the National Science Foundation shows that fewer than 6 percent of American adults can be called scientifically literate. The rest think that DNA is a food additive, Chernobyl is a ski resort, and radioactive milk can be made safe by boiling. *Judith Stone / 2109 Discover Publications*

2. Word Connections
Ignoran sän Parade
You say you don't know a proton from a crouton? Well, you're not the only one. A recent nationwide survey funded by the National Science Foundation shows that fewer than 6 percent of American adults can be called scientifically literate. The rest think that DNA is a food additive, Chernobyl is a ski resort, and radioactive milk can be made safe by boiling.

3. æ, ä, ə
Ignərance än Pərade
You say you don't know a proton from a crouton? Well, you're not the only one. A recent nationwide survey funded by the National Science Foundation shows that fewer than 6 percent of American adults can be called scientifically literate. The rest think that DNA is a food additive, Chernobyl is a ski resort, and radioactive milk can be made safe by boiling.

4. The American T
Ignorants on Parade
You say you don't know a proton from a crouton? Well, you're not the only one. A recent nationwide survey funded by the National Science Foundation shows that fewer than 6 percent of American adults can be called scientifically literate. The rest think that DNA is a food additive, Chernobyl is a ski resort, and radioactive milk can be made safe by boiling.

Review Exercise 16: Ignorance on Parade Explanations

Here, go over each topic, point by point.

1. Two-word phrases, intonation, and phrasing
a **proton** from a **crouton**? *(contrast)*
Well, **you're** not the **only** one. *(contrast)*
A **recent** nationwide **survey** *(modified descriptive phrase)*
National **Science** Foundation *(modified set phrase)*
6 percent of American **adults** *(descriptive phrase with sentence balance)*
scientifically **literate** *(descriptive phrase)*
The **rest** think *(contrast)*
DN**A** *(acronym)*

food additive *(set phrase)*
ski resort *(set phrase)*
radioactive **milk** *(descriptive phrase)*

Ignorance on Parade[stop]

You say you don't know a **pro**ton from a **crou**ton? [pause] **Well,**[pause] **you're** not the **only** one.[pause] A **recent** nationwide **survey** [pause] funded by the National **Science** Foundation [pause] shows that fewer than **6** percent of American **adults** [pause] can be called scientifically **literate**.[stop] The **rest** think[pause] that DNA is a **food** additive,[pause] Chernobyl is a **ski** resort,[pause] and radioactive **milk**[pause] can be made **safe** by **boiling**.

2. Word Connections
Ignoran sän Parade

You sa[y]you don[t]knowa **pro**ton froma **crou**ton? **Well,** you're no[t]the[y]**only** one. A **recen**[t]nationwide-**sur**vey funded by the National**Sci**[y]ence Foundation showzthat fewer thansix percen'v'merica na**dults** can be called scientifically **lit**erate. The **ress**think that Dee[y]εNA[y]iza **foo** dadditive, Cherno**byl**iza **ski** resort, and radi[y]o[w]active **milk** can be made**safe** by boiling.

3. æ, ä, ə
Ignərance än Pərade

You say you dont know ə **pro**tän frəm ə **croo**tän? Well, yer nät thee[y]**only** wən. ə **res**ənt nashənwide **srvey** fəndəd by thə **Næsh**ənəl **Sci**[y]əns **Fæon**dāshən showz thət fewər thən **6** pr senəv əmerəcən **ədəlts** cən be cälld sci[y]əntifəklee **lid**erət. Thə **rest** think thət Dee Yeh **Nay**[y]izə **food** æddətv, Chrnobl izə **skee** rəzort, ən radee[y]o[w]æctəv **milk** cən be made **safe** by **boi**ling.

4. The American T
Ignorants on Parade

You say you don[t] know a **pro**Ton from a **crou**Ton? Well, you're nä[t] the **only** one. A **recen**[t] nation-wide **sur**vey funded by the National **Science** Foundation shows tha[t] fewer than **6** percen of American **adulTs** can be called scienTifically **lid**erə[t]. The **ress** think tha[t] DNA is a **food** addidive, Chernobyl is a **ski** resor[t], and radioakdiv **milk** can be made **safe** by **boi**ling.

5. Combined
Ignərən sän Pərade

You sa[y]you don[t]no wə **pro**tän frəmə **croo**tän?[stop]Well,[pause]yer nät thee[y]**only** wən. [pause]ə **rees**ən[t] nāshənwide **srvey**[pause]fəndəd by thə **Næsh**ənəl **Sci**[y]əns **Fæon**dāshən[pause]shoz thə[t] fewər thən **6** prcenə vəmerəcə nə**dults**[pause]cən be cälld sci[y]əntifəklee **lid**erət.[stop]Thə **ress** think[pause]thə[t] Dee Yeh **Nay**[y]izə **foo** dæddədv,[pause]Chr**nob**ə lizə **skee** rəzort,[pause]ən raydee[y]o[w]æctəv **milk**[pause]cən be made **safe** by **boi**ling.

I told my shrink that I had dreamt I was a teepee and a wigwam.

He said I was too tense.

10
More Reduced Sounds

Unstressed syllables have reduced vowels and are said quickly.

Track 257

There are two sounds that look similar but sound quite different. One is the tense vowel **u**, pronounced *ooh*, and the other is the soft vowel **ü**, whose pronunciation is a combination of *ih* and *uh*. The **u** sound is located far forward in the mouth and requires you to round your lips. The **ü** is one of the four reduced vowel sounds that are made in the throat: The most tense and highest in the throat is **ɛ**; next, slightly more relaxed, is **i**; then **ü**; and deepest and most relaxed is the neutral schwa **ə**. For the reduced semivowel *schwa + R*, the throat is relaxed, but the tongue is tense. (See also Chapters 1, 3, 5, and 12.)

| | Exercise 10-1: Comparing u and ü | | Track 258 |

Look at the chart that follows and repeat each word. We are contrasting the sound u (first and third columns)—a strong, nonreducible sound, ooh, that is made far forward in the mouth, with the lips fully rounded—with the reduced ü sound in the second and fourth columns.

OO,,
OH,,

	u	ü		u	ü
1.	booed	book	11.	Luke	look
2.	boo	bushel	12.	nuke	nook
3.	cooed	could	13.	pool	pull
4.	cool	cushion	14.	pooch	put
5.	food	foot	15.	shoe	sugar
6.	fool	full	16.	suit	soot
7.	gooed	good	17.	shoot	should
8.	who'd	hood	18.	stewed	stood
9.	kook	cook	19.	toucan	took
10.	crew	crook	20.	wooed	would

bük
bük

No lips!

For the *ooh* sound, round your lips like a fish. For the *ü* sound, think of a chicken. Chickens don't have lips, so they certainly can't round them. You have to say **ü** down in the back of your throat.

The lax vowels are produced in the throat and are actually quite similar to each other. Let's practice some lax vowels. (See also Chapter 12 to contrast with tense vowels.) Remember to double the vowel when the word ends in a voiced consonant.

	e	i	ü	ə	ər
1.	end	it	■	un–	earn
2.	bet	bit	book	but	burn
3.	kept	kid	could	cut	curt
4.	check	chick	■	chuck	church
5.	debt	did	■	does	dirt
6.	fence	fit	foot	fun	first
7.	fell	fill	full	■	furl
8.	get	guilt	good	gut	girl
9.	help	hit	hook	hut	hurt
10.	held	hill	hood	hull	hurl
11.	gel	Jill	■	jump	jerk
12.	ked	kid	cook	cud	curd
13.	crest	crypt	crook	crumb	■
14.	let	little	look	lump	lurk
15.	men	milk	■	muck	murmur
16.	net	knit	nook	nut	nerd
17.	pet	pit	put	putt	pert
18.	pell	pill	pull	■	pearl
19.	red	rid	root	rut	rural
20.	said	sit	soot	such	search
21.	shed	shin	should	shut	sure
22.	sled	slim	■	slug	slur
23.	stead	still	stood	stuff	stir
24.	It's stewed.	It'd stick.	It stood.	It's done.	It's dirt.
25.	stretch	string	■	struck	■
26.	tell	tip	took	ton	turn
27.	then	this	■	thus	■
28.	■	thing	■	thug	third
29.	vex	vim	■	vug	verb
30.	wet	wind	would	was	word
31.	yet	yin	■	young	yearn
32.	zen	Zinfandel	■	result	deserve

Tense Vowels

Sound	Symbol	Spelling
ɛi	bāt	bait
ee	bēt	beat
äi	bīt	bite
ou	bōᵘt	boat
ooh	būt	boot
ah	bät	bought
ä + ɛ	bæt	bat
æ + o	bæot	bout

Lax Vowels

Sound	Symbol	Spelling
eh	bɛt	bet
ih	bit	bit
ih + uh	püt	put
uh	bət	but
er	bərt	Bert

Eh (Lax)

Eee (Tense)

Exercise 10-3: Bit or Beat? Track 260

We've discussed intonation in terms of new information, contrast, opinion, and negatives. As you heard on pages 5–6, Americans tend to stretch out certain one-syllable words . . . but which ones? The answer is simple—when a single-syllable word ends in an unvoiced consonant, the vowel is on a single stairstep— short and sharp. When the word ends in a voiced consonant, or a vowel, the vowel is on a double stairstep. (For an explanation of voiced and unvoiced consonants, see page 47.) You can also think of this in terms of musical notes.

Here you are going to compare the four words bit, bid, beat, and bead. Once you can distinguish these four, all of the rest are easy. Repeat.

	single	double
tense	beat	bead
lax	bit	bid

Note *You may hear **tense vowels** called **long vowels**, but this can cause confusion when you are talking about the long, or doubled, vowel before a voiced consonant. Use the rubber band to distinguish: Make a short, sharp snap for the single-note words (beat, bit) and a longer, stretched-out loop for the double-note words (bead, bid).*

Exercise 10-4: Bit or Beat? Bid or Bead? Track 261

Read each column down. Next, contrast the single and double tense vowels with each other, and the single and double lax vowels with each other.

	Tense Vowels		Lax Vowels	
1.	beat	bead	bit	bid
2.	seat	seed	sit	Sid
3.	heat	he'd	hit	hid
4.	Pete	impede	pit	rapid
5.	feet	feed	fit	fin
6.	niece	knees	miss	Ms.
7.	geese	he's	hiss	his
8.	deep	deed	disk	did
9.	neat	need	knit	(nid)
10.	leaf	leave	lift	live

Finally, read all four across.

Track 262

Note *Bear in mind that the single/double intonation pattern is the same for all final voiced and unvoiced consonants, not just **T** and **D**.*

Let's practice tense and lax vowels in context. The intonation is marked for you. When in doubt, try to leave out the lax vowel rather than run the risk of overpronouncing it: l'p in place of lip, so it doesn't sound like leap. Repeat:

	Tense	Lax	
1.	eat	it	I **eat** it.
2.	beat	bit	The **beat** is a bit strong.
3.	keys	kiss	Give me a **kiss** for the keys.
4.	cheek	chick	The chick's **cheek** is soft.
5.	deed	did	He **did** the deed.
6.	feet	fit	These **shoes** fit my **feet**.
7.	feel	fill	Do you feel that we should **fill** it?
8.	green	grin	The Martian's **grin** was **green**.
9.	heat	hit	Last **summer**, the **heat** hit **hard**.
10.	heel	hill	Put your **heel** on the **hill**.
11.	jeep	Jill	Jill's **jeep** is here.
12.	creep	crypt	Let's **creep** near the **crypt**.
13.	leap	lip	He bumped his **lip** when he **leaped**.
14.	meal	mill	She had a **meal** at the **mill**.
15.	neat	knit	He can **knit neatly**.
16.	peel	pill	Don't **peel** that **pill**!
17.	reed	rid	Get rid of the **reed**.
18.	seek	sick	We seek the **sixth** sick sheik's **sheep**.
19.	sheep	ship	There are **sheep** on the **ship**.
20.	sleep	slip	The girl **sleeps** in a **slip**.
21.	steal	still	He still **steals**.
22.	Streep	strip	Meryl **Streep** is in a **comic** strip.
23.	team	Tim	**Tim** is on the **team**.
24.	these	this	**These** are better than **this** one.
25.	thief	thing	The **thief** took my **thing**.
26.	weep	whip	Who **weeps** from the **whips**?

Track 264

In the time you have taken to reach this point in the program, you will have made a lot of decisions about your own individual speech style. Pronunciation of reduced sounds is more subjective and depends on how quickly you speak, how you prefer to express yourself, the range of your intonation, how much you want to reduce certain vowels, and so on.

Exercise 10-6: The Middle "I" List Track 265

The letter I in the unstressed position devolves consistently into a schwa. Repeat.

-ity	ədee	chemistry	hostility	opportunity
-ify	əfái	chronological	humanity	organization
-ited	əd'd	clarity	humidity	partiality
-ible	əbªl	commodity	humility	physical
-ical	əcªl	community	identity	pitiful
-imal	əmªl	communication	imitation	politics
-ization	əzāsh'n	complexity	immaturity	positive
-ication	əcāsh'n	confident	immigration	possible
-ination	ənāsh'n	confidentiality	immunity	possibility
-ifaction	əfæksh'n	contribution	incident	president
-itation	ətāsh'n	creativity	individuality	principle
		credit	infinity	priority
ability		critical	insecurity	psychological
accident		cubicle	instability	publicity
accountability		curiosity	institute	qualify
activity		difficult	investigation	quality
adversity		dignity	invisible	quantity
America		disparity	invitation	radical
analytical		diversity	janitor	reality
animal		Edison	Jennifer	rectify
applicant		editor	legalization	resident
application		electricity	liability	responsibility
article		eligibility	Madison	sacrifice
astronomical		eliminated	maturity	sanity
audible		engineer	medicine	security
auditor		episode	mentality	seminar
authority		equality	majority	seniority
availability		evidence	maximum	severity
beautiful		experiment	Michigan	sensitivity
brutality		facility	minimum	similar
calamity		familiarity	minority	skeptical
California		feasibility	modify	superiority
candidate		flexibility	Monica	technical
capacity		Florida	monitor	testify
celebrity		foreigner	municipality	typical
charity		formality	nationality	uniform
Christianity		fraternity	naturalization	unity
clinical		gravity	necessity	university
clerical		heredity	negative	validity
chemical		hospitality	nomination	visitor

*In the following example, you will see how you can fully sound out a word (such as **to**), reduce it slightly, or do away with it altogether.*

1. . . . easier tū⁽ʷ⁾ənderstand.
2. . . . easier tü⁽ʷ⁾ənderstand.
3. . . . easier tə ənderstand.
4. . . . easier tənderstand.
5. . . . easier dənderstand.

Each of the preceding examples is correct and appropriate when said well. If you have a good understanding of intonation, you might be best understood if you used the last example. How would this work with the rest of our familiar paragraph, you ask? Let's see.

Go through the paragraph that follows and find the three ü's and the five to seven u's. Remember that your own speech style can increase the possibilities. With "to" before a vowel, you have a choice of a strong u, a soft ü, a schwa, or to telescope the two words and eliminate the vowel entirely. Mark the ü and u sounds. The first one is marked for you in blue. (Remember to check the Answer Key on page 218.)

Hello, **my** name is_____. I'm taking American **Accent** Training. There's a **lot** to **learn**, but I **hope** to make it as **enjoyable** as possible. **I** shüd pick **up** on the American **intonation** pattern pretty **easily**, although the **only** way to **get** it is to **practice** all of the time. I ūse the **up** and down, or **peaks** and valleys, **intonation** more than I **used** to. I've been paying attention to **pitch, too**. It's like **walking** down a **stair**case. I've been **talking** to a lot of **Americans** lately, and they tell me that I'm **easier** to under**stand**. **Any**way, I could go **on** and on, but the **important** thing is to **listen** well and sound **good**. **Well**, what do you **think**? **Do** I?

ALL PREFIXES HAVE A SCHWA

Track 268

a-	avert	attend	appellate	attract	apportion	adduce
con/com-	convert	contend	compel	contract	comport	conduct
di/dis/de-	divert	distend	dispel	distract	deport	deduct/deduce
e/ex-	evert	extend	expel	extract	export	educate
in/im-	invert	intend	impel	intractable	import	induce
pro/pre/per-	pervert	pretend	propel	protract	proportion	produce
re-	revert	retain	repel	retract	report	reduce

Exercise 10-9: How Much Wood Would a Woodchuck Chuck? 🔊 Track 269

How fast can you say:

How much wood	hæo məch wüd
would a wood chuck chuck,	wüdə wüdchək chək
if a woodchuck	ifə wüdchəck
could chuck	cüd chəck
wood?	wüd

How many cookies	hæo meny cükeez
could a good cook cook,	cüdə güd cük cük
if a good cook	ifə güd cük
could cook	cüd cük
cookies?	cükeez

In the following two exercises, we will practice the two vowel sounds separately.

Exercise 10-10: Büker Wülsey's Cükbük 🔊 Track 270

Repeat after me.

Booker Woolsey was a good cook. One day, he took a good look at his full schedule and decided that he could write a good cookbook. He knew that he could, and thought that he should, but he wasn't sure that he ever would. Once he had made up his mind, he stood up, pulled up a table, took a cushion, and put it on a bushel basket of sugar in the kitchen nook. He shook out his writing hand and put his mind to creating a good, good cookbook.

Exercise 10-11: A True Fool 🔊 Track 271

Repeat after me.

A true fool will choose to drool in a pool to stay cool. Who knew that such fools were in the schools, used tools, and flew balloons? Lou knew and now you do, too.

YOD DROPPING

🔊
Track 272

People often ask if **Tuesday** and **newspaper** are pronounced **Tiuzday** and **niuzpaper** or **Toozday** and **noozpaper**. Most Americans tend toward the latter, but you can go either way. On some words, however, you cannot add that extra **i** sound, as with **shoes** or **cool**.

What do you call
a boomerang
that doesn't come back?

A stick.

11

"V" as in Victory

P / B / F / V are all popped.

Track 273

When pronounced correctly, **V** shouldn't stand out too much. Its sound, although noticeable, is small. As a result, people, depending on their native language, sometimes confuse **V** with **B** (Spanish, Japanese), with **F** (German), or with **W** (Chinese, Hindi). These four sounds are not at all interchangeable.

The **W** is a semivowel, and there is no friction or contact. The **B**, like **P**, uses both lips and has a slight pop. Americans tend to have a strong, popping **P**. You can check your pronunciation by holding a match, a sheet of paper, or just your hand in front of your mouth. If the flame goes out, the paper wavers, or you feel a distinct puff of air on your hand, you've said **P** not **B**. **B** is the voiced pair of **P**.

Although **F** and **V** are in exactly the same position, **F** is a hiss and **V** is a buzz. The **V** is the voiced pair of **F** (as you saw in Chapter 2, pages 47–48). When you say **F**, it is as if you are *whispering*. So, for **V**, say **F** and simply add some voice to it, which is the whole difference between *fairy* and *very,* as you will hear in our next exercise. (The **F**, too, presents problems to Japanese, who say **H**. To pronounce **F**, the lower lip raises up and the inside of the lip very lightly touches the outside of the upper teeth, and you make a slight hissing sound. *Don't* bite the outside of your lip at all.)

Note In speaking, *of* is reduced to **əv**.

Exercise 11-1: Mind Your Vees 🔊 **Track 274**

Repeat the following words and sounds after me.

	P	B	F	V	W
1.	Perry	berry	fairy	very	wary
2.	pat	bat	fat	vat	wax
3.	Paul	ball	fall	vault	wall
4.	Pig	big	fig	vim	wig
5.	prayed	braid	frayed	▮▮▮	weighed
6.	poi	boy	foil	avoid	▮▮▮
7.	pull	bull	full	▮▮▮	wool
8.	purr	burr	fur	verb	were
9.	pay	bay	fey	vein	way

Exercise 11-2: The Vile VIP Track 275

Repeat after me, focusing on V and W. Of is pronounced uv.

When re**v**ising his **v**isitor's **v**ersion of a plan for a **v**ery **w**ell-pa**v**ed a**v**enue, the VIP **w**as ad**v**ised to re**v**eal none of his moti**v**es. E**v**entually, ho**w**ever, the hapless **v**isitor discovered his knavish vie**w**s and confided that it **w**as **v**ital to revie**w** the plans together to a**v**oid a conflict. The VIP **w**as not con**v**inced, and a**v**erred that he **w**ould ha**v**e it **v**etoed by the **v**ice president. This quite **v**exed the **v**isitor, who then vo**w**ed to in**v**ent an indestructible pa**v**ing compound in order to a**v**enge his good name. The VIP found himself on the **v**erge of a ci**v**il **w**ar **w**ith a **v**isitor **w**ith whom he had previously con**v**ersed easily. It **w**as only due to his insufferable **v**anity that the ine**v**itable di**v**ision arrived as soon as it did. Ne**v**er again did the **v**isitor con**v**erse **w**ith the **v**ain VIP, and they remained di**v**ided forever.

Exercise 11-3: Finding V Sounds Track 276

Underline the five V sounds in this paragraph. The first one is marked for you in blue. Don't forget "of."
(Check Answer Key on page 218.)

Hello, **my** name is_____. I'm taking American **Accent** Training. There's a **lot** to **learn**, but I **hope** to make it as **enjoyable** as possible. I should pick **up** on the American **intonation** pattern pretty **easily**, although the **only way** to **get** it is to **practice all** of the time. I use the **up** and down, or **peaks** and valleys, **intonation** more than I **used** to. I've been paying attention to **pitch, too**. It's like **walking** down a **stair**case. I've been **talking** to a lot of **Americans** lately, and they tell me that I'm **easier** to understand. **Any**way, I could go **on** and on, but the **important** thing is to **listen** well and sound **good**. **Well**, what do you **think**? Do I?

Exercise 11-4: W, V & F Track 277

Repeat the following sentences, focusing on the targeted sounds. Notice that one starts with a W sound and of ends with a V sound.

 Where were we in World War One? On one wonderful Wednesday, we were wandering in Westwood with a wonderful woman from Wisconsin, whose name was Wanda Wilkerson. We had been with Wanda for weeks, and we were wondering when we would wear out our welcome.

"Don't worry," warbled Wanda, waving wildly, "I've been waiting since winter!"

Track 278

Victor Vickerson voted to review the very vilest version of the veto to avoid a controversy. Even Evan reviewed Virginia's available provisions for the vacation as inevitably devoid of value. Evan eventually arrived at the village and saved the day with vast amounts of venison and veal.

Track 279

Fred fried five flat fish on Friday afternoon at four.

	A	B	C	D	E	F	G	H	I	J	K	L	M	N	O
	æ	æo	u	i	ee	ü	ε	a	ə	ä	r	är	o	i	oi
1.	back	bow	booed	Bic	beak	book	beck	bake	buck	Bach	Burke	bark	boat	bite	point
2.	black	blouse	blued	bliss	bleed	books	bled	blade	blood	block	blurred	blarney	bloat	blight	boy
3.	brad	browse	brood	brick	breed	brook	bread	break	brother	brought	fir	far	broke	bright	broil
4.	pat	about	boot	pit	peak	put	pet	paid	putt	pot	pert	part	post	pike	boil
5.	cat	couch	coot	kit	parakeet	cookie	kept	Kate	cut	caught	curt	cart	coat	kite	coin
6.	cad	cowed	cooed	kid	keyed	could	Keds	okayed	cud	cod	curd	card	code	cried	coil
7.	fat	found	food	fit	feet	foot	fed	fade	fun	fog	first	farm	phone	fight	Foyt
8.	flack	flower	fluke	flick	fleet	put	fleck	flake	flood	father	flurry	tar	flow	flight	Floyd
9.	fragile	frown	fruit	frill	free	fructose	French	afraid	from	frog	further	farther	fro	fright	Freud
10.	fallow	foul	fool	fill	feel	full	fell	fail	fuss	fall	furl	Carl	photo	file	foil
11.	gas	gout	gooed	give	geek	good	get	gate	gun	gone	gird	guard	goad	guide	goiter
12.	catch	couch	cool	kick	key	cook	ketch	cake	come	calm	Kirk	carp	coal	kind	coy
13.	lack	loud	Luke	lick	leak	look	lecture	lake	luck	lock	lurk	lark	local	like	lawyer
14.	mallet	mound	mood	mill	meal	wooden	men	main	mother	mom	murmur	march	mobile	mile	Des Moir
15.	pal	Powell	pool	pill	peel	pull	pell	pail	puck	pock	pearl	park	pole	pile	poison
16.	sand	sound	soon	sin	seen	soot	send	same	some	sawn	sir	sorry	sewn	sign	soil
17.	satin	mountain	gluten	mitten	eaten	wouldn't	retina	latent	button	gotten	certain	carton	potent	tighten	ointment
18.	shad	shout	shoed	Schick	sheet	should	shed	shade	shun	shop	insured	sharp	show	shy	■
19.	shack	shower	shooed	shiver	chic	shook	chef	shake	shuck	shock	shirt	shark	shows	shyster	■
20.	shallow	shower	shoot	shift	sheep	sugar	shell	shale	shut	shot	sure	shard	shown	shine	■
21.	chance	chowder	choose	chin	cheek	■	chest	change	chuck	chalk	churn	charge	chose	child	choice
22.	tack	towel	two	tick	teak	took	tech	take	tuck	talk	turkey	tarp	toke	tyke	toy
23.	that	thousand	through	this	these	■	then	they	the	thought	third	cathartic	though	thigh	thyroid
24.	had	how'd	who'd	hid	he'd	hood	hen	hate	hud	hod	heard	hard	hoed	hide	hoi polloi
25.	hat	about	hoot	hit	heat	foot	heck	Hague	hut	hot	hurt	heart	hotel	height	Hoyle
26.	value	vow	review	villain	reveal	■	vegetable	vague	vug	von	verve	varnish	vote	vile	avoid
27.	whack	wow	wooed	wick	weak	would	wed	weighed	what	walk	word	harm	woke	white	woi

12
Tense and Lax Vowels

Move your lips for tense vowels, but not for lax vowels.

Track 281

In this chapter, we tackle tense and lax vowels. This is the difference between **ā**, tense, and **ɛ**, lax; **ē**, tense, and **i**, lax. We will start with tense vowels. (See also Chapters 1, 3, and 10.)

Exercise 12-1: Tense Vowels	Track 282

Don't pay attention to spelling or meaning. Just remember, if you are in the ä column, they all have the same ah sound. Repeat.

	æ	æo	ä	i	ā	ē	ū	ōū
1.	at	out	ought	I'd	ate	eat	ooze	own
2.	bat	about	bought	bite	bait	beat	boot	boat
3.	cat	couch	caught	kite	cane	keys	cool	coat
4.	chat	chowder	chalk	child	chair	cheer	choose	chose
5.	dad	doubt	dot	dial	date	deed	do	don't
6.	fat	found	fought	fight	fate	feet	food	phone
7.	fallow	fountain	fall	file	fail	feel	fool	foal
8.	gas	gown	got	kite	gate	gear	ghoul	go
9.	hat	how	hot	height	hate	heat	hoot	hope
10.	Hal	howl	hall	heil	hail	heel	who'll	hole
11.	Jack	jowl	jock	giant	jail	jeep	jewel	Joel
12.	crab	crowd	crawl	crime	crate	creep	cruel	crow
13.	last	loud	lost	line	late	Lee	Lou	low
14.	mat	mountain	mop	might	mate	mean	moon	moan
15.	gnat	now	not	night	Nate	neat	noon	note
16.	pal	pound	Paul	pile	pail	peel	pool	pole
17.	rat	round	rot	right	rate	real	rule	role
18.	sat	sound	soft	sight	sale	seal	Sue	soul
19.	shall	shower	shawl	shine	shade	she	shoe	show
20.	slap	slouch	slop	slide	slade	sleep	slew	slow
21.	stag	stout	stop	style	stale	steal	stool	stole
22.	strap	Stroud	straw	stride	straight	stream	strew	stroll
23.	tap	town	top	type	tape	team	tool	told
24.	that	thou	thar	thine	they	these	▄▄	though
25.	thang	thousand	thought	thigh	thane	thief	▄▄	throw
26.	van	vow	volume	viper	vain	veal	voodoo	vote
27.	wax	Wow!	wash	wipe	wane	wheel	woo	woe
28.	yank	Yow!	yawn	yikes	Yale	year	you	yo
29.	zap	Zowie!	zombie	xylophone	zany	zebra	zoo	Zoe

Go through the subsequent paragraph and mark all the tense vowels, starting with ā (there are 12 here). The first one is n<u>a</u>me (nɛim, not nɛm). The first ē sound (15) is th<u>e</u> American. (The same 5 æ sounds can be found as in Exercise 3-2, plus the æo of sound and down. Do the marking. Check Answer Key on page 218.)

Hello, **my** nāme is_____. I'm taking American **æccent** Training. There's a **lot** to **learn**, but I **hope** to make it as **enjoyable** as possible. I should pick **up** on thē American **intonation** pattern pretty **easily**, although the **only** way to **get** it is to **practice** all of the time. I use the **up** and down, or **peaks** and valleys, **intonation** more than I **used** to. I've been paying attention to **pitch, too**. It's like **walking** down a **stair**case. I've been **talking** to a lot of **Americans** lately, and they tell me that I'm **easier** to under**stand. Any**way, I could go **on** and on, but the **important** thing is to **listen** well and s**æo**nd **good**. **Well**, what do you **think**? **Do** I?

Tense vowels use the lips and jaw muscles.

These are the lax vowels (as we saw in Chapter 10).

	e	i	ü	ə	ər
1.	end	it	▓	un-	earn
2.	bet	bit	book	but	burn
3.	kept	kiss	could	cut	curt
4.	check	chick	▓	chuck	church
5.	debt	did	▓	does	dirt
6.	fence	fit	foot	fun	first
7.	fell	fill	full	▓	furl
8.	get	gill	good	gut	girl
9.	help	hit	hook	hut	hurt
10.	held	hill	hood	hull	hurl

Soft vowels are subtle variations of sound using the throat muscles.

e slightly tense: **bet**
i more relaxed: **bit**
ü even more relaxed: **put**
ə throat is completely relaxed: **but**

Exercise 12-4: Lax Vowels Practice Paragraph   🔊 Track 285

*Again, go over this paragraph and mark the lax vowels, starting with ɛ. The first one (of about 12 possible) is in **hello** or **American**. The first i sound (of 9 to 22) may be found in **is**. (The numbers are approximations because you may have already reduced the ɛ of **hello** and the i of **is** into schwas.) Do the marking. (Check your answer in the Answer Key on page 218.)*

Hello, **my** name is_____. I'm taking American **Accent** Training. There's **a lot** to learn, but I **hope** to make it as **enjoyable** as possible. I should pick **up** on the American **intonation** pattern pretty **easily**, although the **only** way to **get** it is to **practice** all of the time. I use the **up** and down, or **peaks** and valleys, **intonation** more than I **used** to. I've been paying attention to **pitch, too**. It's like **walking** down a **stair**case. I've been **talking** to a lot of **Americans** lately, and they tell me that I'm **easier** to under**stand**. Anyway, I could go **on** and on, but the **important** thing is to **listen** well and sound **good**. **Well**, what do you **think**? **Do** I?

Exercise 12-5: Take a High-Tech Tack   🔊 Track 286

Repeat the following paragraph and words after me.

Sāy, Rāy, tāke a tack. A high-tack tack? No, Rāy, a high-tech tack, eight high-tech tacks, tāke them. Then find a wāy to māke a plāce for the tacks on the dāy bed. Hey, you lāy the tacks on the pāper plāce mat on the tāble, not on the dāy bed, Rāy. At your āge, why do you always māke the sāme mistākes?

Track 287

late	lack	let	tāke	tack	tech	mate	mat	met
hāil	Hal	hell	fāte	fat	fetch	cane	can	Ken

Exercise 12-6: Pick a Peak   🔊 Track 288

Repeat the following paragraph and words after me. Boldfaced elements represent the ē sound. The i is only marked with underscoring.

People who pick **peaks** **weekly** **seem** to **need** to appear **deep** i̱n order to be disti̱ngui̱shed from **mere** **pea** pi̱ckers. **P**eter, a champi̱on **peak** pi̱cker, thought he'd **be** **even** **neater** i̱f he were the **deepest** **peak** pi̱cker i̱n **P**eoria, **P**hoenix, and New Zealand. On his **peak** **peak**-pi̱cking **week**, though, **P**eter, a **peak** pi̱cker's **peak** pi̱cker, realized that **he** was not **deep**. Thi̱s i̱s not **easy** for a **peak** pi̱cker to admi̱t, and i̱t pi̱tched **P**eter i̱nto a pi̱t of **peak**-pi̱cking despair. He was pi̱tiful for **three** **weeks** and then li̱fted hi̱mself to hi̱therto unrevealed personal **peaks**.

Track 289

eat / it	sheep / ship	seat / sit	neat / nit	feet / fit	sleep / slip

An Australlian tourist steps into the road and a traffic cop yells at him,
"Did you come here to die?!"

"Nah, mate. I came here yesterdie!"

13
The Ridge

The tongue tip touches the ridge in a variety of ways.

THOSE BUMPS AT THE TOP OF YOUR MOUTH

Track 290

Those bumps at the top of your mouth form the alveolar ridge, and it's the location of a lot of activity, including **S, Z, T, D, N, L, Sh, Zh, Ch**, and **J**! (See also the Nationality Guides on page 188.)

Exercise 13-1: It's So Sad Track 291

Repeat the following paragraph.

It's so sad. Sally stole Sammy's snake skin suit and sold it to a salesman from Sonoma. Sid, the salesman, suggested that Sally stop stealing, but Sally simply said, "So!" Sid sighed sadly and stomped off to search for a more suitable subject.

Exercise 13-2: Allz Well That Endz Well Track 292

Repeat the following paragraph.

Zero Zippers is a zillion dollar organization near the Osgood Zoo in Zimbabwe. It zigzagged through an embezzlement scandal and zipped past all reasonable expectations. Zero was in the most desirable zip code in the business zone, but the end result was zilch. As the founder's motto was "Easy come, easy go!", no one resented the bizarre disaster.

Track 293

Make your **T**s crisper (when they are **T**s and not the middle **D**). If the tip of your tongue is even a bit too far forward, it flattens the rest of the tongue. Make sure it's planted right there on the alveolar ridge and that it's clearly popped.

Exercise 13-3: Ted Took Ten Tasty Tacos Track 294

Repeat the following paragraph. Put your hand in front of your mouth when you say the following. You should feel distinct puffs of air against your palm.

Ted took ten tasty tacos from the tidy taco truck on Tuesday at two. It's a tried and true test of temperament to try resisting tasty tacos. Take the taco tasting test ten times to determine your type.

Exercise 13-4: Trudy Tried to Trill in Trinidad Track 295

Repeat the following sentence. Once you've got your tongue tapping on the alveolar ridge, for this next one, you're going to drop away from the ridge. Remember, in American English, the R acts more like a vowel because no two points of the mouth come into contact. With your T tensely poised on the ridge, it's going to release plosively from there, and the back of your tongue will form the R. You'll still feel the puffs of air.

Trudy tried to trill on Trevor's Trail in Trinidad, but tripped up and got off track.

Exercise 13-5: Eddie Oughtta Wait a Little Longer Track 296

Repeat the following sentence.

Eddie ought to try to wait a little longer. (Eddie oughtta tryda way da little longer.)

Exercise 13-6: Little League in Little Italy Track 297

Repeat the following sentence, focusing on the L sounds.

Little Lola played Little League with a little old lady in Little Italy.

Exercise 13-7: No! No! Not Nine! Track 298

Repeat the following paragraph.

No! Not nine new novels! Nine'll never be enough!

Exercise 13-8: Chester's Chocolate Cherries Track 299

Repeat the following paragraph.

Chuck Richards charged Chester a surcharge on the chewy chocolates. Chester chafed and kvetched, but fetched Chuck a chest of riches for his chocolate cherries.

Exercise 13-9: She Should Share Sherman's Shoes Track 300

Repeat the following paragraph.

Shelly and Sherman share a shadowy passion for shoes. Lush, plush shoes in shocking shades of chartreuse. Gosh, why won't she share her shoes with Sherman?

Exercise 13-10: George Judged Jenny's Jewelry Track 301

Repeat the following paragraph.

George judged Jenny's jewelry as just average. Jewelry is Jenny's life. Enjoying ageless gems and jewels cadged from Rogers of Jacksonville, Jenny adjusted George's judgement of her jewelry, as it was not just average—it was a gem jubilee!

Exercise 13-11: Was Your Usual Menage in the Beige Garage? Track 302

Repeat the following paragraph.

It was a beige, beige garage and a vision of precision. The revision of the usual menage's decision was a collision of collusion and illusion.

It was a beizh, beizh garazh and a vizh'n of precizh'n. The revizh'n of the uzhual menazh's decizh'n was a collizh'n of colluzh'n and illuzh'n.

Track 303

> **Ch** and **J** are almost the same sound. The tongue position is the same, and they both **pop**. There's one little difference: **Ch** is **whispered** and **J** is **spoken**.
>
> **Sh** and **Zh** are almost the same. The tongue position is the same, and they both **slide** out. The difference: **Sh** is **whispered** and **Zh** is **spoken**.

In order to make a clear **Ch**, you need to start with a **T** sound, so it sounds like *tch* not *shhh*. The invisible **T** before the **Ch** blocks the air momentarily before the rest of the sound comes out. With the **Sh**, the air flows freely. For **J**, start with a **D**, so **judge** sounds like *djudge*.

Track 304

Unvoiced	Voiced	Unvoiced	Voiced
Ch	**J**	**Sh**	**Zh**
cheese	jeans	she's	Jaque's
in charge	enjoy	insure	usual
much	judge	mush	garage
watch	lodge	wash	rouge
watcher	lodger	washer	was your
patch	page	bash	beige
patches	pages	bashes	beiges
ritual	vigil	vicious	visual
rich	ridge	wish	menage
hatcher	had your	hasher	has your

THE VERB MAP

Track 305

The following is a handy overview of the various verb tenses and verb forms. The **T formation** in each box indicates the more commonly used tenses. The single symbols indicate a completed action, whereas the double symbols indicate two related events. The white symbols are *contrary to fact* and didn't, don't, or won't take place.

Active

	Past	Present	Future
Simple	I did it. ◄	I do it. ●	I will do it. ►
Real Duo	I'd done A before I did B. ◄◄	I've done it. ◄ ●	I'll have done A defore I do B. ► ►
Unreal Duo	If I had done A I would've done B. ◄◄	If I did A I would do B. ◄ ○	If I do A I'll do B. ► ►

To Be

	Past	Present	Future
Simple	I was there. ◄	I am here. ●	I will be there. ►
Real Duo	I'd been there (before then). ◄◄	I've been here (before now). ◄ ●	I'll have been there for an hour (by then). ► ►
Unreal Duo	If I had been there, I'd have done it. ◄◄	If I were there, I would do it. ◄ ○	If I am there, I'll do it. ► ►

Negative

	Past	Present	Future
Simple	I didn't do it.	I don't do it.	I won'tdo it.
Real Duo	I hadn't done A until I did B.	I haven't done it.	I won't have done A before I do B.
Unreal Duo	If I hadn't done A I wouldn't have done B.	If I didn't do A I wouldn't do B.	If I don't do A I won't do B.

Continuous

	Past	Present	Future
Simple	I was doing it.	I'm doing it.	I'll be doing it.
Real Duo	I had been doing A before I did B.	I've been doing A for a long time.	I'll have been doing A for a while. when I start B.
Unreal Duo	If I'd been doing A, I wouldn've been doing B.	If I were doing A, I'd be doing B,	If I'm doing A, I'm doing B.

Questions

	Past	Present	Future
Simple	Did I do it?	Do I do it?	Will I do it?
Real Duo	Had I done A before I idid B?	Have I done A?	Will I have done A before I do B?
Unreal Duo	If I had done A would I have done B?	If I did A would I do B?	If I do A will I do B?

Helping Verbs

	Past	Present	Future
Simple	I had to do it.	I have to do it.	I'll have to do it.
Real Duo	I had had to do A before I had to do B.	I've had many times.	I'll have had to do A before I have to do B.
Unreal Duo	If I had had to do A, I would have had to do B.	If I had to do A, I would have to do B.	If I have to do A, I will have to do B.

Causative

	Past	Present	Future
Simple	I had it done.	I have it done.	I will have it done.
Real Duo	I'd had A done before I had B done.	I've had A done many times.	I'll have had A done by the time I have B done.
Unreal Duo	If I had had A done, I would've had B done.	If I had A done, I would have B done.	If I have A done, I'll have B done.

Passive

	Past	Present	Future
Simple	It was done.	It is done.	It will be done.
Real Duo	A had been done before B was done.	A has been done many times.	A will be done before B is done.
Unreal Duo	If A had been done B would have been done.	If A were done B would be done.	If A is done B will be done.

14

Grammar in a Bigger Nutshell

Even with complex grammar, use the basic rules of intonation.

Track 306

In Chapter 7, we studied compound nouns and complex verb tenses. Now, we are going to put them together and practice the intonation of some complicated sentences.

Exercise 14-1: Compound Nouns and Complex Verbs   **Track 307**

No matter how complex the verb gets, remember to follow the basic Dogs eat bones intonation, where you stress the nouns. For the noun intonation, stick with the basic set phrase or description rule. Let's build up one complex noun for the subject, and another one for the object, starting with The millionaires were impressed by the equipment.

Subject	Object
The **millionaires**	the **equipment**.
The elderly **millionaires**	**eaves**dropping equipment.
The **elderly** Texas **millionaires**	electronic **eaves**dropping equipment.
The two **elderly** Texas **millionaires** . . . **sophisticated** electronic **eaves**dropping equipment.

The two **elderly** Texas millionaires were impressed by the **sophisticated** electronic
eavesdropping equipment.
The two elderly Teksəs millyənair zwerim presst by the səfistəkaydədəlektränik
ēvzdräppiŋə kwipmənt.

zərim prest   **Track 308**
1. The two **elderly** Texas **millionaires**'re impressed by the **sophisticated** electronic **eaves**dropping
   equipment.
   zwərim prest
2. The two **elderly** Texas **millionaires** were impressed by the **sophisticated** electronic **eaves**dropping
   equipment.
   zər beeyingim prest
3. At the moment, the two **elderly** Texas **millionaires**'re being impressed **by** the **sophisticated** electronic **eaves**dropping equipment.
   zəl beeyim prest
4. The two **elderly** Texas **millionaires**'ll be impressed by the **sophisticated** electronic **eaves**dropping
   equipment.
   zəd beeyim prest
5. The two **elderly** Texas **millionaires**'d be impressed by the **sophisticated** electronic **eaves**dropping
   equipment if there were more practical applications for it.

zədəv binim prest

6. The two **elderly** Texas **millionaires**'d've been impressed by the **sophisticated** electronic **eaves**-dropping equipment if there had been more practical applications for it.

zədəv bin so im prest

7. The two **elderly** Texas **millionaires** that've been so impressed by the **sophisticated** electronic **eaves**dropping equipment are now researching a new program.

zəv binim prest

8. The two **elderly** Texas **millionaires**'ve been impressed by the **sophisticated** electronic **eaves**dropping equipment for **a** long time now.

zəd binim prest

9. The two **elderly** Texas **millionaires**'d been impressed by the **sophisticated** electronic **eaves**dropping equipment long before the burglary was thwarted.

zələv bin thərə lee(y)im prest

10. The two **elderly** Texas **millionaires**'ll've been thoroughly impressed by the **sophisticated** electronic **eaves**dropping equipment by the time I've done my presentation.

zädə bee(y)im prest

11. The two **elderly** Texas **millionaires** ought to be impressed by the **sophisticated** electronic **eaves**-dropping equipment.

shüd bee(y)im prest

12. The two **elderly** Texas **millionaires** should be impressed by the **sophisticated** electronic **eaves**-dropping equipment.

shüd•n beetoo(w)im prest

13. The two **elderly** Texas **millionaires** shouldn't be too impressed by the **sophisticated** electronic **eaves**dropping equipment.

shüdəv binim prest

14. The two **elderly** Texas **millionaires** should've been impressed by the **sophisticated** electronic **eaves**dropping equipment.

shüdn•nəv bin thæ dim prest

15. Given the circumstances, the two **elderly** Texas **millionaires** shouldn't've been that impressed by the **sophisticated** electronic **eaves**dropping equipment.

cüdee zəlee bee(y)im prest

16. We think that the two **elderly** Texas **millionaires** could easily be impressed by the **sophisticated** electronic **eaves**dropping equipment.

cüd•n bee(y)im prest

17. No matter what we did, the two **elderly** Texas **millionaires** couldn't be impressed by even the most **sophisticated** electronic **eaves**dropping equipment.

cüdəv binim prest

18. The two **elderly Texas millionaires** could've been impressed by the **sophisticated** electronic **eaves**dropping equipment, but we're not sure.

cüdn•nəv binim prest

19. The two **elderly** Texas **millionaires** couldn't've been impressed by the **sophisticated** electronic **eaves**dropping equipment, because they left after 5 minutes.

myt bee(y)im prest

20. The two **elderly** Texas **millionaires** might be impressed by the **sophisticated** electronic **eaves**dropping equipment this time around.

Exercise 14-1: Compound Nouns and Complex Verbs *continued* **Track 308**

mydəv binim prest

21. The two **elderly** Texas **millionaires** might've been impressed by the **sophisticated** electronic **eaves**dropping equipment, but they gave no indication one way or the other.

məss bee⁽ʸ⁾im prest

22. The two **elderly** Texas **millionaires** must be impressed by the **sophisticated** electronic **eaves**dropping equipment because they are considering a huge order.

məsdəv binim prest

23. The two **elderly** Texas **millionaires** must have been impressed by the **sophisticated** electronic **eaves**dropping equipment because they ordered so much of it.

cən bee⁽ʸ⁾im prest

24. The two **elderly** Texas **millionaires** can be impressed by the **sophisticated** electronic **eaves**dropping equipment because they don't know much about surveillance.

cæn⁽ᵗ⁾ bee⁽ʸ⁾im prest

25. The two **elderly** Texas **millionaires** can't be impressed by the **sophisticated** electronic **eaves**dropping equipment because they invented most of the state-of-the-art technology currently available.

Exercise 14-2: Your Own Compound Nouns **Track 309**

Build up your own compound nouns, both subject and object.

Subject	Object

Exercise 14-3: Your Own Compound Nouns and Complex Verbs   Track 310

Using your compound nouns (from Exercise 14-2), choose a verb and put it through all the changes. Remember that it helps to have a verb that starts with a vowel. Add explanatory words to round out the sentence, complete the thought, and support the verb.

do	1.
did	2.
are doing	3.
will do	4.
would do	5.
would've done	6.
that have done	7.
have done	8.
had done	9.
will've done	10.
ought to do	11.
should do	12.
shouldn't do	13.
should've done	14.
shouldn't have done	15.
could do	16.
couldn't do	17.
could've done	18.
couldn't have done	19.
might do	20.
might've done	21.
must do	22.
must've done	23.
can do	24.
can't do	25.

15

Practical Application

Take everything you've learned and use it.

Listen to the following excerpt* and compare the two versions.

Forty years after the end of World War II, Japan and the U.S. are again engaged in conflict. Trade frictions, which began as minor irritants in an otherwise smooth relationship in the 1960s, have gradually escalated over the years.

The conflict is more dangerous than it appears because its real nature is partially hidden. It masquerades as a banal and sometimes grubby dispute over widgets with the stakes being whether American or Japanese big business makes more money.

In truth, the issue is strategic and geopolitical in nature. Japan is once again challenging the U.S., only this time the issue is not China or the Pacific but world industrial and technological leadership and the military and economic powers, which have always been its corollaries.

*By permission of *U.S. News and World Report*

Fordee yir **zæf**tr^(pause)thee^(y)end'v wrl dwor **too,**^(pause)J'**pæn**'n thə yoo^(w)**ess**^(pause)ärə **gen**in gɛij din^(pause)**cän**fl'ct. ^(stop)**Trəid** fr'ksh'nz,^(pause)w'ch b'gæn'z mynr **rirrət**'nts^(pause)in'n ətherwise^(pause)smooth r'**lɛi**sh'nship in the **näin**teen **siks**deez^(pause)h'v græjəlee^(y)**ɛs**cəladəd^(pause)dover thə **yirz.**

Thə **kän**fl'k d'z mor **dɛin**jer's thəni də**pirz** b'kəzəts **ree**^(y)əl nɛichyr'z pärshəlee **h'dd**'n. It mæskɛr**ɛid** zəzə bə**näl**ən səm**täim**z **grə**bee d'spyu dover **wij**'ts withthə **stɛi**ks be^(y)ing wɛthərə **mɛr**əkəner Jæpə**neez** big **bizn**'s mɛiks mor **mən**ee.

In **truth,** thee^(y)**i**shu^(w)iz strə**teej**əkən jee^(y)opə**lid**əkələn nɛichyer. Jə**pæn**əz wən səgen **chæl**ənjing thə you^(w) **ess,** only **this** täim, thee^(y)**i**shu^(w)iz nät **Chäi**nə or thə Pəs'fək bət wr rolld'in **dəss**tree^(y)l'n tɛknə**läj**əkəl **leed**ershipən the **mil**ətɛree^(y)ənɛkə**näm**ək **pæw**rz, w'ch h'**väw**eez bi n'ts **kor**əlɛreez.

THE LETTER A

Track 312

You've seen many examples of illogical spelling by now, and the letter **A** is a major contributor. **A** can be:

æ cat	ä part	ā make	ə final	ɛ parallel	o war

Note *People who speak Chinese frequently pronounce a, æ, and ɛ the same. The common denominator of the three sounds is ɛ. When a Chinese speaker says* mate, mat, met, *it can sound like* met, met, met. *If this happens to be your case, in order to say common words like* make *and* man *correctly, first practice putting them on the stairsteps and drawing them out. Don't be afraid to exaggerate. You can even draw them out with a final unvoiced consonant.*

Thə prezədənt təmärrou näidiz əxpectədiniz stɛidəv thə yoonyən mesəj tə prəpouz fedrəl səbzədeez tə help lou[(w)]inkəm fæmleez ouvrkəm thə sou-käld dijədəl dəväid. Izidə nəpropree[(y)]ət yusəv gəvrmnt fənz tə hændæot kəmpyudrz ən prəväid innernet æksɛs tə thouz hu cæn[(d)]əford it; ənd if nät, why nät. Will bəgin with Mr. Keez.

I think this iz ənəthər keis whɛer pälətishənz try də jəmpän thə bændwægən əv səmthing thæťs going än in thee[(y)]əcänəmee, sou evreebədeez gənnə think thət they ækchəlee hæv səmthing tə do with thə rəzəlt when they dont. Thɛrz nou need fr this. Wiräl reddy seeing æot thɛr prəpouzəlz fr thə distrəbyushən əv free PeeCees, nät beis dän səm pälətishən meiking ə judgment ən spending tæxpeiyer mənee, bət beis dän thə self-intrst əv thouz hu[(w)]är involvd inə nyu world, ə nyu world ən which p'rtisəpeishən iz thə kee də präfit—ənd in which thɛr iz ækchəlee ə sträng insentiv əmäng thouz hu prtisəpɛidin thə präivət sektər tə giv æksɛss tə indəvijəls sou thət they c'n impruv their äpərtyunədeez fr präfit, fr infərmeishn shɛring. Thæts whəts älredee bin going än—it will kəntinyu. Thɛr iz nou need fr thə gəvərmənt tə prətend thæt it needs tə teik leedership hir. I think thæts jəst pəlidəkəl päsjuring.

Senədər Mə[(k)]kein.

I bəleev th't wee du hæv ə präbləm. æn thædiz thət thɛrizə growing gæp bətween thə hævz ənd hæv-näts in əmɛrəkə, thouz thədr ɛibl də tɛik pärdin this infərmeishn teknäləjee ən thouz th't hævnt. Wee took ə mɛijər step forward when wee dəsaidəd də wäi[(y)]r evree skool ən lybrɛree in əmɛrəkə tə thee[(y)]innərnet. Thætsə güd prougrəm. Wee hæf tə hæv step tu, three, ən four, which meenz güd əkwipmənt, güd teechərz ənd güd clæssroomz. No, I wüdn du[(w)]it d'rektlee. Bət thɛrz läts əv weiz th'chyu kən inkerəj korpəreishnz, who in their own self-intrest, wüd wänt tə prəvaid . . . wüd rəseev tæks bɛnəfits, wüd rəseev kredit, ənd mɛny əthər weiz fr beeing invölvd in thə skoolz, in əpgreiding thə kwälədee əv əkwipmənt th't thei hæv, thə kwälədee əv thə styudənts ənd thɛrby prəvaiding ə məch-needed well-treind wərkfors.

Thæng kyu. Mr. Forbz.

The president tomorrow night is expected in his State of the Union message to propose federal subsidies to help low-income families overcome the so-called digital divide. Is it an appropriate use of government funds to hand out computers and provide Internet access to those who can't afford it, and if not, why not? We'll begin with Mr. Keyes.

"I think this is another case where politicians try to jump on the bandwagon of something that's going on in the economy, so everybody's gonna think that they actually have something to do with the result when they don't. There's no need for this. We're already seeing out there proposals for the distribution of free PCs, not based on some politician making a judgment and spending taxpayer money, but based on the self-interest of those who are involved in a new world, a new world in which participation is the key to profit—and in which there is actually a strong incentive among those who participate on the private sector to give access to individuals so that they can improve their opportunities for profit, for information sharing. That's what's already been going on—it will continue. There is no need for the government to pretend that it needs to take leadership here. I think that's just political posturing."

Senator McCain.

"I believe that we do have a problem. And that is that there is a growing gap between the *haves* and *have-nots* in America, those that are able to take part in this information technology and those that haven't. We took a major step forward when we decided to wire every school and library in America to the Internet. That's a good program. We have to have step two, three, and four, which means good equipment, good teachers, and good classrooms. No, I wouldn't do it directly. But there's lots of ways that you can encourage corporations, who in their own self-interest, would want to provide . . . would receive tax benefits, would receive credit, and many other ways for being involved in the schools, in upgrading the quality of equipment that they have, the quality of the students, and thereby providing a much-needed well-trained workforce."

Thank you. Mr. Forbes.

16
Nasal Consonants

Block the air with your tongue and release it through your nose.

Track 314

We now turn to the three consonants whose sound comes out through the nose—**M**, **N**, and the **NG** combination. They each have one thing in common—their sound is blocked in the mouth in one of three locations. Two of them, **N** and **NG**, you can't even see, as with **R**, so they're hard to pick up on. (See also Chapters 1, 6, 13, and the Nationality Guides.)

m is the easiest and most obvious. Like **b**, the lips come together and the air can't get out, so it has to come out through the nose.

n is in a position similar to **t**, but it can't be at all tense. It has to be completely relaxed, filling the whole mouth, touching the insides of all the teeth, leaving no room for the air to escape, except by the nose.

ng is back in the throat with **g**. The back of the tongue presses back, and, again, the air comes out through the nose.

Exercise 16-1: Nasal Consonants   Track 315

We are going to contrast nasals with regular consonant sounds. Repeat after me.

	Initial		Middle		Final	
m/b	me	bee	llama	lobber	ROM	rob
n/d	knees	deals	Lana	lauder	Ron	rod
ng/g	long eels	geese	longer	logger	wrong	log

Exercise 16-2: Ending Nasal Consonants Track 316

Here we will focus on the final sounds. Repeat after me.

M	N	NG
rumᵊ	runᵊ	rungᵊ
sum/some	sun/son	sung
bum	bun	bung
turn	ton	tongue
dumb	done	dung
psalm	sawn	song

Exercise 16-3: Reading Nasal Consonant Sounds Track 317

We will read the following paragraph. Repeat after me.

The young King Kong can sing along on anything in the kingdom, as long as he can bring a strong ringing to the changing songs. He can only train on June mornings when there is a full moon, but June lends itself to singing like nothing else. Ding Dong, on the other hand, is not a singer; he cannot sing for anything. He is a man often seen on the green lawn on the Boston Open, where no one ever, ever sings.

Exercise 16-4: Finding n and ng Sounds Track 318

Find and mark the final n and ng sounds. (Check the Answer Key on page 218.)

Hello, **my** name is _____. I'm taking American **Accent** Training. There's a **lot** to **learn**, but I **hope** to make it as **enjoyable** as possible. I should pick **up** on the American **intonation** pattern pretty **easily**, although the **only** way to **get** it is to **practice** all of the time. I use the **up** and down, or **peaks** and valleys, **intonation** more than I **used** to. I've been paying attention to **pitch**, **too**. It's like **walking** down a **stair**case. I've been **talking** to a lot of **Americans** lately, and they tell me that I'm **easier** to under**stand**. **Any**way, I could go **on** and on, but the **important** thing is to **listen** well and sound **good**. **Well**, what do you **think**? **Do** I?

17
Throaty Consonants

Throat sounds are formed with the back of the tongue.

Track 319

There are five consonant sounds that are produced in the throat: **h, k, g, ng, er**. Because **R** can be considered a consonant, its sound is included here. For pronunciation purposes, however, elsewhere this book treats it as a semivowel. (See also Chapters 5 and 16, and the Nationality Guides.)

Exercise 17-1: Throaty Consonants	Track 320

Here we will read across the lists of initial, middle, and final consonants.

	Initial	Middle	Final
h	haw	reheat	▬
	hood	in half	▬
	he'll	unhinge	▬
	hat	unheard of	▬
k	caw	accident	rink
	could	accent	rack
	keel	include	cork
	cat	actor	block
g	gaw	regale	rug
	good	ingrate	hog
	geese	agree	big
	gat	organ	log
ng	Long Island	Bronx	wrong
	a long wait	inky	daring
	Dang you!	larynx	averaging
	being honest	English	clung
r	raw	error	rare
	roof	arrow	air
	real	mirror	injure
	rat	carbon	prefer

Exercise 17-2: The Letter X 🔊 Track 321

The letter X can sound like either KS or GZ, depending on the letter that follows the X and where the stress falls.

ks	excite	ɛk**säit**
*Followed by the letter C or other **unvoiced consonants***	extra	ɛk**strə**
	exercise	ɛk**sersiz**
	experience	ɛks**piree**(ʸ)əns
	except	ək**sɛpt**
	execute	ɛk**sekyut**
	excellent	ɛk**sələnt**
gz	example	əg**zæmp**əl
*Followed by a **vowel** and usually stressed on the second syllable*	exist	əg**zist**
	exam	əg**zæm**
	exert	əg**zrt**
	examine	əg**zæmən**
	executive	əg**zɛkyudəv**
	exit	ɛg**zit**
	exactly	əg**zæklee**

Exercise 17-3: Reading the H, K, G, NG, and R Sounds 🔊 Track 322

Repeat after me.

H

"Help!" hissed the harried intern. "We have to hurry! The halfwit who was hired to help her home hit her hard with the Honda. She didn't have a helmet on her head to protect her, so she has to have a checkup ahead of the others."

Track 323

K

The computer cursor careened across the screen, erasing key characters as it scrolled past. The technician was equally confused by the computer technology and the complicated keyboard, so he clicked off the computer, cleaned off his desk, accepted his paycheck, and caught a taxicab for the airport, destination Caracas.

G

Track 324

The Wizard of Og

There was a man named . . .	Og
Who was his best friend?	Dog
Where did he live?	Bog
What was his house made of?	Log
Who was his neighbor?	Frog
What did he drink?	Eggnog
What did he do for fun?	Jog
What is the weather in his swamp?	Fog

NG

Track 325

The stunning woman would not have a fling with the strong young flamingo trainer until she had a ring on her finger. He was angry because he longed for her. She inquired if he were hungry, but he hung his head in a funk. The flamingo trainer banged his fist on the fish tank and sang out, "Dang it, I'm sunk without you, Punkin'!" She took in a long, slow lungful of air and sighed.

R

Track 326

War is horrible. During any war, terrible things occur. The result is painful memories and disfiguring scars for the very people needed to rebuild a war-torn country. The leaders of every country must learn that wars are never won, lives are always lost, and history is doomed to repeat itself unless we all decide to live in harmony with our brothers and sisters.

Exercise 17-4: Glottal Consonant Practice Paragraph Track 327

Go through the paragraph and mark the h, k, g, ng, and r sounds. (Check Answer Key on page 218.)

Hello, **my** name is _____. I'm taking American **Accent** Training. There's a **lot** to **learn**, but I **hope** to make it as **enjoyable** as possible. I should pick **up** on the American **intonation** pattern pretty **easily**, although the **only** way to **get** it is to **practice** all of the time. I use the **up** and down, or **peaks** and valleys, **intonation** more than I **used** to. I've been paying attention to **pitch**, **too**. It's like **walking** down a **stair**case. I've been **talking** to a lot of **Americans** lately, and they tell me that I'm **easier** to understand. **Any**way, I could go **on** and on, but the **important** thing is to **listen** well and sound **good**. **Well**, what do you **think**? **Do** I?

Telephone Tutoring

FINAL DIAGNOSTIC ANALYSIS

Track 328

After a year, you're ready for the final analysis. If you're studying on your own, contact toll-free (800) 457-4255 or go to *AmericanAccent.com* for a referral to a qualified telephone analyst. The diagnostic analysis is designed to evaluate your current speech patterns to let you know where your accent is standard and nonstandard.

The Nasdaq composite index on Monday suffered its biggest loss in three weeks after a wave of selling slammed Internet and other tech shares in Asia and Europe overnight—suggesting many investors are increasingly nervous about tech shares' current heights. The Nasdaq index ended down 141.38 points, or 2.8%, at 4,907.24, though it recovered from a morning sell-off that took it down as much as 209 points from Friday's record high. Biotechnology stocks were particularly hard hit. The broader market was also lower, though the Dow Jones industrial average managed to inch up 18.31 points to 9,37.13.

1. law, job, collar	5. China, dime, fly	9. won, color, Florida	13. about, now, down
2. class, chance, last	6. if, is, been	10. new, blue, through	14. joy, royal, deploy
3. name, date, way	7. eve, ease, bean	11. good, put, could	
4. ten, many, says	8. worm, third, hard	12. won't, know, go	

A	B	C	D	E	F
1. pat	1. bat	1. apparition	1. abolition	1. lap	1. lab
2. fat	2. vat	2. a rifle	2. arrival	2. life	2. live
3. stink	3. zinc	3. graces	3. grazes	3. dice	3. dies
4. sheer	4. girl	4. mesher	4. measure	4. dish	4. deluge
5. ten	5. den	5. latter	5. ladder	5. ought	5. odd
6. cheer	6. jeer	6. nature	6. major	6. etch	6. edge
7. thing	7. the	7. author	7. other	7. breath	7. breathe
8. core	8. gore	8. lacking	8. lagging	8. snack	8. snag
9. yet	9. rice	9. access	9. example	9. box	9. bogs
10. wolf	10. prance	10. association	10. refract	10. way	10. bar
11. her	11. my	11. actual	11. arrive	11. down	11. mutter
12. lice	12. not	12. behind	12. climber	12. ball	12. name
13. plants		13. reflect	13. innate	13. muddle	13. ran
		14. alive	14. singer		14. wrong

1. Sue arranged it.	1. Get a better water heater.
2. She organized her office.	
3. Get your report done.	2. Gedda bedder wädr heedr.
4. Where did you put it?	
5. She's your usual television star.	3. alter later
	4. intern enter
1. Soo⁽ʷ⁾ərɛinj dit.	5. data deter
2. Shee⁽ʸ⁾orgənizdr räfəs.	6. metal metallic
3. Gɛcher r'port dən.	
4. Wɛrjə püd't?	7. bet bed
5. Shezhier yuzhəwᵊl tɛləvizhən stär.	

Chapters 1–17
Review and Expansion

Track 329

We will be reviewing the concepts that form the basis of American speech—intonation, word groups, the staircase, voice quality, and liaisons, as well as pronunciation. Let's briefly review each item in order. This time around, there will be no explanation.

Review Exercise 1-1: Rubber Band Practice with Nonsense Syllables Track 330

1. blah blah blah	1. blah blah blah	1. blah blah blah	1. blah blah blah
2. ding ding ding	2. ding ding ding	2. ding ding ding	2. ding ding ding
A	**B**	**C**	**D**
1. duh duh duh	1. duh duh duh	1. duh duh duh	1. duh duh duh
2. X Y Z	2. unconcerned	2. including	2. educate
3. 8 9 10	3. He sells fish.	3. He's selfish.	3. Softball game
4. Cows give milk.	4. We like Bob.	4. I think so.	4. Bring me some.

Review Exercise 1-2: Noun Intonation 🔊 Track 331

1. Cats eat fish.
2. Boys like toys.
3. Lou lost his mind.
4. Gail earned a fortune.
5. Betty grows tomatoes.
6. Ed found a job.
7. Max cut his finger.
8. Mary flew a kite.
9. Rick passed the test.
10. Our car lost a wheel.

Review Exercise 1-3: Noun and Pronoun Intonation 🔊 Track 332

1. Patrick speaks French.
2. The neighbors sold their car.
3. The police chased the felon.
4. The housekeeper did some laundry.
5. The architect and I designed a house.

1. He speaks it.
2. They sold it.
3. They chased him.
4. She did some.
5. We designed one.

Review Exercise 1-4: Sentence Intonation Test 🔊 Track 333

1. They took it.
2. Mary had a baby.
3. Louis talked on the phone.
4. We forgot about it.
5. She had one.
6. Sam called him.
7. The dogs howled at the moon.
8. Did you order any?
9. We noticed her.
10. The books fell on the floor.

Review Exercise 1-6: Pitch and Meaning Change 🔊 Track 334

1. He looks like Bob.
2. He looks like Bob, but he's not.
3. He knows Bob, but he doesn't trust him.
4. He can't trust him. He can't do it.

Review Exercise 1-7: Individual Practice Track 335

1. Convey the information that it is Bob. ◄
2. Convey the opinion that he only resembles Bob. ◄
3. Convey the different feelings that someone has about Bob. ◄
4. Convey the fact that trust is a problem with Bob. ◄

Review Exercise 1-8: Meaning of "Pretty," "Sort of," "Kind of," and "Little" Track 336

Question: How was it?
Answer: 1. It was pretty expensive. It was pretty expensive.
        2. It was sort of funny. It was sort of funny.
        3. It was kind of rude. It was kind of rude.
        4. It was a little late. It was a little late.

Review Exercise 1-9: Inflection Track 337

1. Her boyfriend almost never sends her flowers, but mine does.
2. Her boyfriend almost never sends her flowers, but her sisters always do.
3. Her boyfriend almost never sends her flowers, but every once in a while he does.
4. Her boyfriend almost never sends her flowers, no matter what!
5. Her boyfriend almost never sends her flowers, but he planted a lot in her garden.
6. Her boyfriend almost never sends her flowers, but he never forgets Mother's Day!
7. Her boyfriend almost never sends her flowers, but he showers her with other gifts.

Review Exercise 1-10: Individual Practice Track 338

1. Indicate that her boyfriend prefers live plants to cut ones. (5) ◄
2. Indicate that her sisters are attentive to her horticultural needs. (2) ◄
3. Indicate that her boyfriend gives her non-floral presents. (7) ◄
4. Indicate that my boyfriend is good in the flower department. (1) ◄
5. Indicate that it is a true rarity for her boyfriend to send flowers. (4) ◄
6. Indicate that there is actually a slim chance that he might send flowers. (3) ◄
7. Indicate that her boyfriend remembers to send flowers to his mother. (6) ◄

Review Exercise 1-11: Translation Track 339

*Translate **Her boyfriend almost never sends her flowers** into your native language.*

Review Exercise 1-12: Create Your Own Intonation Contrast Track 340

Normal intonation _____

Changed intonation _____

Review Exercise 1-13: Variable Stress Track 341

1. How do you know?
2. How do you know?
3. How do you know?
4. How do you know?

Review Exercise 1-14: Make a Variable Stress Sentence 🔊 Track 342

1. _____
2. _____
3. _____
4. _____
5. _____
6. _____
7. _____

Review Exercise 1-15: Application of Stress 🔊 Track 343

Think the United Auto Workers can beat Caterpillar Inc. in their bitter contract battle? Before placing your bets, talk to Paul Branan, who can't wait to cross the picket line at Caterpillar's factory in East Peoria. Branan, recently laid off by a rubber-parts plant where he earned base pay of $6.30 an hour, lives one block from a heavily picketed gate at the Cat complex. Now he's applying to replace one of 12,600 workers who have been on strike for the past five months. "Seventeen dollars an hour and they don't want to work?" asks Branan. "I don't want to take another guy's job, but I'm hurting, too."

Review Exercise 1-17: Staircase Intonation Practice 🔊 Track 344

On a separate piece of paper, draw a staircase and put each word where it belongs.

Review Exercise 1-18: Reading with Staircase Intonation 🔊 Track 345

Think the United Auto Workers can beat Caterpillar Inc. in their bitter contract battle? Before placing your bets, talk to Paul Branan, who can't wait to cross the picket line at Caterpillar's factory in East Peoria. Branan, recently laid off by a rubber-parts plant where he earned base pay of $6.30 an hour, lives one block from a heavily picketed gate at the Cat complex. Now he's applying to replace one of 12,600 workers who have been on strike for the past five months. "Seventeen dollars an hour and they don't want to work?" asks Branan. "I don't want to take another guy's job, but I'm hurting, too."

Review Exercise 1-19: Spelling and Numbers 🔊 Track 346

CEO	See Eee Oh	Catch	See Ei Tee See Aitch
ATM	Ei Tee Em	Nate	En Ei Tee Eee
IRS	Ai Are Ess		
BMW	Bee Em Dubbayou	Area Code	213
JFK	Jay Eff Kay	Zip Code	90291
M&M	emanem	Date	9/15/88

Review Exercise 1-20: Sound/Meaning Shifts 🔊 Track 347

icy	I see.	attic	a tick
achy	a key	comedy	committee
history	his tree	paradise	pair of dice
interest	in trust	selfish	sell fish
orange	arrange	underwear	under where?
eunuch	unique	ambulance	unbalanced

Review Exercise 1-21: Squeezed-Out Syllables — 🔊 Track 348

actually	æk•chully	finally	fine•lee
business	biz•ness	general	gen•r'l
comfortable	c'mf•t'b'l	interest	in•tr'st
different	dif•r'nt	natural	næch•r'l
every	ev•ree	orange	ornj
favorite	fa•vr't	probably	prä•blee
family	fæm•lee	separate	sep•r't
vegetable	vej•t'b'l	several	sev•r'l

Review Exercise 1-22: Syllable Patterns — 🔊 Track 349

1. **la**!   **la**-a . . .
   cat   dog
2. la-**la**   **la**-la
   a dog   hot dog
3. **la**-la-**la**   la-la-**la**   la-**la**-la   **la**-la-la
   Bob's hot dog   a hot dog   a hot dog   hot dog stand
4. **la**-la-la-**la**   la-la-la-**la**   **la**-la-**la**-la
   Spot's a hot dog. It's a hot dog.   Bob likes hot dogs.
   la-la-la-**la**   la-**la**-la-la   **la**-la-la-la
   It's my hot dog.   a hot dog stand   lighthouse keeper

Review Exercise 1-23: Syllable Count Test — 🔊 Track 350

(Check Answer Key on page 218.)

1. confront ____	8. He likes red ones. ____	15. European ____
2. detail ____	9. He bought me one. ____	16. with dignity ____
3. a blind date ____	10. It's very nice. ____	17. popcorn machine ____
4. my date book ____	11. Jim likes hot rods. ____	18. a mortarboard ____
5. consequence ____	12. lake ____	19. robin redbreast ____
6. consequential ____	13. days ____	20. telescope ____
7. Will needs a car. ____	14. It's your birthday? ____	21. telescopic ____

Review Exercise 1-24: Single-Word Phrases — 🔊 Track 351

	Noun	**Adjective**
1.	It's a cat.	It's black.
2.	It's an egg.	It's scrambled.
3.	It's a car.	It's fast.

Review Exercise 1-25: Sentence Stress with Descriptive Phrases — 🔊 Track 352

	Adjective	**Noun and Adjective**
1.	It's black.	It's a black cat.
2.	It's scrambled.	It's a scrambled egg.
3.	It's fast.	It's a fast car.

Review Exercise 1-26: Two Types of Descriptive Phrases — 🔊 Track 353

	Adjective/Noun	**Adverb/Adjective**
1.	It's a black cat.	It's dark black.
2.	It's a scrambled egg.	It's totally scrambled.
3.	It's a fast car.	It's too fast.

Review Exercise 1-27: Descriptive Phrase Story—Snow White & the Seven Dwarves Track 354

Snow White was a beautiful princess. On the castle wall, there was an enchanted mirror owned by an old woman—a wicked witch! "Mirror, mirror, on the wall, who's the fairest of them all?" When the mirror answered, "Snow White," the young girl was banished from her glorious castle to live in the dark woods. She met seven dwarves, and they lived in a small hut. The evil witch tried to kill the poor girl with a poisoned apple, but she was saved by a handsome prince. They had a beautiful wedding and lived happily ever after.

Review Exercise 1-28: Sentence Stress with Set Phrases Track 355

	Noun	Noun/Adjective	Set Phrase
1.	It's a cat.	It's wild.	It's a wildcat.
2.	It's an egg.	It's a timer.	It's an egg timer.
3.	It's a car.	It's a crash.	It's a car crash.

Review Exercise 1-29: Making Set Phrases Track 356

Make your own set phrases.

Review Exercise 1-30: Set Phrase Story—Our Mailman Track 357

Our mailman loves junk food. At dinnertime, he has potato chips and a hot dog. He puts some soy sauce on his eggplant, but it gives him a stomachache. For dessert, he has a watermelon, a grapefruit, and some ice cream. Afterward, he leaves the dinner table and goes to the bookshelf in his bedroom. He takes down a notebook and does his homework. He puts a clean pillowcase on his pillow, covers up with the bedspread, and goes to dreamland.

Review Exercise 1-31: Contrasting Descriptive and Set Phrases Track 358

	Descriptive Phrase	Set Phrase
1.	It's a black cat.	It's a wildcat.
2.	It's a scrambled egg.	It's an egg timer.
3.	It's a fast car.	It's a car crash.

Review Exercise 1-32: Two-Word Stress Track 359

	Descriptive Phrase	Set Phrase
1.	a rocky garden	a rock garden
2.	a gilded cage	a bird cage
3.	melted butter	a butter knife
4.	tomato soup	tomato sauce
5.	a baby goat	a scapegoat

Review Exercise 1-33: Nationality Intonation Quiz Track 360

(Check Answer Key on page 219.)

1. a French guy
2. a French restaurant
3. French food
4. a french fry
5. french toast
6. a french horn
7. French-Canadian
8. a French teacher
9. a french door

Review Exercise 1-34: Contrasting Descriptive and Set Phrases   Track 361

Set Phrase	Descriptive Phrase
1. A French teacher . . . . . . teaches French.	A French teacher . . . . . . is from France.
2. A French book . . . . . . teaches the French language.	A French book . . . is on any subject, but it came from France.
3. French food . . . . . . is croissants for breakfast.	A French restaurant . . . . . . serves croissants for breakfast.

Review Exercise 1-35: Contrast of Compound Nouns   Track 362

(Check Answer Key on page 219.)

1. a dark room
2. a darkroom
3. an antique shop
4. an antique dealer
5. an antique chair
6. a new video
7. the video store
8. a coffee table
9. hot coffee
10. a coffeepot

11. a chemistry set
12. a chemical reaction
13. a sixth sense
14. six cents
15. a sixth grader
16. the sixth grade
17. long hair
18. a hairdresser
19. a haircut
20. the wrong station

21. a police station
22. a radio station
23. orange juice
24. a guitar case
25. an electric guitar
26. trick photography
27. a photo-op
28. a wedding ceremony
29. a beautiful ceremony
30. a wedding cake

Review Exercise 1-36: Description and Set Phrase Test   Track 363

(Check Answer Key on page 219.)

1. The schoolkids took the subway downtown for their field trip on urban living.
2. Our local sheriff had a bumper sticker on his back bumper.
3. The homeowners thought they had to pay property taxes to the federal government.
4. There were small tremblers after the earthquake in San Francisco.
5. The Geology Club went on a camping trip to Mount Hood.
6. The award ceremony at the Hilton Hotel lasted for two hours.
7. Bob Smith took his surfboard out on a stormy day near Diamond Head.
8. The boy scouts pitched their pup tents on the mountaintop in the pouring rain.
9. It's a little late to ask the babysitter to stay overnight.
10. The sixth graders were reading comic books and drinking chocolate milk.

Review Exercise 1-38: Consistent Noun Stress in Changing Verb Tenses   Track 364

erode	1. The floods erode the mountains.	th' fl'd zəroud th' mæon[(t)]nz
eroded	2. The floods eroded the mountains.	th' fl'd zəroudəd th' mæon[(t)]nz
are eroding	3. The floods're eroding the mountains.	th' fl'd zr•rərouding th' mæon[(t)]nz
will erode	4. The floods'll erode the mountains.	th' fl'd zələroud th' mæon[(t)]nz
would erode	5. The floods'd erode the mountains.	th' fl'd zədəroud th' mæon[(t)]nz
would have eroded	6. The floods'd've eroded the mountains.	th' fl'd zədəvəroudəd th' mæon[(t)]nz
that have eroded	7. The floods that've eroded the mountains.	th' fl'd zədəvəroudəd th' mæon[(t)]nz
have eroded	8. The floods've eroded the mountains.	th' fl'd zəvəroudəd th' mæon[(t)]nz
had eroded	9. The floods'd eroded the mountains.	th' fl'd zədəroudəd th' mæon[(t)]nz
will have eroded	10. The floods'll've eroded the mountains.	th' fl'd zələvəroudəd th' mæon[(t)]nz
ought to erode	11. The floods ought to erode the mountains.	th' fl'd zädə eeroud th' mæon[(t)]nz
should erode	12. The floods should erode the mountains.	th' fl'dz shüdəroud th' mæon[(t)]nz
should not erode	13. The floods shouldn't erode the mountains.	th' fl'dz shüdn•nəroud th' mæon[(t)]nz
should've eroded	14. The floods should've eroded the mountains.	th' fl'dz shüdəvəroudəd th' mæon[(t)]nz
should not have	15. The floods shouldn't've eroded the mountains.	th' fl'dz shüdn•nəvəroudəd th' mæon[(t)]nz
could erode	16. The floods could erode the mountains.	th' fl'dz cüdəroud th' mæon[(t)]nz

could not erode	17. The floods couldn't erode the mountains.	th' fl'dz cüdn•nəroud th' mæon⁽ᵗ⁾nz
could have eroded	18. The floods could've eroded the mountains.	th' fl'dz cüdəvəroudəd th' mæon⁽ᵗ⁾nz
could not have	19. The floods couldn't've eroded the mountains.	th' fl'dz cüdn•nəvəroudəd th' mæon⁽ᵗ⁾nz
might erode	20. The floods might erode the mountains.	th' fl'dz mydəroud th' mæon⁽ᵗ⁾nz
might have	21. The floods might've eroded the mountains.	th' fl'dz mydəvəroudəd th' mæon⁽ᵗ⁾nz
must erode	22. The floods must erode the mountains.	th' fl'dz məsdəroud th' mæon⁽ᵗ⁾nz
must have	23. The floods must've eroded the mountains.	th' fl'dz məsdəvəroudəd th' mæon⁽ᵗ⁾nz
can erode	24. The floods can erode the mountains.	the fl'dz kənəroud th' mæon⁽ᵗ⁾nz
can't erode	25. The floods can't erode the mountains.	the fl'dz kæn(d)əroud th' mæon⁽ᵗ⁾nz

---

Review Exercise 1-39: Consistent Pronoun Stress in Changing Verb Tenses 🔊 Track 365

present	1. It erodes them.	idəroudz'm
past	2. It eroded them.	idəroud'd'm
continuous	3. It's eroding them.	itsərouding'm
future	4. It'll erode them if it keeps up.	idələroud'm
present conditional	5. It'd erode them if it kept up.	idəroud'm
past conditional	6. It'd've eroded them if it'd kept up.	idəvəroud'd'm
relative pronoun	7. The one that's eroded them is quite odd.	the wənthətsəroud'd'm (is . . .).
present perfect	8. It's eroded them for eons.	itsəroud'd'm
past perfect	9. It'd eroded them before the last ice age.	idəroud'd'm
future perfect	10. It'll've eroded them by the end of the millennium.	idələvəroud'd'm
obligation	11. It ought to erode them.	idädə eeroud'm
obligation	12. It should erode them.	it sh'dəroud'm
obligation	13. It shouldn't erode them.	it sh'dn•nəroud'm
obligation	14. It should have eroded them.	it sh'dəvəroud'd'm
obligation	15. It shouldn't've eroded them.	it sh'dn•nəvəroud'd'm
possibility/ability	16. It could erode them.	it c'dəroud'm
possibility/ability	17. It couldn't erode them.	it c'dn•nəroud'm
possibility/ability	18. It could have eroded them.	it c'dəvəroud'd'm
possibility/ability	19. It couldn't have eroded them.	it c'dn•nəvəroud'd'm
possibility	20. It might erode them.	it mydəroud'm
possibility	21. It might have eroded them.	it mydəvəroud'd'm
probability	22. It must erode them.	it məss dəroud'm
probability	23. It must have eroded them.	it məsdəvəroud'd'm
ability	24. It can erode them.	it c'nəroud'm
ability	25. It can't erode them.	it cæn(d)əroud'm

Review Exercise 1-40: Intonation in Your Own Sentence 🔊 Track 366

On a separate piece of paper, write the Review Exercise (as on pages 101–103).

Review Exercise 1-41: Supporting Words 🔊 Track 367

1. The floods erode the mountains every day.
   th' fləd zəroud th' mæon⁽ᵗ⁾n zevree day
2. The floods eroded th' mountains for centuries.
   th' fləd zəroudəd th' mæon⁽ᵗ⁾nz fr sen chr•reez
3. The floods're eroding the mountains right now.
   th' fləd zr•r'rouding th' mæon⁽ᵗ⁾nz räit næo
4. The floods'll erode th' mountains if this keeps up.
   th' fləd zələroud th' mæon⁽ᵗ⁾nz if this keep səp
5. The floods'd erode the mountains if this kept up.
   th' fləd zədəroud th' mæon⁽ᵗ⁾nz if this kepdəp
6. The floods'd've eroded th' mountains if it'd kept up.
   th' fləd zədəvəroud'd th' mæon⁽ᵗ⁾nz if id kepdəp

7. The floods that've eroded the mountains are over.
   th' fləd zədəvəroud'd th' mæon⁽ᵗ⁾n zr•rovr
8. The floods've eroded the mountains over the years.
   th' fləd zəvəroud'd th' mæon⁽ᵗ⁾n zovr th' yirz
9. The floods'd already eroded the mountains before the last ice age.
   th' fləd zədäreddy əroud'd th' mæon⁽ᵗ⁾nz b'for th' læssdice age
10. The floods'll've totally eroded th' mountains by the next ice age.
    th' fləd zələv toudəlee⁽ʸ⁾əroud'd th' mæon⁽ᵗ⁾nz by th' nex dysage

Review Exercise 1-42: Contrast Practice Track 368

would erode	5. The floods'd erode the mountains.	th' fləd zədəroud th' mæon⁽ᵗ⁾nz
had eroded	9. The floods'd eroded the mountains.	th' fləd zədəroud'd th' mæon⁽ᵗ⁾nz
would have eroded	6. The floods'd've eroded the mountains.	th' fləd zədəvəroud'd th' mæon⁽ᵗ⁾nz
that have eroded	7. The floods that've eroded the mountains.	th' fləd zədəvəroud'd th' mæon⁽ᵗ⁾nz
will erode	4. The floods'll erode the mountains.	th' fləd zələroud th' mæon⁽ᵗ⁾nz
would erode	5. The floods'd erode the mountains.	th' fləd zədəroud th' mæon⁽ᵗ⁾nz
would have eroded	6. The floods'd've eroded the mountains.	th' fləd zədəvəroud'd th' mæon⁽ᵗ⁾nz
have eroded	8. The floods've eroded the mountains.	th' fləd zəvəroud'd th' mæon⁽ᵗ⁾nz
had eroded	9. The floods'd eroded the mountains.	th' fləd zədəroud'd th' mæon⁽ᵗ⁾nz
will have eroded	10. The floods'll've eroded the mountains.	th' fləd zələvəroud'd th' mæon⁽ᵗ⁾nz
would erode	5. The floods'd erode the mountains.	th' fləd zədəroud th' mæon⁽ᵗ⁾nz
ought to erode	11. The floods ought to erode the mountains.	th' fləd zädə eeroud th' mæon⁽ᵗ⁾nz
can erode	24. The floods can erode the mountains.	the flədz c'nəroud th' mæon⁽ᵗ⁾nz
can't erode	25. The floods can't erode the mountains.	the flədz cæn(d)əroud th' mæon⁽ᵗ⁾nz

Review Exercise 1-43: Yes, You Can or No, You Can't? Track 369

I can tell you.	I k'n tell you	positive
I can't tell you.	I kæn⁽ᵗ⁾tell you	negative
I can tell you.	I kææn tell you	extra positive
I can't tell you.	I kæn⁽ᵗ⁾tell you	extra negative

Review Exercise 1-44: Building an Intonation Sentence Track 370

I saw him. ❖ I saw him again. ❖ I saw him at work again. ❖ I think I saw him at work again. ❖ I really think I saw him at work again. ❖ I really think I saw him at work again in the yard. ❖ I really think I saw him at work again in the yard behind the house.

Review Exercise 1-45: Building Your Own intonation Sentences Track 371

On a separate piece of paper, build up your own sentences.

Review Exercise 1-46: Regular Transitions of Nouns and Verbs Track 372

Nouns		Verbs	
an accent	æks'nt	to accent	æksɛnt
a contract	käntræct	to contract	k'ntrækt
an insert	insert	to insert	insert
an object	äbjekt	to object	əbjɛct
progress	prägr's	to progress	pr'gress

Review Exercise 1-47: Regular Transitions of Adjectives and Verbs Track 373

Nouns/Adjectives		Verbs	
alternate	ältern't	to alternate	älternɛit
estimate	est'm't	to estimate	est'mɛit
separate	sepr't	to separate	sepɛrɛit

Review Exercise 1-48: Regular Transitions of Adjectives and Verbs Track 374

1. Would you please alternate seats with the other alternate?
2. They signed a contract in order to contract their services.
3. Who could object to progress?
4. The unidentified flying object progressed slowly across the night sky.
5. We need a written estimate in order to estimate the payment.

Review Exercise 1-51: Extended Listening Practice 🔊 **Track 375**

(Check Answer Key on page 219.)

1. _____.

2. _____.

3. _____.

Review Exercise 1-53: Reduced Sounds 🔊 **Track 376**

To	Looks Like . . .	Sounds Like . . .
unvoiced	The president hoped to veto the bill.	th' prezədnt houptə veetou th' bill
	Deposit it to my account, please.	d'päz'di(t)t' myə kæon(t), pleez
voiced	Their boss told them to wait.	thɛr bäss toldəmdə wɛit
	The coach showed us how to pitch.	the coch showdəs hæodə pitch
At	Everyone stared at the mess.	everyone stɛrdə(t)th' mess
unvoiced	Stay at my house for a while.	stayə(t) my hæos frə while
voiced	Jim looked at his watch impatiently.	jim lük d'diz wätchim pɛish'ntlee
	He's at his brother's.	heez'diz brəthrz
It	They said it took too long.	they sedi(t)tük too läng
unvoiced	Do you think it turned out?	dyu thing kit turn dæot
voiced	Let's keep it in perspective.	lets keepidin perspekd'v
	Can we keep it for another day?	kwee keepi(t) frə n'ther day
For	This'll do for now.	thissəl du fr næo
	The students all worked for hours.	th' studn tsäll wrkt frhæwrz
From	We learned it from the coach.	we lrn di(t) frm th' coch
	The tourists came from all over.	the tr•rists came frəmällovr
In	We made it just in time.	we meidit jəsdin time
	The place was in an uproar.	th' pleiswəzinənəp roar
An	It was an odd remark.	it wəzənäd rəmärk
	He's an open book to me.	heezə noupən bük tə me
And	Everyone sat and chatted for a while.	evreewən sæ(t)n chædəd frə wyəl
	It was getting later and later.	it w'z gedding leidr'n leidr
Or	We had two or three options.	we hæd tu(w)r three(y)äpsh'nz
	No one could see or hear anything.	nou w'n küd see(y)r hirenny thing
Are	The neighbors are complaining again.	th' neibrzr k'mplay ningə gen
	Whose shoes are these?	hooz shoozr theez
Your	The door's on your left.	th' door zänyr left
	Are you on your way yet?	är yu(w)änyr way yet
One	There's another one later.	therzə nəthr w'n leidr
	One of them is outside.	w'n'v'm'z æo(t)side
The	The other one's in here.	thee(y)əthr w'n zin hir
	Did he pass the test?	didee pæss th' test
A	Let's take a cab.	lets teikə cæb
	What's the tallest building in America?	wts th' täll'st bilding inəmerəkə
Of	Would you like a piece of pie?	Jläikə peesə pie
	They'll be gone for a couple of weeks.	thell be gän frə couplə weeks
Can	Do you think you can do it?	dyu thing kyu k'n du(w)'t
	Can you believe it?!	k'new b'leevit
Had	We think he'd never done it before.	we thing keed never dənit b'for
	They'd always done it that way.	they däweez dənit thæt way
Would	Why would he tell her?	wy woody teller
	I don't know if he'd agree.	äi dou nou if heedə gree

Review Exercise 1-53: Reduced Sounds *continued* Track 376

To	Looks Like . . .	Sounds Like . . .
Was	Who was on the phone?	hoo w'zän th' foun
	The drummer was off beat.	th' drəmr w'zäf beet
What	Let's see what he wants.	let see wədee wänts
	Who knows what it is?	hoo nouz w'd'd'z
Some	Some of it got in my eyes.	s'm'v't gädin my äiz
	Somebody took my place.	s'mb'dee tük my pleis

Review Exercise 1-54: Intonation and Pronunciation of "That" Track 377

Relative Pronoun	The grapes that he bought were sweet.	th' greips the dee bät wr sweet
Conjunction	We hope that you'll be there.	we houp the chüll bee there
Demonstrative	Don't do that!	doun(t)du thæt
Combination	I know that you'll like that car that you bought.	äi nou the chüll like thæt cär the chew bät

Review Exercise 1-55: Crossing Out Reduced Sounds Track 378

Think the United Auto Workers can beat Caterpillar Inc. in their bitter contract battle? Before placing your bets, talk to Paul Branan, who can't wait to cross the picket line at Caterpillar's factory in East Peoria. Branan, recently laid off by a rubber-parts plant where he earned base pay of $6.30 an hour, lives one block from a heavily picketed gate at the Cat complex. Now he's applying to replace one of 12,600 workers who have been on strike for the past five months. "Seventeen dollars an hour and they don't want to work?" asks Branan. "I don't want to take another guy's job, but I'm hurting, too."

Review Exercise 1-56: Reading Reduced Sounds Track 379

Th'nk th' Unit'd Auto Wrkrs c'n beat Cat'pill'r Inc. 'n their b'tter contract battle? B'fore plac'ng y'r bets, talk t' Paul Bran'n, who can't wait t' cross th' p'cket line 't Cat'pill'r's factry 'n East Peoria. Bran'n, rec'ntly laid off by' r'bb'r-parts plant where he 'rned base pay'v $6.30'n hour, l'ves w'n block fr'm' heav'ly p'ck't'd gate 't th' Cat complex. Now hes 'pplying t' r'place w'n'v 12,600 wrkrs who h've b'n on strike f'r th' past five m'nths. "Sev'nteen doll'rs 'n hour 'nd they dont want t' work?" asks Bran'n. "I dont want t' take 'n'ther guys job, b't I'm h'rting, too."

Review Exercise 1-57: Phrasing Track 380

Statement	Birds lay eggs.
Clauses	As we all know, birds lay eggs.
Listing	Birds lay eggs, build nests, and hunt for food.
Question	Do birds lay eggs?
Repeated Question	Do birds lay eggs?!!
Tag Question	Birds lay eggs, don't they?
Tag Statement	Birds lay eggs, DON'T they!
Indirect Speech	He asked if birds laid eggs.
Direct Speech	"Do birds lay eggs?" they inquired.

Review Exercise 1-60: Tag Endings Track 381

(Check Answer Key on page 219.)

1. There's none left. Is there!
2. That was fun, _____ !
3. You don't have a clue, _____ !
4. He wouldn't forget, _____ ?
5. They can do it over, _____ ?
6. She had to do it, _____ ?
7. She'd rather do it, _____ ?
8. She'd better do it, _____ !
9. She'd never do it, _____ ?
10. She'd never done it, _____ ?

Review Exercise 2-1: Spelling and Pronunciation 🔊 Track 382

Buddy.   Buddy forgot.   He said OK, buddy forgot.   He said OK, but he forgot.

Review Exercise 2-4: Consonant / Vowel Liaison Practice 🔊 Track 383

(Check Answer Key on page 219.)

1. I think he's on his way. _____
2. He put it in an umbrella stand. _____
3. We bought it in Italy. _____

Review Exercise 2-8: Consonant / Consonant Liaison Practice 🔊 Track 384

(Check Answer Key on page 219.)

1. Nick Clark hopes to put ten dollars down. _____
2. But Tom makes so much juice. _____
3. Bob's dog got some bones. _____

Review Exercise 2-9: Vowel / Vowel Liaison Practice 🔊 Track 385

(Check Answer Key on page 219.)

1. Can you see it through to the end? _____
2. Be available for the other opportunity in my office. _____
3. He always wants to offer to go over it again. _____

Review Exercise 2-11: T, D, S, or Z + Y Liaison Practice 🔊 Track 386

(Check Answer Key on page 219.)

1. We're glad that your homework's done. _____
2. Would you help me with this? _____
3. Do you miss your old friends? _____
4. Where's your brother? _____

Review Exercise 2-12: Finding Liaisons and Glides 🔊 Track 387

Think the United Auto Workers can beat Caterpillar Inc. in their bitter contract battle? Before placing your bets, talk to Paul Branan, who can't wait to cross the picket line at Caterpillar's factory in East Peoria. Branan, recently laid off by a rubber-parts plant where he earned base pay of $6.30 an hour, lives one block from a heavily picketed gate at the Cat complex. Now he's applying to replace one of 12,600 workers who have been on strike for the past five months. "Seventeen dollars an hour and they don't want to work?" asks Branan. "I don't want to take another guy's job, but I'm hurting, too."

Review Exercise 2-13: Practicing Liaisons 🔊 Track 388

Think the(y)Unite däuto Workers can beat Caterpillr rinc. in their bitter contract battle? Before placing your bets, talk to Paul Branan, who can't wait to cross the picket ly n't Caterpillar's factree yineest Pe(y)ori(y)a. Branan, recently lay däff bya rubber-parts plant wheree(y)earned base pay'v siks thirdy (y)a næ(w)er, live zw'n block froma heavily picketed gate a(t)the Cat complex. Nowee zapplying to replace w'n'v twelv thæoz'n siks hundred workers who(w)v binän strike for the past five months. "Seventeen dollar sa næ(w)er and they don't want to work?" asks Branan. "I don't wan(t) to take another guy's job, b'dime hurting, too."

Review Exercise 3-1: Word-by-Word and in a Sentence Track 389

	Stressed	**Unstressed**		
that	thæt	th't	thət	We think th't we can get there in time.
than	thæn	th'n	thən	It's harder th'n she thought.
as	æz	'z	əz	It was'z flat'z a pancake.
at	æt	't	ət	We jumped't the chance.
and	ænd	'nd	ənd	The speaker went on'n on.
have	hæv	h'v	həv	How h'v you been?
had	hæd	h'd	həd	I wish we h'd been there.
can	cæn	c'n	cən	Let me know if you c'n be there.

Review Exercise 3-3: Vowel-Sound Differentiation Track 390

	æ	ä	ə	ou	a	ε
1.	ask	often	under	over	April	ever
2.	back	ball	bunch	both	baby	bend
3.	cap	cop	cup	cope	cape	kept
4.	dash	dot	does	don't	date	desk
5.	fast	fall	fun	photo	fail	fell

Review Exercise 3-4: Finding the æ, ä, ə Sounds Track 391

Think thə United äuto Workers can beat Cæterpillar Inc. in their bitter contract battle? Before placing your bets, talk to Paul Branan, who can't wait to cross the picket line at Caterpillar's factory in East Peoria. Branan, recently laid off by a rubber-parts plant where he earned base pay of $6.30 an hour, lives one block from a heavily picketed gate at the Cat complex. Now he's applying to replace one of 12,600 workers who have been on strike for the past five months. "Seventeen dollars an hour and they don't want to work?" asks Branan. "I don't want to take another guy's job, but I'm hurting, too."

Review Exercise 3-5: Reading the æ Sound Track 392

Fæst Dæncing Næncy

We plan to have a dance on the last Saturday in January. It's the last chance for a dance. We practice at a dance class with Max and Nancy. Max dances fast, but Nancy dances best. We are happy about the dance, but Max is sad that Sally can't dance. Her ankle is in a cast!

Review Exercise 3-6: Reading the ä Sound Track 393

Päul's Täll Däughter

Tom watches Paul's tall daughter play softball and volleyball. Paul's daughter is called Molly. Molly starts playing softball in March and ends in August. She plays volleyball in October. Tom is Molly's godfather. They have a lot in common. Tom bought Molly a ball. When Molly saw the ball, she tossed it in the air. "Thanks a lot, Tom!"

Review Exercise 3-7: Reading the ə Sound Track 394

S'nday 'n M'nday

Monday is such a wonderful day. But Sunday is much more wonderful than Monday! We have so much fun on Sunday, and we must run on Monday. What trouble . . . Doug must run on Sunday and Monday. Doug has no fun.

Review Exercise 4-1: Stressed and Unstressed T Track 395

paternal   pattern   critique   critic

Review Exercise 4-3: Rule 1—Top of the Staircase Track 396

1. Tell Tina's tailor to take two tucks in the top of Tim's trousers tomorrow.
2. We try and try, but Todd still tells us to try harder.
3. Terry had a tingling in her toes until the doctor took her temperature.

Review Exercise 4-4: Rule 2—Middle of the Staircase Track 397

1. What a totally naughty little daughter!   wədə toudəlee nädee liddle dädr
2. Matty got a little cottage in the city.   mædee gädə liddle cäd'j in th' siddee
3. Letty bought a lot of bottles for Katie.   lɛdee bädə lädə bädlz fr keidee

Review Exercise 4-5: Rule 3—Bottom of the Staircase Track 398

1. Matt got to put Jim's pet rat back in the cage.   mæ(t)gä(t)t' pü(t) jimz pe(t)ræ(t)bæck in th' keij
2. Pat set the date with Kate.   pæ(t)se(t)th' dei(t)with kei(t)
3. It's not what they went for.   its nä(t)wə(t) they wen(t) for

Review Exercise 4-6: Rule 4—"Held T" Before N Track 399

1. Whitney saw lightning on the mountain.   wi(t)nee sä li(t)ning än the mæon(t)n
2. He was certainly a frightening accountant.   he w'z sr(t)nlee(y)əfri(t)ning əkæon(t)n(t)
3. That was a rotten way to shorten the curtain!   thæt w'z'rä(t)n weid' shor(t)n th' kr(t)n

Review Exercise 4-7: Rule 5—The Silent T Track 400

1. We had twenty interviews on May 22.   we hæd twenny innerviewzän may twenny sek'nt
2. They don't even want a percentage.   they doe neev'n wänə prsen'j
3. We took advantage of the interruption.   we tükəd væn'j'v the(y)innerəpshən

Review Exercise 4-10: T Combinations in Context Track 401

1. But he said that it's OK.   bədee sed thədit sou kei
2. It's not what you want, but it's what you get.   its nät wəchew wänt, bədits wəchew get
3. What a way to get what he wants!   wədə weidə get wədee wänts

Review Exercise 4-11: Voiced and Unvoiced Sounds with T Track 402

paw	pod	pot	bah	bawd	bought
par	pard	part	bar	bard	Bart
pall	palled	palt	ball	balled	Balt

Review Exercise 5-2: Sounds Comparing L with T, D, and N Track 403

Beginning				Middle			End			
lab	nab	tab	dab	Ellie	any	Eddie	bill	bin	bit	bid
lot	not	tot	dot	caller	Conner	cotter	sill	sin	sit	sid
lie	night	tie	die	alley	Annie's	at ease	bowl	bone	boat	bode

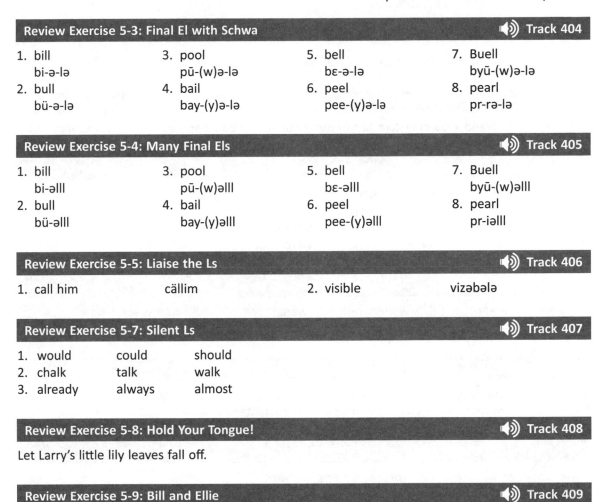

Review Exercise 5-3: Final El with Schwa 🔊 Track 404

1. bill
   bi-ə-lə
2. bull
   bü-ə-lə
3. pool
   pū-(w)ə-lə
4. bail
   bay-(y)ə-lə
5. bell
   bɛ-ə-lə
6. peel
   pee-(y)ə-lə
7. Buell
   byū-(w)ə-lə
8. pearl
   pr-rə-lə

Review Exercise 5-4: Many Final Els 🔊 Track 405

1. bill
   bi-əlll
2. bull
   bü-əlll
3. pool
   pū-(w)əlll
4. bail
   bay-(y)əlll
5. bell
   bɛ-əlll
6. peel
   pee-(y)əlll
7. Buell
   byū-(w)əlll
8. pearl
   pr-iəlll

Review Exercise 5-5: Liaise the Ls 🔊 Track 406

1. call him   cällim
2. visible   vizəbələ

Review Exercise 5-7: Silent Ls 🔊 Track 407

1. would   could   should
2. chalk   talk   walk
3. already   always   almost

Review Exercise 5-8: Hold Your Tongue! 🔊 Track 408

Let Larry's little lily leaves fall off.

Review Exercise 5-9: Bill and Ellie 🔊 Track 409

Bill still calls Ellie all the time. He'll really be glad when she calls back, but it may be a while. He slowly dials the telephone for the twelfth time. *Trill, trill, trill.* No luck. Well, Ellie will feel ill when Bill is in the hospital. He might fall from the windowsill. "Ellie? Hello! Are you well?" Saved by the bell!

Review Exercise 5-11: Final L Practice 🔊 Track 410

	üll	ell	æwl	ell	ale	oll	eel	dl
1.	bull	ball	bowel	bell	bale	bowl	Beal	bottle
2.	pull	pall	Powell	pell	pail	pole	peel	poodle
3.	full	fall	foul	fell	fail	foal	feel	fetal

Review Exercise 5-12: A Frontal Lobotomy? 🔊 Track 411

I'd rather have a frontal lobotomy than a bottle in front of me, chortled the gentle little man, or was it the little gentleman? But anyway, it'll take a battle to test his mettle. What'll he do to get a handle on the whole kit and caboodle? I don't want to meddle, but what if he flies off the handle again? Out of luck, that's what!

Review Exercise 5-13: Speed-reading 🔊 Track 412

Repeat the paragraph from Review Exercise 1-55 as quickly as possible.

Review Exercise 5-14: Tandem Reading	Track 413

Repeat the paragraph from Review Exercise 1-55 along with me.

Review Exercise 6-1: R Location Practice	Track 414

g, gr, Greg, grin, grand, gray, cray, care, core, corner, curl, girl, urban, her, earn, earth, world, were, word

Review Exercise 6-2: Double Vowel Sounds with R	Track 415

	är	ɛr	or	eer	er
1.	ä + er	ɛ + ər	o + ər	e + ər	ər + ər
2.	hä•ərd	shɛ•ər	mo•ər	he•ər	wər•ər
3.	hard	share	more	here	were

Review Exercise 6-3: How to Pronounce Troublesome Rs	Track 416

1. were	wər•ər	3. world/whirled	were rolled	5. where/wear wɛər
2. word	wər•ərd	4. wore/war	woər	

Review Exercise 6-4: Zbignlew's Epsilon List	Track 417

embarrass	character	any	vocabulary	said	paragraph
Paris	necessary	says	parallel	guarantee	area

Review Exercise 6-5: R Combinations	Track 418

	ər	är	ɛr	or	eer	æwr
1.	earn	art	air	or	ear	hour
2.	hurt	heart	hair	horse	here	how're
3.	were	far	where	wore	we're	power

Review Exercise 6-6: Roy the Rancher	Track 419

Roy's car will arrive around three in the afternoon. Gary will rest before they ride around the ranch together in the Ford. Gary's a grape grower in Northern California, and Roy's a rancher in Southern California. They were friends in Paris at the Sorbonne for four years. Roy and Gary had an orange grove and an apple orchard in Barstow, but the oranges were horrible and the apple trees were worse. They roamed around Europe for several years until Gary's marriage. He married Sarah in Bakersfield and had four children: Rachel, Rudy, Randy, and Harry. Harry was a fairly rude boy, and he created rather a lot of trouble between Gary and Sarah. Gary ordered Harry to shape up or forget working in the yard for extra money. Harry said he was sorry, and the group became friends again. After a long separation, Gary heard from his friend, Roy. Roy was driving through Fresno and wanted to get together with Gary's family. Everyone gathered around the fireplace to wait for Gary's old friend. Gary, Sarah, Rachel, Rudy, Randy, and Harry are sitting in a row near the garage. Roy's car will arrive around three in the afternoon.

Review Exercise C: Modifying Descriptive Phrases	Track 420

	Descriptive Phrase	**Modified Description**
1.	It's a black cat.	It's a dark black cat.
2.	It's a scrambled egg.	It's a totally scrambled egg.
3.	It's a fast car.	It's a really fast car.

Review Exercise D: Modifying Set Phrases Track 421

Set Phrase	Modified Set Phrase
1. It's a wildcat.	It's a fierce wildcat.
2. It's an egg timer.	It's a plastic egg timer.
3. It's a car crash.	It's a catastrophic car crash.

Review Exercise E: Two- and Three-Word Set Phrases Track 422

Two-Word Set Phrase	Three-Word Set Phrase
1. It's a wildcat.	It's a wildcat preserve.
2. It's an egg timer.	It's an egg timer bell.
3. It's a car crash.	It's a car crash report.

Review Exercise F: Three-Word Phrase Summary Track 423

Modified Description	Modified Set Phrase	Three-Word Set Phrase
1. a dark black cat	a fierce wildcat	a wildcat preserve
2. a totally scrambled egg	a plastic egg timer	an egg timer bell
3. a really fast car	a catastrophic car crash	a car crash report

Review Exercise I: Multiple Modifiers with Set Phrases Track 424

Modified Set Phrase	Remodified Set Phrase
1. It's a fierce wildcat.	It's an astonishingly fierce wildcat.
2. It's a plastic egg timer.	It's an old plastic egg timer.
3. It's a catastrophic car crash.	It's a truly catastrophic car crash.

Review Exercise J: Compound Intonation of Numbers Track 425

1. How old is she?
   She's thirteen. thirtéen
   She's thirty. thírdy

2. How long has it been?
   Thirteen years.
   Thirty years.

3. How old is she?
   She's thirteen years old.
   She's thirty years old.

Review Exercise K: Modifying Three-Word Set Phrases Track 426

Three-Word Set Phrase	Modified Three-Word Set Phrase
1. It's a wildcat preserve.	It's a new wildcat preserve.
2. It's an egg timer bell.	It's a loud egg timer bell.
3. It's a car crash report.	It's a graphic car crash report.

Review Exercise L: Three-Word-Phrase Story—The Amazing Rock Soup Track 427

A tired young hiker was striding through the thick, dark forest when he came upon a gnarled old crone standing before a small stone hut in a sunny little clearing. "My poor old stomach is really very empty," he thought. "I hope this old landlady can spare a little food." Sensing what he was about to say, she snapped, "No! I have barely enough for myself!" "My good woman," he said, "On the contrary! I'd like to cook you a sumptuously rich dinner . . . of rock soup!" She was naturally very suspicious, but she let him in. He boiled some clear, fresh water, added three clean rocks, and hung the dented old kettle in the old fireplace. He tasted the mysterious liquid concoction. "This is truly delicious," he declared, "but it would be so much better with just one little vegetable." She begrudgingly gave him a small limp carrot and two dry onions. "Yum," he said happily. "But if only . . ." Bit by bit, he cajoled the lonely housewife into making a savory stewpot. The two of them sat down, smiled at each other, and enjoyed a fabulous dinner together.

Review Exercise M: Building Up to Five-Word Phrases Track 428

1. It's a house.
2. It's old.
3. It's really old.
4. It's an old house.
5. It's a really old house.
6. It's a lighthouse.
7. It's an old lighthouse.
8. It's a really old lighthouse.
9. He's a lighthouse keeper.
10. He's an old lighthouse keeper.
11. He's a really old lighthouse keeper.

Review Exercise 7-1: The Thing Track 429

This is the thing that they told them about this Thursday. This thing or that thing? This thing. Actually, there are two of them. Both of these things were with the three other things there in the theater. They're worth three thousand dollars. Ruth and her mother think that they are worth more than that, though, unless they break, and then they are worthless. Altogether worthless to them. That would bother Ruth's brother, mother, and father on their birthday, the thirtieth of this month. Ruth, Ethel, and Beth have a rule of thumb about birthdays, which is to stay together, through thick and thin, whether it's worth it or not. And that's the thing.

Noun Intonation Summary Track 430

Rule 1: New Information

Noun | Verb | Noun—*Bob studies English.*   Pronoun | Verb | Noun—*He studies English.*

Rule A: Descriptive Phrases

pretty good	a good shot	a pretty good shot
really long	a long talk	really very long
fairly rubbery	a rubber hose	a long rubber hose

Rule B: Compound Nouns

a snapshot	a snapshot collection
a talkshow	a talkshow host
a rubber band	a rubber band box
a good snapshot	a good snapshot collection
a funny talkshow	a funny talkshow host
a cheap rubber band	a cheap rubber band box
a really good snapshot	a really good snapshot collection
a super funny talkshow	a super funny talkshow host
a very cheap rubber band	a very cheap rubber band box

Rule C: Descriptive Phrases with Sentence Balance

The Great Wall	pretty good
The Great Wall of China	a pretty good shot
seventeen	fourteen
seventeen dollars	fourteen years
seventeen dollars an hour	fourteen years old
seventeen dollars and ten cents an hour	fourteen and a half years old

Rule 2: Old Information

Pronoun | Verb | Pronoun—*He studies it.*   Noun | Verb | Pronoun—*Bob studies it.*

Rule 3: Contrast

We need a red pen. (new information)   We need a red pen. (not a blue one)

Rule 4: Opinion

I should go **jogging**. (new info)—I **should** go jogging . . . (opinion indicating the opposite)

pretty **good** (new info)—**pretty** good (just OK); I think **so** (confident)—I **think** so (not sure)

Rule 5: Negation (Can't)

I can do it.	I k'n do it	(positive) I can do it.	I kææn do it	(extra positive)
I can't do it.	I kæn(t)do it	(negative) I can't do it.	I kæn(t)do it	(extra negative)

Review Exercise 8-1: Comparing **u** and **ü**   🔊 Track 431

u	ü	u	ü
soon	book	Luke	look
cooed	could	wooed	would
shoed	should	tool	took

Review Exercise 8-2: Lax Vowels   🔊 Track 432

e	i	ü	ə	ər
held	hill	hook	hug	her
bet	bit	book	but	burn
kept	kiss	could	cut	curt

Review Exercise 8-4: Bit or Beat? Bid or Bead?   🔊 Track 433

Tense Vowels		Lax Vowels	
beat	bead	bit	bid
seat	seed	sit	Sid
heat	he'd	hit	hid

Review Exercise 8-5: Tense and Lax Vowel Review Exercise   🔊 Track 434

	Tense	Lax	
1.	even	if	Even if it's raining, they'll go.
2.	bean	been	We've been growing beans.
3.	deal	dill	You made a deal for dill pickles.

Review Exercise 8-6: Middle "I" List   🔊 Track 435

similar	typical	president	episode	beautiful	ability
animal	chemistry	experiment	security	technical	monitor

Review Exercise 8-10: **ü** Paragraph   Track 436

You could've pushed, you could've pulled. You should've pushed and pulled, by hook or by crook, to take a good look at that book. It stood a full foot tall, propped up on the cushion at the Book Nook. Now, I'm all shook up, sugar!

Review Exercise 8-11: **u** Paragraph   Track 437

As a rule, you and Sue Woo are truly too cool—if only you knew how cool you two choose to be at school or at the movies. Lou blew his cool on Tuesday while perusing the newspaper for the truth about who flew the coop from the boot camp, including the lieutenant. Who knew the truth?

Review Exercise 9-1: Mind Your Vees Track 438

P	B	F	V	W
Perry	berry	fairy	very	wary
pat	bat	fat	vat	wax
Paul	ball	fall	vault	wall

1. Peter picked a peck of pickled peppers.
2. It's important to provide perfect principles for young people.
3. Hopscotch, lollipops, hoolahoops, and popsicles keep a little nipper happy.
4. Laptop computers put payroll, payables, and spreadsheets at our fingertips.
5. It's impossible to predict population patterns.

1. Betty bought a bit of better butter.
2. Ben believes Bill broke Bob's box.
3. Billions of bagels are being baked in Brooklyn.
4. Babies babble and blow bubbles.
5. Bananas come from Cuba.

1. What were the women doing in the woods?
2. How would I know?
3. When was Willy's worst weekend?
4. Why would we wear warm wool?
5. Where were we when we woke up?

1. Fred forgot to fry fish on Friday.
2. Few friends fail to fight.
3. Freedom fighters fight for freedom.
4. Only a fool feeds fugu to friends.
5. Feel free to laugh if it's funny.

1. It's evident that Vera was very valuable.
2. Cliff Claven was available for every version.
3. The navy revoked his visa for obvious reasons.
4. Beavers give the environment very valuable dams.
5. Caves leave me cold, but I love to dive.

Review Exercise 10-1: S or Z? Track 439

s	z	s	z
ice	eyes	dust	does
ace	A's	race	rays
fleece	fleas	muscle	muzzle

Review Exercise 10-2: Sally at the Seashore Track 440

It's so silly to see Sally sell seashells at the seashore. Sally and her sister, Sue, can sell seventy-six apiece every Saturday and Sunday in August and September, but their price must decrease or their sales will sink.

Review Exercise 10-3: Fuzzy Wuzzy Track 441

Fuzzy Wuzzy was a bear. Fuzzy Wuzzy had no hair. Fuzzy Wuzzy wasn't fuzzy, was he!

Review Exercise 11-1: Tense Vowels Track 442

	æ	æo	ä	i	a	e	u	ou
1.	ask	out	ought	I'm	ape	eel	oops	own
2.	bake	about	boss	bike	bathe	bean	boost	both
3.	camp	cow	cough	kind	case	keep	coop	code

Review Exercise 11-3: Lax Vowels Track 443

e	i	ü	ə	ər
wed	which	would	what	work
bet	bit	book	but	burn
kept	kiss	could	cut	curt

Review Exercise 11-7: Compound Nouns and Complex Verbs   **Track 444**

invendə
1. The wily old lighthouse keepers invent a highly lucrative money-laundering scheme once a season.
invenədə
2. The wily old lighthouse keepers invented a highly lucrative money-laundering scheme last year.
zərinvending
3. The wily old lighthouse keepers're inventing a highly lucrative money-laundering scheme again.
zəlinvendə
4. The wily old lighthouse keepers'll invent a highly lucrative money-laundering scheme if they aren't afraid of being caught and sent to prison.
zədinvendə
5. The wily old lighthouse keepers'd invent a highly lucrative money-laundering scheme if they weren't afraid of being caught and sent to prison.
zədəvinvenədə
6. The wily old lighthouse keepers'd've invented a highly lucrative money-laundering scheme if they hadn't been afraid of being caught and sent to prison.
zədəvinvenədə
7. The wily old lighthouse keepers that've invented a highly lucrative money-laundering scheme are languishing in Club Fed at the moment.
zəvinvenədə
8. The wily old lighthouse keepers've invented a highly lucrative money-laundering scheme for the tenth year in a row.
zədinvenədə
9. The wily old lighthouse keepers had invented a highly lucrative money-laundering scheme long before multilevel marketing became popular.
zələvinvenədə
10. The wily old lighthouse keepers'll've invented a highly lucrative money-laundering scheme by the time they get back from checking their off-shore bank accounts.
zädə invendə
11. The wily old lighthouse keepers ought to invent a highly lucrative money-laundering scheme to handle the overflow cash from their many nefarious enterprises.
shüdin vendə
12. The wily old lighthouse keepers should invent a highly lucrative money-laundering scheme to stash their ill-gotten gains.
shüdn•nin vendə
13. The wily old lighthouse keepers shouldn't invent a highly lucrative money-laundering scheme in this anti-crime climate.
shüdə vinvendə
14. The wily old lighthouse keepers should've invented a highly lucrative money-laundering scheme while they were in the witness protection plan.
shüdn•nəvin venedə
15. The wily old lighthouse keepers shouldn't've invented a highly lucrative money-laundering scheme while they were being monitored by the FBI.
cüdin vendə
16. The wily old lighthouse keepers could invent a highly lucrative money-laundering scheme once a year for a hundred years and never run out of ideas.
cüdn•nin vendə
17. The wily old lighthouse keepers couldn't invent a highly lucrative money-laundering scheme even if their lives depended on it.
cüdə vinvenədə
18. The wily old lighthouse keepers could've invented a highly lucrative money-laundering scheme if they'd had a laptop and a bank account.

cüdn*nəvin venəd suchə

19. Even those wily old lighthouse keepers couldn't've invented such a highly lucrative money-laundering scheme without outside help.

mydin vendə

20. The wily old lighthouse keepers might invent a highly lucrative money-laundering scheme unless they're kept under house arrest.

mydəvin vendədə

21. The wily old lighthouse keepers might've invented a highly lucrative money-laundering scheme while they were waiting for trial.

məssdin vendə

22. The wily old lighthouse keepers must invent a lot of highly lucrative money-laundering schemes.

məssdəvin vendədə

23. The wily old lighthouse keepers must've invented a highly lucrative money-laundering scheme while they were out on parole.

cənin vent

24. The wily old lighthouse keepers can invent hundreds of highly lucrative money-laundering schemes.

kændin vendɛnee

25. The wily old lighthouse keepers can't invent any more highly lucrative money-laundering schemes.

Review Exercise 11-8: Your Own Compound Nouns Track 445

On a separate piece of paper, build up your own compound nouns, both subject and object.

Review Exercise 11-9: Your Own Compound Nouns and Complex Verbs Track 446

On a separate piece of paper, write out your own sentences.

Review Exercise 12-1: Nasal Consonants Track 447

	Initial		**Middle**		**Final**	
m/b	more	bore	summing	subbing	jam	jab
n/d	nine	dine	Anna	adder	pawn	pod
ng/g	bring each	geese	singer	cigar	ring	rig

Review Exercise 12-2: Ending Nasal Consonants Track 448

M	**N**	**NG**
rumª	runª	rungª
some	son	sung
hum	hun	hung

Review Exercise 12-3: Reading Nasal Consonant Sounds Track 449

Some young men wanted to fling a ring along the rim of the fountain, but we told them to clam up and clean up their game. One was a well-mannered young man with the name Dan Wang. He said, "Yes, ma'am."

Review Exercise 13-1: Throaty Consonants — Track 450

	Initial	Middle	Final
h	how	rehire	▬▬
k	cow	accent	sink
g	go	regard	drag
ng	bring in	thanks	sing
r	row	mirror	car

Review Exercise 13-2: The Letter X — Track 451

ks		gz	
excite	ɛksäit	example	əgzæmpəl
extra	ɛkstrə	exactly	əgzæklee
except	əksɛpt	examine	əgzæmən
excellent	ɛksələnt	exit	ɛgzit

Review Exercise 13-3: Reading the H, K, G, NG, and R sounds — Track 452

Dr. Baxter's exact experience was such that when the good doctor traveled to the Sahara, he inhaled the arid air, picked up his still packed bags, and headed for the bar. It was time to examine the sorry situation, which was exactly the case with Dr. Igor Baxter, an English historian with a peg leg and a unquenchable thirst for Mexican rum. Baxter had had a pair of strange experiences in the area, but he was still game to accomplish his goal in the exiled purgatory of the great, dry Sahara. When he saw that his patients were to be camels, however, he packed up and took off for green England, without a single pang of regret.

Nationality Guides

- Intonation
- Liaisons
- Word endings
- Pronunciation
- Location in the mouth
- Particular difficulties

No matter what language you speak, you will have different sounds and rhythms from a native speaker of American English. These Nationality Guides will give you a head start on what to listen for in American English from the perspective of your own native language. In order to specifically identify what you need to work on, this section can be used in conjunction with the *diagnostic analysis.* The analysis provides an objective rendering of the sounds and rhythms based on how you currently speak, as well as specific guidelines for how to standardize your English; call (800) 457-4255 for a private consultation.

Each section will cover *intonation, word connections, word endings, pronunciation, location of the language in the mouth,* as well as particular difficulties to work through and solutions to common misperceptions.

Most adult students rely too heavily on spelling. It's now your job to listen for pure sound and reconcile that to spelling—not the other way around. This is the same path that a native speaker follows.

As you become familiar with the major characteristics and tendencies in American English, you will start using that information in your everyday speech. One of the goals of the diagnostic analysis is to show you what you already know so you can use the information and skills in English as *transfer skills,* rather than *newly learned skills.* You will learn more readily, more quickly, and more pleasantly—and you will retain the information and use the accent with less resistance.

Read all the nationality guides—you never know when you'll pick up something useful for yourself. Although each nationality is addressed individually, there are certain aspects of American English that are difficult for everyone, in this order:

Nouns generally indicate new information and are stressed.

1. Pitch changes and meaning shifts of intonation
2. Regressive vocalization with a final voiced consonant *(bit/bid)*
3. Liaisons
4. R & L
5. æ, ä, ə (including the æo in *ow)*
6. Tense & lax vowels (i/ē and ü/ū)
7. Th
8. B, V & W

Ideally, you would have learned intonation before you learned grammar, but since that didn't happen, you can now incorporate the intonation into the grammar that you already know. When you first start listening for intonation, it sounds completely random. It shifts all around even when you use the same words. So, where should you start? In basic sentences with a *noun-verb-noun* pattern, the nouns are usually stressed. Why? Because nouns carry the new information. Naturally, contrast can alter this, but noun stress is the default. Listen to native speakers and you will hear that their pitch goes up on the noun most of the time.

Pronouns indicate old information and are unstressed.

You will, however, also hear verbs stressed. When? The verb is stressed when you replace a noun with a pronoun. Because *nouns are new information* and *pronouns are old information*—and we don't stress old information—the intonation shifts over to the verb. Intonation is the most important part of your accent. Focus on this, and everything else will fall into place with it.

CHINESE
Intonation

There are several immediately evident characteristics of a Chinese accent. The most notable is the lack of speech music, or the musical intonation of English. This is a problem because, in the English language, *intonation* indicates meaning, new information, contrast, or emotion. Another aspect of speech music is *phrasing,* which tells if it is a statement, a question, a yes/no option, a list of items, or where the speaker is in the sentence (introductory phrase, end of the sentence, etc.). In Chinese, however, a change in tone indicates a different vocabulary word. (See also Chapter 1.)

In English, Chinese speakers have a tendency to increase the *volume* on stressed words but otherwise give equal value to each word. This atonal volume increase will sound aggressive, angry, or abrupt to a native speaker. When this is added to the tendency to lop off the end of each word, and almost no word connections at all, the result ranges from choppy to unintelligible.

In spite of this unpromising beginning, Chinese learners have a tremendous advantage. Here is an amazingly effective technique that radically changes how you sound. Given the highly developed tonal qualities of the Chinese language, you are truly a "pitch master." In order for you to appreciate your strength in this area, try the four *ma* tones of Mandarin Chinese. (Cantonese is a little more difficult since it has eight to twelve tones and people aren't as familiar with the differentiation.) These four tones sound identical to Americans—*ma, ma, ma, ma.*

Take the first sentence in Exercise 1-11, *It sounds like* **rain,** and replace *rain* with *ma*[1]. Say *It sounds like ma*[1]. This will sound strangely flat, so then try *It sounds like ma*[2]. This isn't it either, so go on to *It sounds like ma*[3] and *It sounds like ma*[4]. One of the last two will sound pretty good, usually *ma*[3]. You may need to come up with a combination of *ma*[3] and *ma*[4], but once you have the idea of what to listen for, it's really easy. When you have that part clear, put *rain* back in the sentence, keeping the tone:

Important Point
In English, a pitch change indicates the speaker's intention. In Chinese, a pitch change indicates a different word.

The four "ma" tones of Mandarin Chinese

ma[1] —
ma[2] ╱
ma[3] ╲╱
ma[4] ╲

It sounds like *ma*[3].
It sounds like *rain*[3].

If it sounds a little short *(It sounds like ren),* **double** the sound:

It sounds like

When this exercise is successful, go to the second sentence, *It **sounds** like rain,* and do the same thing:

It *ma*[3] like rain.
It *sounds*[3] like rain.

Then, contrast the two:

It sounds like *rain*[3].
It *sounds*[3] like rain.

From this point on, you only need to periodically listen for the appropriate *ma,* substituting it in for words or syllables. You don't even need to use the rubber band since your tonal sophistication is so high.

Chinese Intonation Summary
1. Say the four **ma**'s.
2. Write them out with the appropriate arrows.
3. Replace the stressed word in a sentence with each of the four **ma**'s.
4. Decide which one sounds best.
5. Put the stressed word back in the sentence, keeping the tone.

Goal
To get you to use your excellent tone control in English.

The main point of this exercise is to get you listening for the tone shifts in English, which are very similar to the tone shifts in Chinese. The main difference is that Americans use them to indicate stress, whereas in Chinese they are fully different words when the tone changes.

A simple way to practice intonation is with the sound that American children use when they make a mistake—**uh**-*oh*. This quick note shift is completely typical of the pattern, and once you have mastered this double note, you can go on to more complex patterns. Because Chinese grammar is fairly similar to English grammar, you don't have to worry too much about word order.

Liaisons

Chinese characters start with consonants and end with either a vowel or a nasalized consonant (n or ng).

All of the advantages that you have from *intonation* are more than counter-balanced by your lack of *word connections*. The reason for this is that Chinese characters (words or parts of words) start with consonants and end with either a vowel or a nasalized consonant, **n** or **ng**. There is no such thing as a final **t**, **l**, or **b** in Chinese. To use an example we've all heard of, *Mao Tse Tung*. This leads to several difficulties:

• No word endings
• No word connections
• No distinction between final voiced or unvoiced consonants.

It takes time and a great deal of concentration, but the lack of word endings and word connections can be remedied. Rather than force the issue of adding on sounds that will be uncomfortable for you, which will result in overpronunciation, go with your strengths—notice how in *speech,* but not *spelling,* Americans end their words with vowel sounds and start them with consonants, just as in Chinese! It's really a question of rewriting the English script in your head that you read from when you speak. (See also Chapter 2.)

Goal
To get you to rewrite your English script and to speak with sound units rather than word units.

Liaisons or *word connections* will force the final syllable to be pronounced by pushing it over to the beginning of the next word, where Chinese speakers have no trouble—not even with **L**.

Written English	Chinese Accent	American (with Liaisons)
Tell him	teo him	tellim
Pull it out	puw ih aw	pü li dout

Because you are now using a natural and comfortable technique, you will sound smooth and fluid when you speak, instead of that forced, exaggerated speech of people who are doing what they consider unnatural. It takes a lot of correction to get this process to sink in, but it's well worth the effort. Periodically, when you speak, write down the exact sounds that you made, then write it in regular spelling, so you can *see* the Chinese accent and the effect it has on meaning *(puw ih aw* has no meaning in English). Then convert the written English to spoken American *(pull it out* changes to *pü li dout)* to help yourself rewrite your English script.

When you don't use liaisons, you also lose the underlying hum that connects sentences together. This *coassonance* is like the highway and the words are the cars that carry the listener along.

The last point of intonation is that Chinese speakers don't differentiate between voiced and unvoiced final consonants—*cap* and *cab* sound exactly the same. For this, you will need to go back to the staircase. When a final consonant is voiced, the vowel is lengthened, or doubled. When a final consonant is unvoiced, the vowel is short, or single.

Additionally, the long **a** before an **m** is generally shortened to a short **ɛ**. This is why the words *same* and *name* are particularly difficult, usually being pronounced *sem* and *nem.* You have to add in the second half of the sound. You need *nay + eem* to get *name.* Doubled vowels are explained on pages 5–6 and page 10.

Pronunciation

Goal
For you to hear the actual vowel and consonant sounds of English, rather than a Chinese perception of them.

The most noticeable nonstandard pronunciation is the lack of final **L**. This can be corrected by either liaisons, or by adding a tiny schwa after it (l^uh or l^ə) in order to position your tongue correctly. This is the same solution for **n** and **ng**. Like most other nationalities, Chinese learners need to work on **th** and **r**, but fortunately, there are no special problems here. The remaining major area is **ā**, **ɛ**, and **æ**, which sound the same. *Mate, met, mat* sound like *met, met, met.* The **ɛ** is the natural sound for the Chinese, so working from there, you need to concentrate on Chapters 1 and 3. In the word *mate,* you are hearing only the first half of the **ɛi** combination, so double the vowel with a clear *eet* sound at the end (even before an unvoiced final consonant). Otherwise, you will keep saying *meh-eht* or *may-eht.*

It frequently helps to know exactly how something would look in your own language—and in Chinese, this entails characters. The characters on the left are the sounds needed for a Chinese person to say both the long **i** as in *China* and the long **ā** as in *made* or *same.* Read the character, and then put letters in front and in back of it so you are reading half alphabet, half character. An **m** in front and a **d** in back of the first character will let you read *made.* A **ch** in front and **na** in back of the second character will produce *China.* It's odd, but it works. (See also Chapter 3.)

ā made
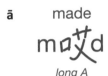
long A

A word that ends in *–ail* is particularly difficult for Chinese speakers since it contains both the hard **ɛi** combination and a final **L** (Chapter 1). It usually sounds something like *feh-o.* You need to say *fail* as if it had three full syllables—*fay-yə-l^ə.* (See also Chapter 6.)

L China

long I

Another difficulty may be **u, v, f,** and **w.** The point to remember here is that **u** and **w** can both be considered *vowels* (i.e., they don't touch anywhere in the mouth), whereas **v** and **f** are *consonants* (your upper teeth touch your lower lip). **ū,** as in *too* or *use,* should be no problem. Similar to **ū,** but with a little push of slightly rounded lips is **w,** as in *what* or *white.* The letters **f** and **v** have basically the same sound, but **f** is unvoiced and **v** is voiced. Your lower lip should come up a little to meet your top teeth. You are not biting down on the outside of your lip here; the sound is created using the inside of your lower lip. Leave your mouth in the same position and make the two sounds, both voiced and unvoiced. Practice words such as *fairy, very,* and *wary.* (See also Chapter 11.)

u, v, f, w
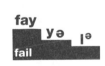

There is another small point that may affect people from southern mainland China who use **l** and **n** interchangeably. This can be corrected by working with **l** words and pinching the nose shut. If you are trying to say *late* and it comes out *Nate,* hold your nose closed and the air will be forced out through your mouth. (See also Chapter 6.)

æ The **æ** sound doesn't exist in Chinese, so it usually comes out as **ā** or **ɛ**, so *last* sounds like *lost* or *name* sounds like *nem.* You need to work on Chapter 3, which drills this distinctively American vowel. (See also Chapters 3, 10, and 12.)

ä	Because of spelling, the **ä** sound can easily be misplaced. The **ä** sound exists in Chinese, but when you see an **o**, you might want to say **ō**, so *hot* sounds like *hōht* instead of *häht*. Remember, most of the time, the letter **o** is pronounced *ah*. This will give you a good reference point for whenever you want to say **ä** instead of **ō**: *astronomy, cäll, läng, prägress*, etc. (See also Chapters 3, 10, and 12.)
o	Conversely, you may pronounce the letter **o** as *ä* or *ə* when it should be an *o*, as in *only, most, both*. Make sure that the American **o** sounds like *ou: ounly, moust, bouth*. (See also Chapters 3, 10, and 12.)
ə	The schwa is typically overpronounced based on spelling. Work on Chapter 1, "American Intonation," and Chapter 3, "Cat? Caught? Cut?." If your intonation peaks are strong and clear enough, then your valleys will be sufficiently reduced as well. Concentrate on smoothing out and reducing the valleys and *ignore spelling!* (See also Chapters 3, 10, and 12.)
ü	The **ü** sound is generally overpronounced to *ooh*. Again, spelling is the culprit. Words such as *smooth, choose,* and *too* are spelled with two **o**'s and are pronounced with a long **ū** sound, but other words such as *took* and *good* are spelled with two **o**'s but are pronounced halfway between *ih* and *uh*; **tük** and **güd**. (See also Chapters 10 and 12.)
i	In most Chinese dictionaries, the distinction between **i** and **ē** is not made. The **ē** is generally indicated by **i**, which causes problems with final consonants, and the **ih** sound is overpronounced to *eee*. Practice these four sounds, remembering that *tense vowels* indicate that you tense your lips or tongue, while *lax vowels* mean that your lips and tongue are relaxed and the sound is produced in your throat. *Unvoiced* final consonants (**t, s, k, p, ch, f**) mean that the vowel is short and sharp; *voiced* final consonants (**d, z, g, b, j, v**) mean that the vowel is doubled. Work on *Bit or Beat? Bid or Bead?* in Chapter 18. (See also Chapter 12.)
r	Chinese speakers usually pronounce American **r** as **ä** at the end of a word *(car* sounds like *kaaah)* or almost a **w** in the beginning or middle *(grow* sounds like *gwow)*. The tongue should be curled back more, and the **r** produced deep in the throat. (See also Chapter 5.)
th	If you pronounce **th** as **t** or **d** (depending if it's voiced or unvoiced), then you should allow your tongue tip to move about a quarter of an inch forward, so the very tip is just barely between your teeth. Then, from this position you make a sound similar to **t** or **d**. (See also Chapter 8.)
n	Chinese will frequently interchange final **n** and **ng**. The solution is to add a little schwa at the end, just like you do with the **el**: men³, thing³, call³. This will make the tongue position more apparent, as you can see on page 84.
sh	Some people pronounce the **sh** in a particularly Chinese-sounding way. It seems that the tongue is too curled back, which changes the sound. Make sure that the tongue is flat, the tongue tip is just at the ridge behind the top teeth, and that only a thin stream of air is allowed to escape. (See also Chapter 13.)
t	American English has a peculiar characteristic in that the **t** sound is, in many cases, pronounced as a **d**. (See also Chapter 4.)

Final Consonants One of the defining characteristics of Chinese speech is that the final consonants are left off *(hold* sounds like *ho)*. Whenever possible, make a liaison with the following word. For example, *hold* is difficult to say, so try *hold on = hol dän*. Pay particular attention to Chapter 2.

Location of the Language

Chinese, like American English, is located in the *back of the throat.* The major difference between the two languages is that English requires that the speaker use the *tongue tip* a great deal: **l, th**, and final **t, d, n, l**. Chapter 13, "The Ridge," will help a great deal with this.

JAPANESE

Intonation

Although Chinese and Japanese are both Asian languages and share enormously in their written characters, they are opposites in terms of intonation, word-endings, pronunciation, and liaisons. Whereas the Chinese stress every word and can sound aggressive, Japanese speakers give the impression of stressing no words and sounding timid. Both impressions are, of course, frequently entirely at odds with the actual meaning and intention of the words being spoken. Chinese speakers have the advantage of *knowing* that they have a tonal language, so it is simply a question of transferring this skill to English.

Japanese, on the other hand, almost always insist that the Japanese language "has no intonation." Thus, Japanese speakers in English tend to have a picket fence intonation: | | | | | | | | | | . In reality, the Japanese language does express all kinds of information and emotion through intonation, but this is such a prevalent myth that you may need to examine your own beliefs on the matter. Most likely, you need to use the rubber band extensively in order to avoid volume increases rather than on changing the pitch. (See also Chapter 1.)

One of the major differences between English and Japanese is that there is a fixed word order in English—a verb grid—whereas in Japanese, you can move any word to the head of a sentence and add a topic particle *(wa* or *ga).* Following are increasingly complex verbs with adverbs and helping verbs. Notice that the positions are fixed and do *not* change with the additional words.

	auxiliary	negative	perfect auxiliary	adverb	passive	continuous	main verb
Draw!							
							Draw!
He draws.							
He							draws.
He does draw.							
He	does						draw.
He is drawing.							
He	is						drawing.
He is not drawing.							
He	is	**not**					drawing.
He is not always drawing.							
He	is	not		always			drawing.
He is not always being drawn.							
He	**is**	not		always	being		drawn.
He has not always been drawn.							
He	has	not		always	been		drawn.
He has not always been being drawn.							
He	has	not		always	been	being	drawn.
He will not have always been being drawn.							
He	will	not	have	always	been	being	drawn.

Liaisons

Whereas the Chinese drop word endings, Japanese totally overpronounce them. This is because in the katakana syllabary, there are the five vowels sounds, and then consonant-vowel combinations. In order to be successful with word connections, you need to think only of the final consonant in a word, and connect that to the next word in the sentence. For example, for *What time is it?* instead of *Whato täimu izu ito?* connect the two **T**'s and let the other consonants move over to connect with the vowels: *w'täi mi zit?* Start with the held **t** in Chapter 4 and use that concept for the rest of the final consonants. (See also Chapter 2.)

Written English	The only way to get it is to practice all of the time.
American accent	Thee(y)only way də geddidiz də præctisälləv th' time.
Japanese accent	Zä ondee weh tsu getto itto izu tsu pudäctees odu obu zä taimu.

Pronunciation

æ The æ doesn't exist in Japanese; it usually comes out as **ä**, so *last* sounds like *lost*. You need to raise the back of your tongue and drop your jaw to produce this sound. Work on Chapter 3, which drills this distinctively American vowel. (See also Chapters 3, 10, and 12.)

ä The **ä** sound is misplaced. You have the **ä** sound, but when you see an **o**, you want to say **o**, so *hot* sounds like *hohto* instead of *haht*. Here's one way to deal with it. Write the word *stop* in katakana—the four characters for *su + to + hold + pu*, so when you read it, it sounds like *stohppu*. Change the second character from *to* to *tä*: *su + tä + hold + pu*, it will sound like *stop*. This will give you a good reference point for whenever you want to say **ä** instead of **o**; *impossible, call, long, problem*, etc. (See also Chapters 3, 10, and 12.)

o You may pronounce the letter **o** as **ä** or **ə** when it should be an **o**, as in *only, most, both*. Make sure that the American **o** sounds like *ou: ounly, moust, bouth*. This holds true for the diphthongs as well—*oi* sounds like *ou-ee*.

t<u>ou</u>n	t<u>o</u>ne	n<u>ou</u>t	n<u>o</u>te	h<u>ou</u>m	h<u>o</u>me
<u>ou</u>nli	<u>o</u>nly	c<u>ou</u>l	c<u>oa</u>l	j<u>ou</u>k	j<u>o</u>ke

Another way to develop clear strong vowels instead of nonstandard hybrids is to understand the relation between the American English spelling system and the Japanese katakana sounds. For instance, if you're having trouble with the word *hot*, say *ha, hee, hoo, heh, hoh* in Japanese, and then go back to the first one and convert it from *ha* to *hot* by adding the held **t** (Chapter 4). Say *hot* in Japanese, *atsui*, then add an **h** for *hatsui* and then drop the *-sui* part, which will leave *hot*. (See also Chapters 3, 10, and 12.)

ə The schwa is typically overpronounced, based on spelling. Concentrate on smoothing out and reducing the valleys and *ignore spelling!* (See also Chapters 3, 10, and 12.)

ü Distinguishing tense and lax vowels is difficult, and you'll have to forget spelling for **ū** and **ü**. They both can be spelled with *oo* or *ou*, but the lax vowel **ü** should sound much closer to *i* or *uh*. If you say *book* with a tense vowel, it'll sound like *booque*. It should be much closer to *bick* or *buck*. (See also Chapters 10 and 12.)

i Similarly, you need to distinguish between **e** and **i**, as in *beat* and *bit*, on page 136. Also, tone down the middle **i** in the multisyllabic words on page 138; otherwise, *similar* **sim'lr** will sound like *see-mee-lär*. Most likely, you overpronounce the lax vowel **i** to *eee*, so that *sit* is mispronounced as *seat*. Reduce the lax **i** almost to a schwa; *sit* should sound like *s't*. In most Japanese dictionaries, the distinction between **i** and **ē** is not made. Practice the four sounds—*bit, beat, bid, bead*—remembering that *tense vowels* indicate that you tense your lips or tongue, while *lax vowels* mean that your lips and tongue are relaxed and the sound is produced in your throat. *Unvoiced* final consonants (**t, s, k, p, ch, f**) mean that the vowel is short and sharp; *voiced* final consonants (**d, z, g, b, j, v**) mean that the vowel is doubled. Work on *Bit or Beat? Bid or Bead?* in Chapter 10. (See also Chapter 12.)

	single	double
tense	beat	bead
lax	bit	bid

The Japanese R = The American T

ベリ バラ ビラ	Betty bought a bit of		アイ ニーダ ラァダ タイム	I need a lot of time.
アイ バラ バイク	I bought a bike.		マイ マロウ	my motto
クディ ドゥイッ	Could he do it?		ミリン	meeting
ウィ アラ ゴウ	We ought to go.		アイム ナラン タイム	I'm not on time.

The Japanese **r** is a consonant. This means that it touches at some point in the mouth. Japanese speakers usually trill their r's (tapping the ridge behind the top teeth), which makes it sound like a **d** to the American ear. The tongue should be curled back, and the **r** produced deep in the throat—*not* touching the top of the mouth. The Japanese pronunciation of **r** is usually just an **ä** at the end of a word (*car* sounds like *caaah*) or a flap in the beginning or middle (*area* sounds like *eddy-ah*).

L	Japanese speakers often confuse the **el** with **r** or **d**, or drop the schwa, leaving the sound incomplete. (See also Chapter 6.)
th	The *th* sound is mispronounced *s* or *z*, depending if it is voiced or unvoiced. (See also Chapter 8.)
v	**v** is mispronounced either as a simple *bee,* or if you have been working on it, it may be a combination such as *buwee*. You need to differentiate between the four sounds of **p/b/f/v**. The plosives **b/p** pop out; the sibilants **f/v** slide out. **b/v** are voiced; **f/p** are unvoiced. **b/v** are the *least* related pair. The root of the problem is that you need a good, strong **f** first. To the American ear, the way the Japanese say *Mount Fuji* sounds like *Mount Hooji*. Push your bottom lip up with your finger so that it is *outside* your top teeth and make a sharp popping sound. (See also Chapter 11.) Practice these sounds:

F	V	B		F	V	B
fat	vat	bat		ferry	very	berry
face	vase	base		effort	ever	Ebber
fear	veer	beer		foul	vowel	bowel

Once you have the **f** in place, simply allow your vocal cords to vibrate and you will then have a **v**.

	whispered	spoken
popped	P	B
hissed	F	V

w	The **w** is erroneously dropped before **ü**, so *would* is shortened to *ood*. Since you can say *wa, wi, wo* with no problem, use that as a starting point; go from *waaaaa, weeeeeeee, woooooo* to *wüüüüü*. It's more a concept problem than a physical one. (See also Chapter 11.)
n	Japanese will frequently interchange final **n** and **ng**. Adding the little schwa at the end will clear this up by making the tongue position obvious, as in Chapter 6. (See also Chapter 17.)
z	**z** at the beginning of a word sounds like *dz*. (*zoo* sounds like *dzoo*). For some reason, this is a tough one. In the syllabary, you read *ta, chi, tsu, teh, toh* for unvoiced and *da, ji, dzu, de, do* for voiced. Try going from unvoiced *sssssue* to *zzzzzzzoo*, and don't pop that **d** in at the last second. (See also Chapter 9.)
si	The **si** combination is mispronounced as *shi*, so *six* comes out as *shicks*, and I don't even want to say what *city* sounds like! Again, this is a syllabary problem. You read the **s** row as *sa, shi, su, seh, soh*. You just need to realize that since you already know how to make a hissing *s* sound, you are capable of making it before the *i* sound. (See also Chapter 10.)

Location of the Language

Japanese is *more forward* in the mouth than American English and there is much *less lip movement.*

SPANISH
Intonation

Spanish-speaking people (bearing in mind that there are 22 Spanish-speaking countries) tend to have strong intonation, but it's usually toward the end of a phrase or sentence. It is very clear sometimes in Spanish that a person is taking an entire phrase pattern and imposing it on the English words. This can create a subtle shift in meaning, one that the speaker is completely unaware of. For example,

Spanish	English with a Spanish Pattern	Standard English Pattern
Quiero comer *álgo.*	I want to eat *só*mething.	I want to *éat* something.

This is a normal stress pattern in Spanish, but it indicates in English that either you are willing to settle for less than usual or you are contrasting it with the possibility of *nothing.*

Spanish has five pure vowels sounds—*ah, ee, ooh, eh, oh*—and Spanish speakers consider it a point of pride that words are clearly pronounced the way they are written. The lack of the concept of schwa or other reduced vowels may make you overpronounce heavily in English. You'll notice that I said the *concept* of schwa—I think that every language has a schwa, whether it officially recognizes it or not. The schwa is just a neutral vowel sound in an unstressed word, and at some point in quick speech in any language, vowels are going to be neutralized. (See also Chapter 1.)

Liaisons

In Spanish, there are strong liaisons—*el hombre* sounds like *eh lombre*—but you'll probably need to rewrite a couple of sentences in order to get away from word-by-word pronunciation. Because consonant clusters in Spanish start with an epsilon sound *(español* for *Spanish, estudiante* for *student),* this habit carries over into English. Rewriting expressions to accommodate the difference will help enormously. (See also Chapter 2.)

With Epsilon	Rewritten	With Epsilon	Rewritten
I estudy	ice tudy	excellent espeech	excellence peech
in espanish	ince panish	my especialty	mice pecialty
their eschool	theirss cool	her espelling	herss pelling

Word Endings

In Spanish, words end in a vowel (**o** or **a**), or the consonants **n, s, r, l, d**. Some people switch **n** and **ng** *(I käng hear you)* for either *I can hear you* or */ can't hear you.* Another consequence is that final consonants can get dropped in English, as in *short* (**shor**) or *friend* (**fren**). (See also Chapters 4 and 16.)

Pronunciation

With most Spanish speakers, the **s** is almost always unvoiced, **r** is trilled, **l** is too short and lacks a schwa, **d** sounds like a voiced **th**, and **b** and **v** are interchangeable. Spanish speakers also substitute the **ä** sound whenever the letter **a** appears, most often for **œ**, **ä**, and **ə**. Bear in mind that there are six different pronunciations for the letter **a** as in Chapter 3. Knowing these simple facts will help you isolate and work through your difficulties. (See also Chapter 1.)

The Spanish S = The American S, But . . .

In Spanish, an **s** always sounds like an **s**. (In some countries, it may be slightly voiced before a voiced consonant such as in *mismo.)* In English, a final –**s** sounds like **z** when it follows a voiced consonant or a vowel (*raise* **raz**, *runs* **rənz**). The most common verbs in English end in the **z** sound—*is, was, does, has,* etc. Double the preceding vowel and allow your vocal cords to vibrate. (See also Chapter 9.)

The Spanish R = The American T

Beri bara bira	Betty bought a bit of	ai nira lara taim	I need a lot of time.
¡Ai Caracól!	I caught a cold.	mai marou	my motto
Curi du it?	Could he do it?	mirin	meeting
ui ara gou	We ought to go.	aim naran taim	I'm not on time.

In Spanish, **r** is a consonant. This means that it touches at some point in the mouth. Spanish speakers usually roll their r's (touching the ridge behind the top teeth), which makes it sound like a **d** to the American ear. The tongue should be curled back, and the **r** produced deep in the throat—*not* touching the top of the mouth. The Spanish pronunciation of **r** is usually the written vowel and a flap **r** at the end of a word (*feeler* is pronounced like *feelehd*) or a flap in the beginning or middle (*throw* sounds like *tdoh*). In English, the pronunciation of **r** doesn't change if it's spelled **r** or **rr**. (See also Chapter 5.)

The -ed Ending

You may have found yourself wondering how to pronounce *asked* or *hoped*; if you came up with *as-ked* or *ho- ped,* you made a logical and common mistake. There are three ways to pronounce the -*ed* ending in English, depending what the previous letter is. If it's voiced, -*ed* sounds like **d**: *played* pleid. If it's unvoiced, -*ed* sounds like **t**: *laughed* læft. If the word ends in **t** or **d**, -*ed* sounds like *əd: patted* pædəd. (See also Chapter 4.)

The Final T

The **t** at the end of a word should not be heavily aspirated. Let your tongue go to the **t** position, and then just stop. It should sound like *hä^t*, not *hä*, or *häch*, or *häts*. (See also Chapter 4.)

The Spanish D = The American Th (voiced)

The Spanish **d** in the middle and final positions is a fricative **d** *(cada* and *sed).* If you are having trouble with the English **th**, substitute in a Spanish **d**. First, contrast *cara* and *cada* in Spanish, and then note the similarities between *cara* and *caught a,* and *cada* and *father.* (See also Chapters 1 and 8.)

ca**d**a	fa**th**er	bei**d**	ba**th**e

The Spanish of Spain Z or C = The American Th (unvoiced)

The letters **z** and **c** in most Spanish-speaking countries sound like **s** in English (not in Andalusia, however). The **z** and **c** from Spain, on the other hand, are equivalent to the American unvoiced **th**. When you want to say *both* in English, say *bouz* with an accent from Spain. (See also Chapters 1 and 8.)

bou**z**	bo**th**	gra**c**ias	gra**th**ias	ui**z**	wi**th**

The Spanish I = The American Y (not J)

In most Spanish-speaking countries, the **y** and **ll** sounds are equivalent to the American **y**, as in *yes* or in liaisons such as *the$^{(y)}$other one. Jes, I jelled at jou jesterday* can be heard in some countries such as Argentina for *Yes, I yelled at you yesterday.*

hielo	yellow (not jello)	ies	yes	iu	you

The Doubled Spanish A Sound = The American O, AL, or AW Spelling

Because of spelling, the **ä** sound can easily be misplaced. The **ä** sound exists in Spanish, but it is represented with the letter **a**. When you see the letter **o**, you pronounce it **o**, so *hot* sounds like *hoht* instead of *haht*. Remember, most of the time, the letter **o** is pronounced *ah*. You can take a sound that already exists in Spanish, such as *jaat* (whether it means anything or not) and say it with your native accent—*jaat* with a Spanish accent more or less equals *hot* in English. This will give you a good reference point for **ä** instead of **o**: *astronomy, call, long, progress,* etc. Focus on Chapter 3, differentiating *æ, ä, ə.*

j<u>aa</u>t	hot	c<u>aa</u>l	call	s<u>aa</u>	saw

The Spanish O = The American OU

You may pronounce the letter **o** as **ä** or **ə** when it really should be an **o**, as in *only, most, both.* Make sure that the American **o** sounds like ou, *ounly, moust, bouth.* This holds true for the diphthongs as well—**oi** sounds like *ou-ee.*

<u>ou</u>nli	<u>o</u>nly	j<u>ou</u>p	h<u>o</u>pe	n<u>ou</u>t	n<u>o</u>te

æ	The **æ** sound doesn't exist in Spanish, so it usually comes out as **ä**, so *last* sounds like *lost.* You need to work on Chapter 3, which drills this distinctively American vowel. (See also Chapters 10 and 12.)
ə	The schwa is typically overpronounced, based on spelling. Work on Chapter 1, "The American Sound" and Chapter 3, "Cat? Caught? Cut?." If your intonation peaks are strong and clear enough, then your valleys will be sufficiently reduced as well. Concentrate on smoothing out and reducing the valleys and *ignore spelling!* (See also Chapters 10 and 12.)
ü	The **ü** sound is generally overpronounced to *ooh.* Again, spelling is the culprit. Words such as *smooth, choose,* and *too* are spelled with two **o**'s and are pronounced with a long **ü** sound, but other words, such as *took* and *good,* are spelled with two **o**'s but are pronounced halfway between *ih* and *uh;* **tük** and **güd.** (See also Chapters 10 and 12.)
i	Spanish speakers overpronounce the lax vowel **i** to *eee,* so *sit* comes out as *seat.* In most Spanish dictionaries, the distinction between **i** and **ē** is not made. Practice the four sounds—*bit, beat, bid, bead*—remembering that *tense vowels* indicate that you tense your lips or tongue, while *lax vowels* mean that your lips and tongue are relaxed and the sound is produced in your throat. *Unvoiced* final consonants (**t, s, k, p, ch, f**) mean that the vowel is short and sharp; *voiced* final consonants (**d, z, g, b, j, v**) mean that the vowel is doubled. Work on *Bit or Beat? Bid or Bead?* in Chapter 10. Reduce the soft **i** to a schwa; *sit* should sound like *s't.* (See also Chapter 12.)

	single	double
tense	beat	bead
lax	bit	bid

Also, watch out for cognates such as *similar,* pronounced *see-mee-lär* in Spanish, and **si•m'•lr** in American English. Many of them appear in the Middle "I" List on page 138.

l	The Spanish **l** lacks a schwa, leaving the sound short and incomplete to the American ear. Contrast similar words in the two languages and notice the differences. (See also Chapter 6.)

Written	Pronounced	Spanish
ball	bä-uhl	bal

v	A Spanish speaker usually pronounces **v** and **b** the same (*I have trouble with my bowels* instead of *I have trouble with my vowels*). You need to differentiate between the four sounds of **p/b/f/v**. The plosives **b/p** pop out; the sibilants **f/v** slide out. **b/v** are voiced; **f/p** are unvoiced, **b/v** are the *least* related pair. Push your bottom lip up with your finger so that it is *outside* your top teeth and make a sharp popping sound. (See also Chapter 11.) Practice these sounds:

F	V	B	F	V	B
fat	vat	bat	ferry	very	berry
face	vase	base	effort	ever	Ebber
fear	veer	beer	foul	vowel	bowel

Once you have the **f** in place, simply allow your vocal cords to vibrate and you will then have a **v**.

	whispered	spoken
popped	P	B
hissed	F	V

n	The final **n** is often mispronounced *ng—meng* rather than *men.* Put a tiny schwa at the end to finish off the **n, men^ə** or **thing^ə**, as explained in Chapter 6. (See also Chapter 17.)
w	The **w** sound in Spanish can sound like a **gw** *(I gwould do it).* You need to practice **g** in the throat, rounding your lips for **w**. You can also substitute in a Spanish **ū**, as in *will uil.* (See also Chapter 11.)
h	The Spanish **h** is silent, as in *hombre,* but Spanish speakers often use a stronger fricative than Americans would. The American **h** is equivalent to the Spanish **j**, but the air coming out shouldn't pass through a constricted throat—it's like you're steaming a mirror—*hat, he, his, her, whole, hen,* etc. In some Spanish-speaking countries, the **j** is fricative and in others it is not. Also, there are many words in which the **h** is completely silent, as in *hour, honest, herb,* as well as in liaisons with object pronouns such as *her* and *him (tell her* sounds like *teller).* (See also Chapter 17.)
ch	In order to make the **ch** sound different from the **sh**, put a **t** in front of the **Ch**. Practice the difference between *wash* **wäsh** / *watch* **watch**, or *sharp* **sharp** / *charm* **chärm**. (See also Chapter 13.)
p	The American **p** is more strongly plosive than its Spanish counterpart. Put your hand in front of your mouth—you should feel a strong burst of air. Practice with *Peter picked a peck of pickled peppers.* (See also Chapter 11.)
j	In order to make a clear **j** sound, put a **d** in front of the **j**. Practice *George* **djordj**. (See also Chapter 13.)
sh	There was a woman from Spain who used to say, "Es imposible que se le quite el acento a uno," pronouncing it, "Esh imposhible que se le quite el athento a uno." In her particular accent, **s** sounded like **sh**, which would transfer quite well to standard American English. What it also means is that many people claim it is impossible to change the accent, but, as we all know, that is not the case.

Location of the Language

Spanish is very far forward with much stronger use of the lips.

INDIAN

Intonation

Of the many and varied Indian dialects (Hindi, Telugu, Punjabi, etc.), there is a common intonation transfer to English—sort of a curly, rolling cadence that flows along with little relation to meaning. It is difficult to get the average Indian learner to change pitch. Not that people are unwilling to try or difficult to deal with; on the contrary, in my experience of working with people from India, I find them incredibly pleasant and agreeable. This is part of the problem, however. People agree in concept, in principle, in theory, in every aspect of the matter, yet when they *say* the sentence, the pitch remains unchanged.

I think that what happens is that, in standard American English, we raise the pitch on the beat, while Indians drop their pitch on the beat. Also, the typical Indian voice is much higher pitched than Americans are accustomed to hearing. In particular, you should work on the voice quality exercise in Chapter 1.

Of the three options (*volume, length, pitch*), you can raise the volume easily, but it doesn't sound very good. Since volume is truly the least desirable and the most offensive to the listener, and since pitch has to be worked on over time, lengthening the stressed word is a good stopgap measure. Repeating the letter of a stressed word will help a lot toward changing a rolling *odabah odabah odabah* intonation to something resembling peaks and valleys.

The **oooonly** way to **geeeeeeee**didiz to **præœœœœœœœœœk**tis all of the time.

One thing that works for pitch is to work on the little sound that children make when they make a mistake: "uh-oh!" The first sound is on a distinctly higher level than the second one. Because it's a nonsense syllable, it's easier to work with as you're focusing on pure pitch change and not a real word.

Since so much emotion is conveyed through intonation, it's vital to work with the various tone shifts in Chapter 1.

It's necessary to focus on placing the intonation on the correct words (nouns, compound nouns, descriptive phases, etc.), as well as contrasting, negating, listing, questioning, and exclaiming.

Intonation is also important in numbers, which are typically difficult for Indian speakers. There are both intonation and pronunciation differences between **13** and **30**. The number **13** should sound like **thr-*teen*,** while **30** sounds like ***thr-dee;* 14** is **for-*teen*,** and **40** is ***for-*dee.** (See also Chapter 1.)

Liaisons

Liaisons shouldn't be much of a problem for you once the pattern is pointed out and reinforced. (See also Chpater 2.)

Pronunciation

One way to have an accent is to leave out sounds that should be there, but the other way is to put in sounds that don't exist in that language. Indians bring a rich variety of voiced consonants to English that contribute to the heavy, rolling effect.

| **t** | For the initial **t** alone, there are eight varieties, ranging from plosive to almost swallowed. In American English, **t** at the top of a staircase is a sharp **t,** and **t** in the middle is a soft **d.** Indians tend to reverse this, using the popping British **t** in the middle position (**water**) and a **t**-like sound in the beginning. (*I need two* sounds like *I need doo.*) The solution is to substitute *your th*—it will sound almost perfect (*I need thoo* sounds just like *I need two*). Another way is to separate the **t** from the rest of the word and whisper it. **T + aim = time.** Bit by bit, you can bring the whispered, sharply popped **t** closer to the body of the word. A third way is to imagine that it is actually **ts,** so you are saying *tsäim,* which will come out sounding like *time.* (See also Chapter 4.) |

T	D	T	D
tennis	*Dennis*	*ten*	*den*
time	*dime*	*to*	*do*

The final **t** is typically too plosive and should be held just at the position before the air is expelled.

p   This is similar to the initial **t,** in that you probably voice the unvoiced **p** so it sounds like a **b.** Start with the **m,** progress to the **b,** and finally whisper the **p** sound. (See also Chapter 11.)

M	B	P	M	B	P
men	Ben	pen	mull	bull	pull
mail	bail	pail	mossy	bossy	possible
met	bet	pet	mile	bile	pile

æ	The **æ** sound usually sounds like **ä**. You might refer to *the last class*, but it will sound like *the lost closs*. You should raise the back of your tongue and make a noise similar to that of a lamb. (See also Chapters 3, 10, and 12.)
ä	Because of spelling, the **ä** sound can easily be misplaced. The **ä** sound exists in the Indian languages, but is represented with the letter **a**. When you see the letter **o**, you pronounce it **o**, so *John* sounds like *Joan* instead of *Jahn*. Remember, most of the time, the letter **o** is pronounced *ah*. You can take a sound that already exists in your language, such as *tak* (whether it means anything or not) and say it with your native accent—*tak* with an Indian accent more or less equals *talk* in English. This will give you a good reference point for whenever you want to say **ä** instead of **o**; *astronomy, call, long, progress,* etc. Focus on Chapter 3, differentiating **œ, ä, ə**. (See also Chapters 3, 10, and 12.)

h<u>aa</u>t   h<u>o</u>t   c<u>aa</u>l   c<u>a</u>ll   s<u>aa</u>   saw

o	You may pronounce the letter **o** as **ä** or **ə** when it really should be an **ö**, as in *only, most, both*. Make sure that the American **o** sounds like *ou, ounly, moust, bouth*. This holds true for the diphthongs as well—**oi** should sould like *ou-ee*. (See also Chapters 3, 10, and 12.)

<u>ou</u>nli   <u>o</u>nly   h<u>ou</u>p   h<u>o</u>pe   n<u>ou</u>t   n<u>o</u>te

r	Indians tend to have a British **r**, which means that it is either a flap at the beginning or middle of a word or it is reduced to **ä** at the end of a word. You need to understand that the American **r** is not a consonant (i.e., it doesn't touch at any two points in the mouth)—it is much closer to a vowel in that the tongue curls back to shape the air flow. (See also Chapter 5.)
th	The American **th**, both voiced and unvoiced, usually sounds like a **d** when said by an Indian speaker; *thank you* sounds like *dank you*. Also you must distinguish between a voiced and an unvoiced **th**. The voiced ones are the extremely common, everyday sounds—*the, this, that, these, those, them, they, there, then;* unvoiced are less common words—*thing, third, Thursday, thank, thought*. (See also Chapter 8.)

Indians usually reverse **v/w**: *These were reversed > Dese ver rewersed*. It should be a simple thing to simply reverse them back, but for some reason, it's more problematic than that. Try substituting in the other word in actual sentences. (See also Chapter 11.)

He vent to the store.	He closed the went.
I'll be back in a vile.	It was a while attack.

v	Think of the **w**, a "double **u**," or even as a "single **u**"; so in place of the **w** in *want*, you'd pronounce it *oo-änt*. There can be NO contact between the teeth and the lips for **w**, as this will turn it into a consonant. Feel the **f/v** consonants, and then put *oo* in place of the **w** (*oo-ile* for *while*). Conversely, you can substitute *ferry* for *very* so that it won't come out as *wary*. Because of the proximity of the consonants, **f** and **v** are frequently interchanged in English (*belief/believe, wolf/wolves*). Consequently, *It was ferry difficult* is easier to understand than *It was wary difficult*. Practice Exercise 11-1 to distinguish among **p/b**, **f/v**, and **w**.

F	V	W	F	V	W
fence	vent	went (oo-ent)	first	verse	worse (oo-rs)
face	vase	waste (oo-aste)	file	vile	while (oo-ile)

L	The **L** is too heavy, too drawn out, and is missing the schwa component. (See also Chapter 6.)

Location of the Language

Far forward and uttered through rounded lips.

RUSSIAN
Intonation

Russian intonation seems to start at a midpoint and then cascade down. The consequence is that it sounds very downbeat. You definitely need to add a lilt to your speech—more peaks, as there're already *plenty* of valleys. To the Russian ear, English can have a harsh, almost metallic sound due to the perception of nasal vibrations in some vowels. This gives a clarity to American speech that allows it to be heard over a distance. When Russian speakers try to imitate that "loudness" and clarity, without the American speech music, instead of the intended pronunciation, it can sound aggressive. On the other hand, when Russians do not try to speak "loud and clear," it can end up sounding vaguely depressed. (See also Chapter 1.)

Liaisons

Word connections should be easy since you have the same fluid word/sound boundaries as in American English. The phrase *dosvedänyə* sounds like *dos vedanya*, whereas you know it as *do svedanya*. It won't be difficult to run your words together once you realize it's the same process in English. (See also Chapter 2.)

Pronunciation

Although you have ten vowels in Russian, there are quite a few other vowels out there waiting for you.

æ   The æ sound doesn't exist in Russian, so *last* is demoted to the lax ɛ, *lest*. In the same way, Russian speakers reduce *actually* to *ekchually*, or *matter* to *metter*. Drop your jaw and raise the back of your tongue to make a noise like a goat: æ! Work on Chapter 3, which drills this distinctively American vowel. (See also Chapters 10 and 12.)

ä   The ä sound exists in Russian, but is represented with the letter **a**. Bear in mind that there are six different pronunciations of the letter **a**, as you can see on page 158. Because of spelling, the ä sound can easily be misplaced. When you see the letter **o**, you pronounce it *o*, so *job* sounds like *jobe* instead of *jääb*. Remember, most of the time, the letter **o** is pronounced *ah*. Take a sound that already exists in Russian, such as *baab* (whether it means anything or not) and say it with your native accent; *baab* with a Russian accent more or less equals *Bob* in English. This will give you a good reference point for whenever you want to say ä instead of **o**: *biology, call, long, problem,* etc. Focus on Chapter 8, differentiating œ, ä, ə. (See also Chapters 10 and 12.)

o   Conversely, you may pronounce the letter **o** as ä or ə when it really should be an ō, as in *only, most, both* (which are exceptions to the spelling rules). Make sure that the American **o** sounds like *ou, ounly, moust, bouth*. This holds true for the diphthongs as well—**oi** should sound like *ou-ee*. (See also Chapters 3, 10, and 12.)

t<u>ou</u>n	tone	n<u>ou</u>t	n<u>o</u>te	h<u>ou</u>m	h<u>o</u>me
<u>ou</u>nli	<u>o</u>nly	c<u>ou</u>l	c<u>oa</u>l	OK	<u>ou</u>kei

ə   The schwa is often overpronounced to ä, which is why you might sound a little like Count Dracula when he says, *I vänt to säck your bläd* instead of *I wänt to sək your bləd*. Don't drop your jaw for the neutral schwa sound; it's like the final syllable of *spasiba* **sp'sibə**, not **sp'sibä**. Similarly, in English, the schwa in an unstressed syllable is completely neutral; *famous* is not **fay-moos**, but rather **fay-m's**. (See also Chapters 3, 10, and 12.)

ü   Distinguishing tense and lax vowels is difficult, and you'll have to forget spelling for **u** and **ü**. They both can be spelled with *oo* or *ou,* but the lax vowel **ü** should sound much closer to *i* or *uh*. If you say *book* and *could* with a tense vowel, it'll sound like *booque* and *cooled*. It should be much closer to *bick* or *buck*. (See also Chapters 10 and 12.)

i Similarly, you need to distinguish between **ee** and **ih**, as in *beat* and *bit* (Chapter 12), as *his big sister* is mispronounced as *heez beeg seester* or with the extra **y**, *hyiz byig systr*. Frequently, Russian speakers transpose these two sounds, so while the lax vowel in *his big sister* is overpronounced to *heez beeg seester,* the tense vowel in *She sees Lisa,* is relaxed to *shi siz lissa*. Also, tone down the middle **i** in the multisyllabic words on page 138; otherwise, *similar* **sim'lr** will sound like **see-mee-lär**. (See also Chapter 10.)

-y Russian speakers often mispronounce the final **-y** as a short **-i**, so that *very funny* sounds like *verə funnə*. Extend the final sound out with three **e**'s: *vereee funneee*. (See also Chapter 12.)

The Russian R = The American T

The Cyrillic **r** is a consonant. This means that it touches at some point in the mouth. Russian speakers usually roll their **r**'s (touching the ridge behind the top teeth), which makes it sound like a **d** to the American ear. The American **r** is not really a consonant anymore—the tongue should be curled back, and the **r** produced deep in the throat—*not* touching the top of the mouth. The Russian pronunciation of **r** is usually the written vowel and a flap **r** at the end of a word (*feeler* sounds like *feelehd*) or a flap in the beginning or middle (*throw* sounds like *tdoh*). (See also Chapter 4.)

бэри бара бира	Betty bought a bit of	аин ира лара таим	I need a lot of time.
аи бара баик	I bought a bike.	маи мароу	my motto
уэира сэкен	Wait a second.	мирин	meeting
уи ара гоу	We ought to go.	аин наран таим	I'm not on time.
юв гара пэира гэрит	You've got to pay to get it.	бюрафли	beautifully

Another major point with the American **r** is that sometimes the preceding vowel is pronounced, and sometimes it isn't. When you say *wire,* there's a clear vowel plus the **r**—*wy•r*; however, with *first,* there is simply no preceding vowel. It's **frst**, not **feerst** (Exercises 5-2 and 5-3).

t At the beginning of a word, the American **t** needs to be more plosive—you should feel that you are "spitting air." At the end of the word, it is held back and not aspirated (See also Chapter 4.)

eh One of the most noticeable characteristics of a Russian accent is the little **y** that is slipped in with the *eh* sound. This makes a sentence such as *Kevin has held a cat* sound like *Kyevin hyes hyeld a kyet*. This is because you are using the back of the tongue to "push" the vowel sound out of the throat. In English, you need to just allow the air to pop through directly after the consonant, between the back of the tongue and the soft palate: **k•æ**, not **k•yæ**. (See also Chapters 10 and 12.)

h Another strong characteristic of Russian speech is a heavily fricative **h**. Rather than closing the back of the throat, let the air flow unimpeded between the soft palate and the back of your tongue. Be sure to keep your tongue flat so you don't push out the little **y** mentioned above. Often, you can simply drop the **h** to avoid the whole problem. For *I have to,* instead of *I hhyef to,* change it to *I y'v to*. (See also Chapter 17.)

v The **v** is often left unvoiced, so the common word *of* sounds like *oaf*. Allow your vocal cords to vibrate. (See also Chapter 11.)

sh There are two **sh** sounds in Russian, **ш** and **щ**. The second one is closer to the American **sh**, as in *щиуз* for *shoes,* not *шуз*. (See also Chapter 13.)

th You may find yourself replacing the voiced and unvoiced **th** sounds with **t/d** or **s/z**, saying *dä ting* or *zä sing* instead of *the thing*. This means that your tongue tip is about a half inch too far back on the alveolar ridge (the bumps behind the teeth). Press your tongue against the *back* of the teeth and try to say *dat*. Because of the tongue position, it will sound like *that*. (See also Chapter 8.)

-ing   Often the **-ing** ending is not pronounced as a single **ng** sound, but rather as **n** and **g**, or just **n**. There are three nasals, **m** (lips), **n** (tongue tip and alveolar ridge), and **ng** (soft palate and the back of the tongue). It is not a hard consonant like **g**, but rather a soft nasal. (See also Chapter 16.)

FRENCH

Intonation

The French are, shall we say, a linguistically proud people. More than working on accent or pronunciation, you need to "believe" first. There is an inordinate amount of psychological resistance here, but the good thing is that, in my experience, you are very outspoken about it. Unlike the Japanese, who will just keep quiet, or Indians, who agree with everything with sometimes no discernible change in their speech patterns, my French students have quite clearly pointed out how difficult, ridiculous, and unnatural American English is. If the American pattern is a stairstep, the Gallic pattern is a fillip at the end of each phrase. (See also Chapter 1.)

Hello, *my* name is Pierre. I live in *Pari*s. Al*lo*, my name is *Pierre*. I live in Par*ee*. I ride the sub*way*.

Liaisons

The French either invented liaisons or raised them to an art form. You may not realize, though, that the rules that bind your phrases together also do so in English. Just remember, in French, it is spelled *ce qu'ils disent,* but you've heard it pronounced colloquially a thousand times, *skidiz*! (See also Chapter 2.)

Pronunciation

th	In French, the **th** is usually mispronounced **s** or **f**, as in *sree* or *free* for *three.* (See also Chapters 1 and 8.)
r	The French **r** is in the same location as the American one, but it is more like a consonant. For the French **r**, the back of the tongue rasps against the soft palate, but for the American **r**, the throat balloons out, like a bullfrog. (See also Chapter 5.)
æ	The **æ** sound doesn't exist in French, so it usually comes out as **ä** or **ɛ**; consequently, *class* sounds like *class,* and *cat* sounds like *ket.* The *in-* prefix, however, sounds like a nasalized **æ**. Say *in* in French and then denasalize it to *æd*. Work on Chapter 3, which drills this distinctively American vowel. (See also Chapters 3, 10, and 12.)
ə	The schwa is typically overpronounced, based on spelling. Work on Chapter 1 for the rhythm patterns that form this sound and Chapter 3 for its actual pronunciation. If your intonation peaks are strong and clear enough, then your valleys will be sufficiently reduced as well. Concentrate on smoothing out and reducing the valleys and *ignore spelling*! (See also Chapters 10 and 12.)
ü	The **ü** sound is generally overpronounced to *ooh,* which leads to *could* being mispronounced as *cooled.* Again, spelling is the culprit. Words such as *smooth, choose,* and *too* are spelled with two **o**'s and are pronounced with a long **ü** sound, but other words such as *look* and *took* are spelled with two **o**'s but are pronounced halfway between *ih* and *uh;* **lük** and **tük**. *Leuc* and *queuc* with a French accent are very close. (See also Chapters 10 and 12.)

French speakers overpronounce the lax vowel **i** to *eee,* so *sit* comes out like *seat.* Reduce the soft **i** to a schwa; *sit* should sound like *s't.* In most French dictionaries, the distinction between **i** and **ē** is not made. Practice the four sounds—*bit, beat, bid, bead*—remembering that *tense vowels* indicate that you tense your lips or tongue, while *lax vowels* mean that your lips and tongue are relaxed, and the sound is produced in your throat. *Unvoiced* final consonants (**t, s, k, p, ch, f**) mean that the vowel is short and sharp; *voiced* final consonants (**d, z, g, b, j, v**) mean that the vowel is doubled. Work on *Bit or Beat? Bid or Bead?* in Chapter 10.

	single	double
tense	beat	bead
lax	bit	bid

Also, watch out for cognates such as *typique/typical,* pronounced **tee•peek** in French and **tí•p'•kl** in American English. Many of them appear in the Middle "I" List in Chapter 10. (See also Chapter 12.)

ä   Because of spelling, the **ä** sound can easily be misplaced. The **ä** sound exists in French, but is represented with the letter **a.** When you see the letter **o,** you pronounce it **o,** so *lot* sounds like *loht* instead of *laht.* Remember, most of the time the letter **o** is pronounced *ah.* You can take a sound that already exists in French, such as *laat* (whether it means anything or not) and say it with your native accent—*laat* with a French accent more or less equals *lot* in English. This will give you a good reference point for whenever you want to say **ä** instead of **o**; *astronomy, call, long, progress,* etc. Focus on Chapter 3, differentiating **æ, ä, ə**. (See also Chapters 10 and 12.)

         h<u>aa</u>t   h<u>o</u>t   c<u>oa</u>l   c<u>a</u>ll   s<u>aa</u>   s<u>aw</u>

o   On the other hand, you may pronounce the letter **o** as **ä** or **ə** when it really should be an **o,** as in *only, most, both.* Make sure that the American **o** sounds like **ou,** *ounly, moust, bouth.* This holds true for the diphthongs as well—**oi** sounds like *o-u-ee.* (See also Chapters 3, 10, and 12.)

         <u>ou</u>nli   <u>o</u>nly   l<u>ou</u>n   l<u>oa</u>n   n<u>ou</u>t   n<u>o</u>te

h   French people have the most fascinating floating **h.** Part of the confusion comes from the *hache aspiré,* which is totally different from the American *aitch.* Allow a small breath of air to escape with each *aitch.* (See also Chapter 17.)

in–   The nasal combinations **in–** and **–en** are often pronounced like *œñ* and *äñ,* so *interesting* **in**tr' sting sounds like *æñteresting,* and *enjoy* ɛn**joy** and *attention* ətɛnshən sound like *äñjoy* and *ätäñseeõn.* (See also Chapters 1, 10, and 12.)

Location in the Mouth

Very far forward, with extensive use of the lips.

GERMAN

Intonation

Germans have what Americans consider a stiff, rather choppy accent. The great similarity between the two languages lies in the two-word phrases, where a **hót** dog is food and a *hot* **dóg** is an overheated chihuahua. In German, a *thimble* is called a **fingerhut,** literally a *finger hat,* and a *red* **hat** would be a *rote* **hut,** with the same intonation and meaning shift as in English. (See also Chapter 1.)

Liaisons

German word connections are also quite similar to American ones. Consider how *In einem Augenblick* actually is pronounced *ineine maugenblick*. The same rules apply in both languages. (See also Chapter 2.)

Pronunciation

j	A salient characteristic of German is the unvoicing of **j**, so you might say I *am Cherman* instead of *I am German*. Work with the other voiced pairs (**p/b, s/z, k/g**) and then go on to **ch/j** while working with **J** words such as *just, Jeff, German, enjoy, age,* etc. (See also Chapter 13.)
w	Another difference is the transposing of **v** and **w**. When you say *Volkswagen,* it most likely comes out *Folksvagen*. It works to rewrite the word as *Wolksvagen,* which then will come out as we say: *Volkswagen*. A German student was saying that she was a *wisiting scholar,* which didn't make much sense—say *wisiding* with a German accent—it'll sound like *visiting* in American English. (See also Chapter 11.)
th	In German, the **th** is usually pronounced **t** or **d**. (See also Chapters 4 and 8.)
r	The German **r** is in the same location as the American one, but it is more like a consonant. For the German **r**, the back of the tongue rasps against the soft palate, but for the American **r**, the throat balloons out, like a bullfrog. (See also Chapter 5.)
æ	The **æ** sound doesn't exist in German, so it usually comes out as **ä** or **ɛ**, so *class* sounds like *class*. You need to work on Chapter 12, which drills this distinctively American vowel. (See also Chapters 3, 10, and 12.)
ə	The schwa is typically overpronounced, based on spelling. Work on Chapter 1 for the rhythm patterns that form this sound, and for its actual pronunciation. If your intonation peaks are strong and clear enough, then your valleys will be sufficiently reduced as well. Concentrate on smoothing out and reducing the valleys and *ignore spelling!* (See also Chapters 3, 10, and 12.)
ü	The **ü** sound is generally overpronounced to *ooh,* which leads to *could* being mispronounced as *cooled*. Again, spelling is the culprit. Words such as *smooth, choose,* and *too* are spelled with two **o**'s and are pronounced with a long *u* sound, but other words such as *look* and *took* are spelled with two **o**'s but are pronounced halfway between *ih* and *uh: lük* and *tük*. (See also Chapters 10 and 12.)
i	German speakers overpronounce the lax vowel **i** to *eee,* so *sit* comes out like *seat*. Reduce the soft **i** to a schwa; *sit* should sound like *s't*. In most German dictionaries, the distinction between **i** and **ē** is not made. Practice the four sounds—*bit, beat, bid, bead*—remembering that *tense vowels* indicate that you tense your lips or tongue, while *lax vowels* mean that your lips and tongue are relaxed, and the sound is produced in your throat. *Unvoiced* final consonants (**t, s, k, p, ch, f**) mean that the vowel is short and sharp; *voiced* final consonants (**d, z, g, b, j, v**) mean that the vowel is doubled. Work on *Bit or Beat? Bid or Bead?* in Chapter 10.

	single	double
tense	beat	bead
lax	bit	bid

Also, watch out for words such as *chemical/Chemikalie,* pronounced **ke•mi•kä•lee•eh** in German and **kɛmək³l** in American English. Many of them appear in the Middle "I" List in Chapter 10.

ä   Because of spelling, the **ä** sound can easily be misplaced. The **ä** sound exists in German, but is represented with the letter **a**. When you see the letter **o**, you pronounce it *o*, so *lot* sounds like *loht* instead of *laht*. Remember, most of the time, the letter **o** is pronounced *ah*. You can take a sound that already exists in German, such as *laat* (whether it means anything or not) and say it with your native accent—*laat* with a German accent more or less equals *lot* in American English. This will give you a good reference point for whenever you want to say **ä** instead of **o**; *astronomy, call, long, progress,* etc. Focus on Chapter 12, differentiating **æ, ä, ə**. (See also Chapters 12, 18, and 20.)

h<u>aa</u>t	hot	c<u>oa</u>l	call	s<u>aa</u>	s<u>aw</u>

o   German speakers tend to use the British **o**, which sounds like *ɛo* rather than the American *ou*. Make sure that the American **o**, in *only, most, both,* sounds like *ou: ounly, moust, bouth*. This holds true for the diphthongs as well—**oi** sounds like *o-u-ee*. (See also Chapters 12, 18, and 20.)

<u>ou</u>nli	<u>o</u>nly	l<u>ou</u>n	l<u>oa</u>n	n<u>ou</u>t	n<u>o</u>te

KOREAN

Intonation

While English is a stress-timed language, Korean is a syllable-timed language. Korean is more similar to Japanese than Chinese in that the pitch range of Korean is also narrow, almost flat, and not rhythmical. Many Korean speakers tend to stress the wrong word or syllable, which changes the meaning in English *(They'll sell **fish** and They're **sel**fish.)* Korean speakers tend to add a vowel to the final consonant after a long vowel: **b/v** *(babe/beibu* and *wave/weibu)*, **k/g** *(make/meiku* and *pig/pigu)*, and **d** *(made/meidu.)* Koreans also insert a vowel after **sh/ch/j** *(wash/washy, church/churchy, bridge/brijy)*, and into consonant clusters *(bread/bureadu)*. It is also a common problem to devoice final voiced consonants, so that *dog* can be mispronounced as either *dogu* or *dock*. All this adversely influences the rhythm patterns of spoken English. The different regional intonation patterns for Korean interrogatives also affect how questions come across in English. In standard Korean, the intonation goes up for both *yes/no* questions and *wh* questions (who?, what?, where?, when?, why?); in the Kyungsang dialect, it drops for both; and in the Julia dialect, it drops and goes up for both. In American English, the intonation goes up for *yes/no* and drops down for *wh* questions. (See also Chapter 4.)

Word Connections

Unlike Japanese or Chinese, word connections are common in Korean. The seven final consonants (**m, n, ng, l, p, t, k**) slide over when the following word begins with a vowel. Although a **t** between two vowels in American English should be voiced *(latter/ladder* sound the same), a frequent mistake Korean speakers make is to also voice **k** or **p** between two vowels, so *back up, check up,* and *weekend* are mispronounced as *bagup, chegup,* and *weegend*; and *cap is* sounds like *cab is*. Another liaison problem occurs with a plosive consonant (**p/b, t/d, k/g**) just before a nasal (**m, n, ng**)—Koreans often nasalize the final consonant, so that *pick me up* and *pop music* sound like *ping me up* and *pom music*. (See also Chapter 11.)

Pronunciation

l/r   At the beginning of a word or in a consonant cluster, **l** and **r** are confused, with both being pronounced like the American **d**, which can be written with the letter **t** (*glass* or *grass* sound like either *gurasu* or *gudasu*, and *light* or *right* sound like *raitu* or *daitu*). The final **r** is usually dropped *(car/kaa)*. (See also Chapters 15 and 16.)

f   The English **f** does not exist in Korean, so people tend to substitute a **p**. This leads to words such as *difficult* sounding like *typical* to the American ear. When a Korean speaker says a word from the **F** column, it's likely to be heard by Americans as being from the **P** column. (See also Chapter 19.)

F	P	F	P	F	P
difficult	typical	coffee	copy	half and	happen
calf	cap	deaf	tape	Steph	step
left	leapt	cough	cop	laugh	lap
often	open	fat	pet	informant	important
stuff	stop	after	apter	fossil	possible
enough	and up	friend	planned	free	pre–

æ   The exact **æ** sound doesn't exist in Korean; it's close to **ɛ**, so *bat* sounds like *bet*. You need to raise the back of your tongue and drop your jaw to produce this sound. Work on Chapter 3, which drills this distinctively American vowel. (See also Chapters 12, 18, and 20.)

ä   The *ä* sound is misplaced. You have the **ä** sound when you laugh *hahaha* 하하하, but when you see an **o**, you want to say **ō**, as in *hohoho* 호호호, so *John* sounds like *Joan* instead of *Jähn*. If you're having trouble with the word *hot*, say *ha* 하 in Korean and then add a very slight **t**. (See also Chapters 12, 18, and 20.)

o   You may pronounce the letter **o** as **ä** or **ə** when it really should be an **ō**, as in *only, most, both.* Make sure that the American **o** sounds like ou: *ounly, moust, bouth.* This holds true for the diphthongs as well—*oi* sounds like *o-u-ee.* (See also Chapters 12, 18, and 20.)

<u>tou</u>n	<u>to</u>ne	<u>nou</u>t	<u>no</u>te	<u>hou</u>m	<u>ho</u>me
<u>ou</u>nli	<u>o</u>nly	<u>cou</u>l	<u>coa</u>l	<u>jou</u>k	<u>jo</u>ke

ə   The schwa is typically overpronounced, based on spelling. Concentrate on smoothing out and reducing the valleys and *ignore spelling!* (See also Chapters 12, 18, and 20.)

ü   Distinguishing tense and lax vowels is difficult, and you'll have to forget spelling for **u** and **ü**. They both can be spelled with *oo* or *ou*, but the lax vowel **ü** should sound much closer to *i* or *uh*. If you say *book* with a tense vowel, it'll sound like *booque.* It should be much closer to *bick* or *buck.* (See also Chapters 18 and 20.)

i   Similarly, you need to distinguish between **e** and **i**, as in *beat* and *bit,* on page 136. Tone down the middle **i** in multisyllabic words, as in Chapter 18, otherwise, *beautiful* **byoo•d'•fl** will sound like **byoo-tee-fool.** Most likely, you overpronounce the lax vowel **i** to *eee,* so *sit* is overpronounced to *seat.* Reduce the soft **i** to a schwa; *sit* should sound like *s't.* In most Korean dictionaries, the distinction between **i** and **ē** is not made. Practice the four sounds—*bit, beat, bid, bead*—remembering that *tense vowels* indicate that you tense your lips or tongue, while *lax vowels* mean that your lips and tongue are relaxed and the sound is produced in your throat. *Unvoiced* final consonants (**t, s, k, p, ch, f**) mean that the vowel is short and sharp; *voiced* final consonants (**d, z, g, b, j, v**) mean that the vowel is doubled. Work on *Bit or Beat? Bid or Bead?* in Chapter 18. (See also Chapter 20.)

	single	double
tense	beat	bead
lax	bit	bid

The Korean R = The American T

The Korean **r** is a consonant. This means that it touches at some point in the mouth. Korean speakers usually trill their **r**'s (tapping the ridge behind the top teeth), which makes it sound like a **d** to the American ear. The tongue should be curled back, and the **r** produced deep in the throat—*not* touching the top of the mouth. The Korean pronunciation of **r** is usually just an **ä** at the end of a word *(car* sounds like *caaah)* or a flap in the beginning or middle *(area* sounds like *eddy-ah). (See also Chapter 14.)

베리 바라비라	Betty bought a bit of better butter.	아이 니랄라라 타임	I need a lot of time.
아이 카라콜 드	I caught a cold.	마이 마로우	my motto
쿠리 두잇	Could he do it?	미링	meeting
위 아라 고우	We ought to go.	아임 나란 타임	I'm not on time.

ARABIC

Though there are several dialects in Arabic, from the Levantine dialect of Jordan, Palestine, Lebanon, and Syria to the dialect specific to the Gulf States, as well as the regional differences in Iraq, Egypt, and Libya, there remains a common accent thread in Arabic speakers. Especially noticable in those who have had little prior exposure to English or other Western languages, the accent is typified by a leaden intonation and the lack of several key consonants and vowels. (See also Chapters 3 and 4.)

Intonation

The overall intonation can be perceived as leaden, as it's rather heavy and non-musical. Syllable stress is also an issue as non-standard syllables are stressed, such as in *subséquent* and *dévelopment*. When the Arabic speaker is unaware of the rules of American intonation, there is a tendency to simply guess where intonation goes. As a result, intonation pretty much lands on every other word, greatly confusing the American listener. (See Chapter 4.)

Liaisons

This is a category that causes confusion for Arabic speakers, resulting in comprehension and pronunciation problems. Because Americans tend to connect all their words, many Arabic speakers are not sure where one word ends and the next begins. Relying on the phonetic transcriptions of phrases and sentences teaches the Arabic speaker the construction of American liaisons. Also, simple rules like T + Y = CH is tremendously helpful with high-frequency phrases such as "Got you," pronounced "Gotcha." (See also Chapter 11.)

Pronunciation

There is no ambiguity in pronouncing words in Arabic, and because of that, there's a very strong tendency to carry this purely phonetic concept over to the wilds of English where *-ough* can be pronounced *cough, through, enough, though,* and *thought.* Phonetics are the problem; phonetics are the solution. Because the concept of phonetics is so strong in the Arabic psyche, reliance on the phonetic transcription will be very useful.

Word Endings

Arabic speakers overstress the final consonant. At times it can be surprising to an American listener, as it sounds overly emphatic or emotional. The idea of an "unvoiced" final consonant is new to Arabic speakers. Listening carefully to the exercises dealing with unvoiced final consonants, recording yourself, and repeating, will address this issue. Liaisons will assist with word endings.

The Arabic R

The Arabic **R** is a single trill of the tongue tip on the alveolar ridge, which ends up sounding like a **D** or a middle **T** to the American ear. The final **R** also tends to pick up the preceding vowel, so *her* sounds like *hair, verb* like *vairb, were* like *where.* To the American ear, the initial **R** is like five **D**s fluttered in a row. Making sure that the tongue has no contact with the rest of the mouth is the start of the process for the American **R**.

The Arabic T

All **T**s are popped, regardless of the position in the word. The **T** at the beginning of a word doesn't typically have the necessary puff of air, and a *tssh* sound should be added.

Conversely, middle **T**s should be changed to **D**, as in *authority* (*authoridy*), or dropped completely as in *twenty* or *identity* (*twenny* and *idenadee*).

بِري بارَ بِرُف بِرَر بَرَر	Betty bought a bit of better butter.	آي نِيز لارا تائِم	I need a lot of time.
آي بازَ بايك	I bought a bike.	مائ مازُرو	my motto
كُري ذو وِت؟	Could he do it?	مِيرِنج	meeting
وِي آزا جُو	We ought to go.	آيْمْ نازنْ تائِمْ	I'm not on time.

In particular, the word *To* should be changed to *duh*, as in *day to day* (*day da day*) or *like to mention* (*like duh mention*). The final **T** should be held in for risk of sounding tense or annoyed. The held **T** before **N** is also usually popped, and should be held, instead, as in *important, written, forgotten*.

Although there are two **TH** sounds in Arabic, this often ends up sounding like a **D**. The tongue tip needs to be about a half inch more forward, either against the back of the teeth or on the biting edge, but definitely not on the ridge.

Middle I

Arabic speakers tend to overpronounce this sound, and instead should reduce it to a schwa.

V

The **V** sound doesn't exist in Arabic, and is often replaced with an **F**.

P

The **P** sound doesn't exist in Arabic, and is often replaced with a **B**, resulting in *brivate, broblem, beeble*. A joke making the rounds is *"Officer, may I blease bark here?" "Sure, you can bark anywhere!"*

F	V	B	F	V	B
fat	vat	bat	ferry	very	berry
face	vase	base	effort	ever	Ebber
fear	veer	beer	foul	vowel	bowel

G

The **G** is an interesting and important sound in Arabic, as it's the one dealing with the problematic spelling of Ghaddafi, Khaddafi, Qhaddafi. Given that Arabic is considered a gutteral language, this is a very noticeable sound. Especially the soft **G**, which is hardened, so *bring it* sounds like *bring git*.

THE AMERICAN SOUTH

Granted, the American South, the land of the lilting drawl, encompasses a lot of geography, and to the denizens there are very clear regional distinctions. We are not going to address that here, but rather give some general guidelines on standardizing the accent. Clearly, the predominant characteristic is the duration of the vowels. Clipped Yankee vowel durations can sound snippy, rude, or cold to a southerner, so there may be a little psychological resistance to shortening them up. To a northerner, these shortened vowels sound completely neutral.

Intonation

Word stress can be different from standard speech, with emphasis on the first syllable. (See also Chapter 4.)

Southern	Standard	Southern	Standard	Southern	Standard
Détroit	Detróit	'TV	TV'	dísplay	displáy
pólice	políce	cément	cemént	béhind	behínd
ínsurance	insúrance	úmbrella	umbrélla	récycle	recy'cle
Thánksgiving	Thanksgíving	guítar	guitár	áddress	addréss

Word Endings

A classic southernism is the dropped **g** of **ing**. This can be changed in two ways. The standard way is to bring up the back of the tongue until it meets the soft palate. The other way is the Californian -**een**, so *running* sounds like *runneen*. Practice with *Mr. Manning was being confusing as he was running, jumping, and singing.* (See also Chapter 11.)

The final **D** is dropped in *understand: unnerstan', friend: fren'*, and so on. In terms of vowel duration, the vowels are often lengthened with a lilt, but with final voiced consonants, the last consonant is devoiced, so that *job* sounds more like *jop*, and and *did* like *dit*.

The -ed Ending

When there is a voiced consonant followed by -**ed**, you need vocalize the **D**. Otherwise, it can sound like a **T**, such as *The deer was **killt** as it crossed the tracks.* (See also Chapter 14.)

Pronunciation

Consonants are similar to standard American, but vowels tend to be doubled or even tripled. If you just change the long **I** from **ah** to **äi**, round off the final **R** and don't add an extra syllable after the **æ** sound, you'll make a major change in how you sound. (See also Chapter 3.)

The Southern R

The Southern **R** (or lack thereof) is most noticeable at the end of a word, where it sounds more like a schwa than an **R**, as *Put the paypuh upstayuhz*. Use a growly *RRRR* to finish off these words, so it sounds like *Put the paperrrr upstairrrrrs*. Make sure that *sure* doesn't sound like *shore*. Don't let *hair* and *there* become *hayuh* and *they-uh*. Practice with *Therrrrre arrrre fourrrrr shorrrrrrt hairrrrrs overrrrr therrrrrre.* Yes, you'll sound a little like a pirate.

You'll also want to make a clear distinction between *card* (**cärd**) / *cord* (**kord**), *far* (**fär**) / *for* (**for**), *farm* (**färm**) / *form* (**form**). (See also Chapter 15.)

æ	Resist adding an extra syllable to *cat* (*cayut*), *can* (*cayan*), *pan* (*payan*). Make sure that *can't* doesn't sound like *cain't* and the **æo** in *about* doesn't come out as *abat*. Practice: *Jack sat back, drank from his glass, and laughed about how it sounded . . .* (See also Chapters 12, 18, and 20.)
Long i	This is a classic sound associated with the South, where *My eye* sounds like *Mah aahh*. What's going on is that the first half of the **äi** sound is elongated and the second half gets dropped off. Practice these sentences: *I'm tired. I'd like a nice slice of lime pie.* (See also Chapters 12, 18, and 20.)

ü	The **ü** sound can either be elongated from *book* to *buuhk*, or turned into an *ih* sound, a *good cook* sounds like a *gid kick*. (See also Chapters 18 and 20.) Practice with this sentence: *I took a good look at the cook book*. A Northerner was driving through the South and heard advertisements on the radio, and was surprised that someone was selling an automobile and four guitars. Listening further, he realized of course, that it was a car with four good tires.
ih	The **ih** sound can go in three directions. Words like *pin* are often pronounced *pen, again / agin, get / git*. Also, **ih** can sound like *æ, thing / thang* and *drink / drank*. For this, try saying it *theeng* and *dreenk*. Third, it can also turn into a lilting **E** sound, with *Bill* sounding like *Beel*. Practice this sentence: *Bill filled his thin pen again*. (See also Chapters 18 and 20.)
ε	Resist adding an extra syllable to *bed* (*beyed*), *pet* (*peyet*), *next* (*nayext*). Practice with this sentence: *Jeb gets to help the next pet*. (See also Chapters 12, 18, and 20.)
o	Try not rounding and extending the **ah** sound so much, so *dog* doesn't sound like *dawg*, nor *talk* like *tawk*. Practice this sentence: *Bob talked about John's dog all along the walk with Tom*. This should all have the same **ah** sound in every word: *Bahb tahkt about Jahnz dahg ahl alahng the wahk with Tahm*. Think of a ventriloquist's dummy, where your jaw just clacks up and down. (See also Chapters 12, 18, and 20.)
ee	Make sure that the **ee** sound doesn't relax into the **ih**, so *I feel good* doesn't sound like *I fill good*. (See also Chapter 20.)
ə	As you saw in the **R** section, this neutral vowel is commonly used to replace **-er** and **-or**. Practice saying *favrrr* (*favor*) instead of *favuh*, and *rathrrrr* (*rather*) instead of *rathuh*. Practice sentence: *Her cars were over there*. (See also Chapters 12, 18, and 20.)
oi	This should be two full vowels. The southern *boy* almost sounds like *boa*. Practice with *Joy's boy toy foiled the royal oil ploy*. (See also Chapter 20.)
Z	The **Z** sound (spelled with an **S**) turns to a **D** before **N**. *That dudn't make sense. It just idn't right. It's a good bidness, innit? That wadn't what happened*. Practice putting in buzzy **Z**s: *He duzzzzen know, duzzzzy? It wazzzzen any good, wuzzzzzzit?* (See also Chapter 17.)
L	Make sure to pronounce the **L** in *help* and *values* so that it doesn't sound like *Hep yoursef*, and *va-yoos*.

Vocabulary

Modal stacking is particular to the South. **I used to could do it. You might could send them an email. You might should tell her about it**. Leave either one of them off.

Y'all can be changed to **you guys, everyone, everybody** or just plain **you**. (Make sure to say **everybody**, not **ever'body**).

Fixing to is more readily recognizable as **getting ready to.**

Done can be omitted in **I done told you about it!** or **I done had lunch**.

Make sure to change **doin' good** to **doing well**.

AFRICAN LANGUAGES
Intonation

Given that Africa is a continent with a very high linguistic diversity, there are an estimated 1500–2000 African languages. We will not be able to address all of that here, but will find some commonalities to help you study. The Niger–Congo language family is the largest group of Africa in terms of the number of languages. The vast majority of languages of this family are tonal, such as Yoruba and Igbo, Ashanti, and Ewe. Intonation can go in a couple of different directions—if a speaker is from an Anglophone region or a Francophone one—but often the speaker ends up with a rather flat, atonal speech pattern. Intonation is the pitch change that creates the speech music of English. Let's use the visual metaphor of the staircase. When you want a syllable to stand out, just raise your pitch. This way, your greeting will sound like a friendly *Hello!* and not like a robotic *Heh. Low.* Make sure you understand the difference between pitch change and volume.

The Intonation of a Basic Sentence

One of the most common sentence types is SVO (Subject Verb Object), which is Noun Verb Noun. The easiest rule to remember is stress the noun, and don't stress any of the other words: *Dogs eat bones*. Be careful—if you don't use this pitch change, you can sound rude, aggressive, or overly emphatic: Dogs eat bones! After you've introduced the nouns, you're going to start replacing them with pronouns—and the intonation pattern will change. If you listen carefully, you'll hear that *them*, *him*, and *her* are shortened to *'em* and *'er*. This means that *Tell her* sounds like *Teller*, *Get him* sounds like *Geddim*, and *Make them* sounds like *Make 'em*.

Descriptions Versus Compound Nouns

An adjective and a noun form a description. Stress the noun: *a good **plan**, a long **walk**, a sharp **knife***. Two nouns form a compound noun. Stress the first noun: *a **data** base, a **credit** card, a **coffee** cup*. The interesting thing is, even though the words may be exactly the same, the meaning will be totally different. For example, *dark **room*** is any room that is dark, but a ***dark**room* is specifically for photograpy. A ***green** house* is any house that is painted green, but a ***green**house* is made of glass to protect plants.

Vowel Durations & Linking

You may have a tendency to clip your words into a shorter vowel duration. The downside of this is that it makes you seem upset or impatient. If you say words one by one, this will make you sound pedantic, aloof, or overly serious. It's important to let the words flow together, and realize that this is in no way substandard or unacceptable. There are four rules for linking words.

Consonant Vowel

When a word ends in a consonant and the next word starts with a vowel, the consonant links to the vowel:

Jum pover

Consonant Consonant

When a word ends in a consonant and the next word starts with a similar consonant, they link together:

Get-together

Vowel Vowel

When a word ends in a vowel and the next word starts with a vowel, they are joined by **W** or **Y** depending on if the vowel is rounded or not:

Go(w)on / He(y)is

T / D / S / Z + Y

When a word ends in **T**, **D**, **S**, or **Z** and the next word starts with **Y**, a new sound is formed: **Ch**, **J**, **Sh**, **Zh**. Canchoo?, Didja?, pressure, casual

æ ä ə

These are The Big 3 Vowels: **æ** because it's so distinctly American, **ä** because it Americanizes all of the **O**, **AL**, and **AW** words, and **ə** because it's the most common sound in English. The basic rule is based on one syllable words or a stressed syllable.

A = æ Jack sat back and laughed at Sally's last chance to dance.
O = ä Bob talked about John's dog all along the walk with Tom.
U = ə Someone must run a bunch of stuff.

Bob talked about John's dog all along the walk with Tom should all have the same *ah* sound in every word: Bahb tahkt about Jahnz dahg ahl alahng the wahk with Tahm.
   Think of a ventriloquist's dummy, where your jaw just clacks up and down.
   Of course, the schwa is the tricky bit, as it can be represented by any of the vowels or even an absent vowel: *banana, deny, Mississippi, potato, lettuce, prism* or *chasm* (before the **M**)

ĭ and ē

These are commonly known as the short **I** and and the long **E**. Make sure the *ih* sound is very lax and muted, while the *ee* sound is clear and distinct:

ĭ The big pig didn't fit in his rig.   **ē** We need Lee's three free cheesy meat deals.

ŭ and ū

The **ŭ** sound is actually much closer to the **ih** sound, and you'll notice that they're grammatically related: **will > would, fill > full**.

ŭ I took a good look at the cook book.   **ū** Sue knew who threw Lou's shoes.

The Letter A

Amazingly, this one little letter has six different pronunciations: **æ, ā, ä, ə, ɛ, o** (*chance, change, charge, ago, parent, war*). You may be only using the **ä** sound.

The Letter T

There are actually seven different ways to pronounce the letter **T**: popped, **D**, held final, held before **N**, held before a throat consonant, silent with **N**, silent. (*Ted, later, hot, gotten, what was, Internet, listen*).

TH

The schwa (**ə**) is the most common sound in English, followed by **TH**, which is used in super high-frequency words indicating number, person, location, direction, and time (*the, they, them, there, this, that, these, those, then*, etc.). This was traditionally taught as a breathy sound, but it's actually a plosive (popping sound).

Middle T

This can be a very quick fix if you are willing to make the change. Generally speaking, the middle **T** sounds like **D**, which is why *metal* and *medal* sound the same.

L & R

If you say *la-la-la*, be aware of the tongue touching the top of the mouth, as this will help you understand that the position of the **L** is very far forward in the mouth. For the final **L**, touch the tongue to the alveolar ridge . . . and do NOT round your lips.

For the **R**, put out your hand with the palm up and say *aaaaah*. Then, make a tight fist and say *RRRRR*. The tongue should replicate the hand position and hunch back, creating the throaty, rhotic **R** sound.

F / V / P / B / W

These five sounds all involve the lower lip. **F** & **V** are in the same position (top teeth against the bottom lip). **F** is whispered and **V** is spoken. **P** & **B** are in the same position (both lips together). **P** is whispered and **B** is spoken. **W** also uses both lips, but they don't touch.

S & Z

The letter **S** actually sounds like **Z** most of the time: *his, was, does, goes, has*. It's a clear **S** at the beginning of a word (*see*), after an unvoiced consonant (*lets*), or when spelled with a **C** (*ice*).

Nasals

The nasals are positioned at the three areas where the air can be blocked and redirected out the nose:
Lips: **M**; Tongue Tip: **N**; Soft Palate: **NG**.

Answer Key

Exercise 1-5: Regular English
1. Bob lost his job.
2. Scott taught a lot.
3. Don bought a bike.

Exercise 1-10: Sentence Intonation Test
1. **Sam** sees **Bill**.
2. She **wants** one.
3. **Betty** likes **English**.
4. They **play** with them.
5. **Children** play with **toys**.
6. **Bob** and I call you and **Bill**.
7. You and **Bill** read the news.
8. It **tells** one.
9. **Bernard** works in a restaurant.
10. He **works** in one.
11. He **sees** him.
12. **Mary** wants a **car**.
13. She **likes** it.
14. They **eat** some.
15. Len and **Joe** eat some **pizza**.
16. We **call** you.
17. You **read** it.
18. The **news** tells a **story**.
19. **Mark** lived in **France**.
20. He **lived** there.

Exercise 1-23: Can or Can't Quiz
1. A   4. D   7. C
2. B   5. A   8. B
3. C   6. D   9. A

Exercise 1-24: Application of Stress
Hello, **my** name is _____. I'm taking American **Accent** Training. There's a **lot** to **learn**, but I **hope** to make it as **enjoyable** as possible. I should pick **up** on the American **intonation** pattern pretty **easily**, although the **only** way to **get** it is to **practice** all of the time. I use the **up** and down, or **peaks** and valleys, intonation more than I **used** to. I've been paying attention to **pitch, too.** It's like **walking** down a **stair**case. I've been **talking** to a lot of **Americans** lately, and they tell me that I'm **easier** to under**stand**. **Any**way, I could go **on** and on, but the **important** thing is to **listen** well and sound **good. Well,** what do you **think**? **Do** I?

Exercise 1-27: Sounds of Empathy
1. B   4. A   7. C   10. A   13. A   16. B   19. C
2. B   5. B   8. C   11. C   14. C   17. A   20. B
3. B   6. A   9. B   12. A   15. B   18. A   21. B

Exercise 1-34: Regular Transitions of Adj. and Verbs
1. You need to in**sert** a paragraph here on this newspaper **in**sert.
2. How can you ob**ject** to this **ob**ject?
3. I'd like to pre**sent** you with this **pre**sent.
4. Would you care to **elabor**eit on his **elabor**'t explanation?
5. The manufacturer couldn't re**call** if there'd been a **re**call.
6. The religious **con**vert wanted to con**vert** the world.
7. The political **re**bels wanted to re**bel** against the world.
8. The mogul wanted to re**cord** a new **re**cord for his latest artist.
9. If you per**fect** your intonation, your accent will be **per**fect.
10. Due to the drought, the fields didn't pro**duce** much **pro**duce this year.
11. Unfortunately, City Hall wouldn't per**mit** them to get a **per**mit.
12. Have you heard that your as**soci**'t is known to asso**ciet** with gangsters?
13. How much do you **estim**eit that the **estim**'t will be?
14. The facilitator wanted to se**pareit** the general topic into **sepr**'t categories.

Exercise 1-44: Making Set Phrases
1. a **chair**man
2. a **phone** book
3. a **house** key
4. a **base**ball
5. a **door**bell
6. the **White** House
7. a **movie** star
8. the **Bullet** train
9. a **race** car
10. a **coffee** cup
11. a **wrist**watch
12. a **beer** bottle
13. a **high** chair
14. a **hunting** knife
15. a **dump** truck
16. a **jelly**fish
17. a **love** letter
18. a **thumb**tack
19. a **lightning** bolt
20. a **pad**lock

Exercise 1-50: Contrast of Compound Nouns
1. The **White** House
2. a white **house**
3. a **dark**room
4. a dark **room**
5. Fifth **Avenue**
6. **Main** Street
7. a main **street**
8. a hot **dog**
9. a **hot**dog
10. a **baby** blanket
11. a baby's **blanket**
12. a baby **bird**
13. a **black**bird
14. a black **bird**
15. a **green**house
16. a green **house**
17. a green **thumb**
18. a **parking** ticket
19. a one-way **ticket**
20. an unpaid **ticket**
21. **convenience** store
22. convenient **store**
23. to pick **up**
24. a **pick**up truck
25. six years **old**
26. a **six**-year-old
27. six and a **half**
28. a **sugar** bowl
29. a wooden **bowl**
30. a large **bowl**
31. a **mixing** bowl
32. a **top** hat
33. a nice **hat**
34. a straw **hat**
35. a **chair**person
36. Ph.**D.**
37. **IBM**
38. **MIT**
39. **USA**
40. AS**AP**
41. a **door**knob
42. a glass **door**
43. a locked **door**
44. **ice** cream
45. I **scream.**
46. **elem**entary
47. a **lémon** tree
48. **Water**gate
49. the back **gate**
50. the final **year**
51. a **year**book
52. United **States**
53. New **York**
54. **Long** Beach
55. Central **Park**
56. a raw **deal**
57. a **deal** breaker
58. the bottom **line**
59. a **bottom** feeder
60. a new **low**

Exercise 1-51: Description and Set Phrase Test
1. He's a nice **guy.**
2. He's an **American** guy from San **Francisco.**
3. The **cheerleader** needs a **rubber** band to hold her **ponytail.**
4. The executive **asst.** needs a **paper** clip for the final **report.**
5. The **law** student took an **English** test in a foreign **country.**
6. The **policeman** saw a red **car** on the freeway in Los **Angeles.**
7. My old **dog** has long **ears** and a **flea** problem.
8. The new **teacher** broke his **coffee** cup on the first **day.**
9. His best **friend** has a broken **cup** in his other **office.**
10. Let's play **football** on the **weekend** in New **York.**
11. "Jingle Bells" is a nice **song.**
12. Where are my new **shoes?**
13. Where are my **tennis** shoes?
14. I have a **headache** from the **heat** wave in South Carolina.
15. The **newlyweds** took a long **walk** in **Long** Beach.
16. The little **dog** was sitting on the **sidewalk.**
17. The famous **athlete** changed clothes in the **locker** room.
18. The **art** exhibit was held in an empty **room.**
19. There was a class **reunion** at the **high** school.
20. The **headlines** indicated a new **policy.**
21. We got **online** and went to AmericanAccent dot **com.**
22. The **stock** options were listed in the company **directory.**
23. All the **second**-graders were out on the **playground.**

Exercise 1-53: Phrasal Verb Quiz
1. The plane **took off.** The **take**off was worse than the landing.
2. **Clean**up on aisle five! Please **clean up** the mess on aisle five.
3. Why is he **showing off**? He's such a **show-off**!

4. We need to **check in**! What time is **check-in**?
5. We missed the **cut-off** time by five minutes! Why did they have to **cut** it **off** so early?!!
6. The kids were playing **dress up**. The adults had to **dress up** for the dinner party.
7. The teachers **handed out** the tests, but missed giving us one of the most important **handouts**.
8. The workers wanted jobs, not **handouts**.
9. **Wake up**! We missed the **wake-up** call!
10. We had such a nice **get-together**. We should **get together** again soon!
11. He gave him the **go-ahead** to get started. He said, "**Go ahead**! It's fine!"
12. It was such a **letdown** to lose in the finals. We felt that we'd **let down** the whole school.
13. B **goes between** A and C.
14. He was a reluctant **go-between** for the warring factions.
15. They wanted to **try out** for the team, but they missed the **tryouts**.
16. Could you **pick me up** at 5:00, please? And bring me a coffee, as I'll need a **pick-me-up**!
17. It's freezing, we need to **warm up**! Let's do some **warm-up** exercises before we start yoga.
18. **Back up**, you're standing too close to the edge. If you fall off, we'll need a **backup** plan!
19. I **took out** cash from the ATM, so let's order **takeout**.
20. Darn, I **mixed up** millions and billions on the math test. What a **mix-up**!

Exercise 2-4: Consonant/Vowel Liaison Practice
1. ree donly
2. fä läff
3. fällo wə pän
4. cə min
5. cä lim
6. se lit
7. ta kout
8. fa də way
9. sik so
10. eh may

Exercise 2-8: Consonant/Consonant Liaison Practice
1. businessteal
2. credi⁽ᵗ⁾check
3. the topfile
4. sellnine newcars
5. sitdown
6. someplan znee dluck
7. che⁽ᶜᵏ⁾cashing
8. let⁽ᵗ⁾themma⁽ᵏ⁾conditions
9. hadthe
10. bothdays

Exercise 2-9: Vowel/Vowel Liaison Practice
1. go⁽ʷ⁾ɛnywhere
2. so⁽ʷ⁾änest
3. through⁽ʷ⁾är
4. you⁽ʷ⁾är
5. he⁽ʸ⁾iz
6. do⁽ʷ⁾äi
7. I⁽ʸ⁾æskt
8. to⁽ʷ⁾open
9. she⁽ʸ⁾äweez
10. too⁽ʷ⁾äffen

Exercise 2-11: T, D, S, or Z + Y Liaison Practice
1. dijoo
2. hoozhier
3. jesjer
4. jesjer
5. misshue
6. tisshue
7. gächer
8. wherzhier
9. c'ngræjəläshunz
10. hæjer

Exercise 2-12: Finding Liaisons and Glides
Hello, **my** name-is _____. I'm taking-American-Accent-Training. There's-a **lot-to learn**, but-I **hope** to make-it-as-en**joy**able-as possible. I should pick-**up**-on-the⁽ʸ⁾American-into**na**tion pattern pretty⁽ʸ⁾**easi**ly, although the⁽ʸ⁾**only** way-də **get**-it-is-to **prac**tice-all-of the time. I⁽ʸ⁾use the⁽ʸ⁾**up**-and-down, or **peaks**-and valleys,-into**na**tion more than-I⁽ʸ⁾**used**-to. I've-been paying-attention-to **pitch**,-**too**. It's-like-**walk**ing down-a **stair**case. I've-been-**talk**ing to⁽ʷ⁾a lot-of-A**mer**icans-lately, and-they tell me that-I'm-**easi**er to⁽ʷ⁾under**stand**. Any**way**,-I could go⁽ʷ⁾ **on**-and-on, but-the⁽ʸ⁾im**por**tant-thing-is-to **lis**ten-well-and-sound **good**. Well, what-do-you **think**? **Do**⁽ʷ⁾I?

Exercise 2-19: Punctuation & Phrasing
1. D   2. B   3. C   4. B

Exercise 2-20: Tag Endings
1. isn't he
2. can't he
3. does she
4. didn't they
5. do you
6. is it
7. aren't I
8. will you
9. doesn't he
10. don't we
11. haven't we
12. didn't we
13. didn't we
14. hadn't we
15. hadn't we
16. wouldn't we
17. hasn't it
18. could you
19. won't you
20. shouldn't he
21. shouldn't he
22. did I
23. will I
24. don't you
25. aren't you
26. didn't you
27. did you
28. isn't it

Exercise 3-2: Finding æ, ä, and ə Sounds
Hᵊllo, **my** name is _____. I'm taking əmerəcən **æc**sənt Training. There's ə **lät** tə **learn**, bət I **hope** tə make ət əs ənjoyəbələs **pässə**bəl. I should pick **əp** än the əmerəcən əntənashən pættern pretty **ea**səly, ä⁽ᵊ⁾lthough the **only** way tə **get** ət əs tə **præc**təss ä⁽ᵊ⁾ll əv thə time. I use the **əp** ənd down, ər **peaks** ənd **væl**leys, intənashən more thən I **used** to. I've been paying əttenshən tə **pitch, too**. It's like **wälk**ing down ə **stair**case. I've been **talk**ing to ə **lät** əf **ame**rəcəns lately, ənd they tell me thət I'm **easi**er tə ənder**stænd**. **Any**way, I could go **än** ənd än, bət the im**por**tant thing əs tə **lis**sən we⁽ᵊ⁾ll ənd sound **good**. **We**⁽ᵊ⁾ll, what də yə **think**? **Do** I?

Exercise 3-9: Extended Listening Practice
1. Take it! tay•kit
2. Thank you. thæng•kiu
3. I need a cup of coffee. äi•nee•də•kə•pə•kä•fee
4. What did he do? wə•di•dee•doo
5. Can we go get it now? kwee•go•geh•dit•næo
6. Where did you learn to speak English so well? where•jə•lrrn•də•spee•king•glish•so•well
7. I'm going to have to think about it. äi•mə•nə•hæf•tə•thing•kə•bæou•dit
8. Sorry, I'm a little late. sä•ree, äi•mə•li•də•late
9. Try to get another one. try•də•ge•də•nə•thr•wən
10. Why don't you turn it on? wyn•chə•tr•ni•dän
11. Could/Can you hold on to this for a sec? kyu•hol•dän•də•this•frə•sec

Exercise 4-14: Finding American T Sounds
Hello, **my** name is _____. I'm taking American **Accen**⁽ᵗ⁾ Training. There's a **lo**⁽ᵗ⁾ to **learn**, bud I **hope** to make id as en**joy**able as possible. I should pick **up** on the American into**na**tion **pad**dern **prid**dy **easi**ly, although the **only** way də **ged**didis də **prac**tice all of the time. I use the **up** and down, or **peaks** and valleys, into**na**tion more than I **use**⁽ᵗ⁾to. I've been paying attention to **pitch, too**. It's like **walk**ing down a **stair**case. I've been **talk**ing to a **läd**dəv Americans la⁽ᵗ⁾ely, and they tell me the dime **easi**er də under**stand**. **Any**way, I could go **on** and on, bu⁽ᵗ⁾ the im**por**⁽ᵗ⁾n⁽ᵗ⁾ thing is də **lis**sen well and sound **good**. **Well**, wha⁽ᵈ⁾ do you **think**? **Do** I?

Exercise 4-15: Rhyme Time
1. No	11. No	21. Yes	31. Yes	41. Yes
2. No	12. No	22. No	32. Yes	42. Yes
3. Yes	13. Yes	23. Yes	33. Yes	43. Yes
4. Yes	14. Yes	24. No	34. No	44. Yes
5. Yes	15. Yes	25. No	35. No	45. Yes
6. Yes	16. No	26. No	36. Yes	46. Yes
7. No	17. Yes	27. No	37. No	47. Yes
8. No	18. No	28. Yes	38. No	48. No
9. No	19. No	29. No	39. No	49. Yes
10. No	20. Yes	30. No	40. No	50. Yes

Exercise 5-7: Finding the R Sounds
Hello, **my** name is _____. I'm taking American **Accent** Training. The<u>r</u>e's a **lot** to lea<u>r</u>n, but I **hope** to make it as en**joy**able as possible. I should pick **up** on the Ame<u>r</u>ican intonation patte<u>r</u>n p<u>r</u>etty **easi**ly, although the **only** way to **get** it is to p<u>r</u>actice all of the time. I use the **up** and down, o<u>r</u> **peaks** and valleys, **intonation** mo<u>r</u>e than I **used** to. I've been paying attention to **pitch, too**. It's like **walk**ing down a **stair**case. I've been **talk**ing to a lot of Ame<u>r</u>icans lately, and they tell me that I'm **easi**e<u>r</u> to unde<u>r</u>**stand**.

217

Anyway, I could go **on** and on, but the imp**or**t**ant** thing is to **lis**ten well and sound **good. Well,** what do you **think? Do** I?

Exercise 6-6: Finding L Sounds
He**ll**o, **my** name is _____. I'm taking American **Accent** Training. There's a **lot** to **learn,** but I **hope** to make it as en**joy**ab**le** as possib**le**. I should pick **up** on the American intonation pattern pretty eas**i**ly, although the on**ly** way to **get** it is to **prac**tise a**ll** of the time. I **use** the **up** and down, or **peaks** and va**ll**eys, **intonation** more than I **used** to. I've been paying attention to **pitch, too.** It's **like walk**ing down a **stair**case. I've been **talk**ing to a **lot** of Americans **late**ly, and they te**ll** me that I'm **easi**er to under**stand. Any**way, I could go **on** and on, but the imp**or**t**ant** thing is to **lis**ten we**ll** and sound **good. We**ll,** what do you **think? Do** I?

Exercise 7-8: Writing Your Own Phonetics
1. bä bry tsa ledder
2. bä bro də ledder
3. bä bi zrydi ngə ledder
4. bä bəl ry də ledder
5. bä bədry də ledderif
6. bä bə də ri(t)n nə ledder
7. thə gäi thə dəz ri(t)n nə ledder
8. bä bə zri(t)n nə ledder
9. bä bə dri(t)n nə ledder
10. bä bə lə vri(t)n nə ledder
11. bä bädə ry də ledder
12. bäb shüdry də ledder
13. bäb shüdn ry də ledder
14. bäb shüdə vri(t)n nə ledder
15. bäb shüdnə vri(t)n nə ledder
16. bäb cüdry də ledder
17. bäb cüdn dry də ledder
18. bäb cüdə vri(t)n nə ledder
19. bäb cüdn nəvri(t)n nə ledder
20. bäb my(t) ry də ledder
21. bäb my də vri(t)n nə ledder
22. bäb məs dry də ledder
23. bäb məs də vri(t)n nə ledder
24. bäb cən ry də ledder
25. bäb cæn(t) ry də ledder

Exercise 8-1: Targeting the TH Sound
Hello, **my** name is _____. I'm taking American **Accent** Training. **There**'s a **lot** to **learn,** but I **hope** to make it as en**joy**able as possible. I should pick **up** on **the** American intonation pattern pretty easily, al**though** the **only** way to **get** it is to **prac**ti**se** all of **the** time. I use **the up** and down, or **peaks** and valleys, **intonation** more **than** I **used** to. I've been paying attention to **pitch, too.** It's like **walk**ing down a **stair**case. I've been **talk**ing to a lot of Americans lately, and **they** tell me **that** I'm **easi**er to under**stand. Anyway, I could go **on** and on, but **the** imp**or**t**ant** **th**ing is to **lis**ten well and sound **good. Well,** what do you **think? Do** I?

Exercise 9-5: Finding S and Z Sounds
Hello, **my** name iz _____. I'm taking American **Ac**s**ent** Training. There'**z** a **lot** to **learn,** but I **hope** to make it a**z** en**joy**able a**z** po**ss**ible. I should pick **up** on the American intonation pattern pretty eaz**i**ly, although the **only** way to **get** it i**z** to **prac**ti**s**e all of the time. I u**ze** the **up** and down, or **peaks** and valley**z**, intonation more than I **u**s**ed** to. I've been paying attention to **pitch, too.** It'**s** like **walk**ing down a **s**tair**ca**s**e**. I've been **talk**ing to a lot of American**z** lately, and they tell me that I'm **eaz**ier to under**s**tand. Any**way, I could go **on** and on, but the imp**or**t**ant** thing i**z** to **lis**ten well and **s**ound **good. Well,** what do you **think? Do** I?

Review Exercise B (Ch. 1–9): Intonation Review Test
1. Los **Angeles**
2. paper **bag**
3. **lunch** bag
4. **convenience** store
5. convenient **store**
6. **home**work
7. good **writer**
8. apple **pie**
9. **pine**apple
10. all **things**
11. **every**thing
12. **moving** van
13. new **paper**
14. **news**paper
15. glass **eyes**
16. **eye**glasses
17. high **chair**
18. **high**chair
19. **base**ball
20. blue **ball**

Exercise 10-8: Finding Reduced Sounds
Hello, **my** name is _____. I'm taking American **Accent** Training. There's a **lot** to **learn,** but I **hope** to make it as en**joy**able

as possible. I **shüd** pick **up** on the American intonation pattern pretty ea**si**ly, although the **only** way to **get** it is to practice all of the time. I **üse** the up and down, or **peaks** and valleys, intonation more than I used **tü**. I've been paying attention to **pitch, tü**. It's like **walk**ing down a **stair**case. I've been **talk**ing **tü** a lot of Americans lately, and they tell me that I'm **easier tü** understand. Any**way, I** c**üd** go **on** and on, but the imp**or**t**ant** thing is to **lis**ten well and sound **güd. Well,** what do you **think? Dü** I?

Exercise 11-3: Finding V Sounds
Hello, **my** name is _____. I'm taking American **Accent** Training. There's a **lot** to **learn,** but I **hope** to make it as en**joy**able as possible. I should pick **up** on the American intonation pattern pretty ea**si**ly, although the **only** way to **get** it is to **prac**tice all of the time. I use the **up** and down, or **peaks** and valleys, intonation more than I **used** to. I**'ve** been paying attention to **pitch, too.** It's like **walk**ing down a **stair**case. I**'ve** been **talk**ing to a lot of Americans lately, and they tell me that I'm **easi**er to understand. Any**way, I could go **on** and on, but the imp**or**t**ant** thing is to **lis**ten well and sound **good. Well,** what do you **think? Do** I?

Exercise 12-2: Tense Vowels Practice Paragraph
Hello, **my** name is _____. I'm t**a**king American **æk**s**ent** Tr**ai**ning. There's a **lot** to learn, but I **hope** to m**a**ke it as en**joy**able as possible. I should pick **up** on th**e** American intonation p**æ**ttern pretty **ea**sily, although th**e only way** to **get** it is to **præc**tice all of the time. I use th**e up** an d**æo**n, or **peaks** and v**æ**lleys, inton**a**tion more than I **used** to. I've been p**a**ying attention to **pitch, too.** It's like **walk**ing d**æo**n a **stair**case. I've been **talk**ing to a lot of Americans l**a**tely, and th**a**y tell m**e** that I'm **ea**si**e**r to underst**æ**nd. Any**wa**y, I could go **on** and on, but th**e** import'nt thing is to **lis**ten well and s**æ**ond **good. Well,** what d' you **think? Do** I?

Exercise 12-4: Lax Vowels Practice Paragraph
Hello, **my** name is _____. I'm taking **ə**mer**ə**c**ən** **Acc**ə**nt** Training. There's **ə** **lot** t**ə** learn, b**ət** I **hope** t**ə** make it **əs** en**joy**ab°l **əs** poss**ə**bəl. I should pick **ə**p on the **ə**mer**ə**c**ən** int**ə**nashən pattern pritty **ea**s**ə**ly, although the only way t**ə get** it is t**ə prac**t**əs** all **ə**v th**ə** time. I use the **up ə**n down, or **peaks ə**n valleys, int**ə**nashən more than I **used** to. I've bin p**a**ying **ə**ttenshən t**ə pitch, too.** It's like **walk**ing down **ə** st**ə**rcase. I've bin **talk**ing to **ə** lot **ə**v **ə**mer**ə**c**ə**ns lately, **ə**nd they tell me th**ə**t I'm **easi**er to **ə**nder**stand.** ɛny**way, I could go **on** **ə**nd on, b**ə**t the import'nt thing i**s** to **lis**t**ə**n wɛll **ə**nd sound **good. Wɛll,** wh**ə**t d' you **think? Do** I?

Exercise 16-4: Finding n and ŋ Sounds
Hello, **my** **n**ame is _____. I'm taki**ŋ** America**n** **Acc**e**nt** Training. There's a **lot** to lear**n**, but I **hope** to make it as e**n**joyable as possible. I should pick **up** o**n** the America**n** into**n**ation pattern pretty easily, although the **only** way to **get** it is to **prac**tice all of the time. I use the **up** a**n**d dow**n**, or **peaks** a**n**d valleys, into**n**ation more tha**n** I **used** to. I've bee**n** paying atte**n**tio**n** to **pitch, too.** It's like walki**ŋ** dow**n** a staircase. I've bee**n** talki**ŋ** to a lot of America**n**s lately, a**n**d they tell me that I'm **easi**er to u**n**der**stand.** Any**way, I could go **on** a**n**d o**n**, but the imp**or**t**ant** thing is to **lis**ten well a**n**d sou**n**d **good. Well,** what do you **think? Do** I?

Exercise 17-4: Glottal Consonant Practice Paragraph
Hello, **my** **n**ame is _____. I'm taki**ŋ** Amerikan **A**kcent Training. The**re**'s a lot to lear**n**, but I **hope** to make it as enjoyable as possible. I should pick **up** on the Amerikan intonation pattern pretty easily, although the only way to get it is to prak**tice all of the time. I use the up and down, or peaks and valleys, intonation more than I used to. I've been paying attention to pitch, too. It's like walki**ŋ** down a stair**k**ase. I've been **talki**ŋ to a lot of Amerikans lately, and they tell me that I'm **easi**er to unde**r**stand. Any**way, I kould go **on** and on, but the imp**or**t**ant** thi**ŋ** is to **lis**ten well and sound **good. Well,** what do you **think? Do** I?

Review Exercise 1-23: Syllable Count Test

1. 2	4. 3	7. 4	10. 4	13. 1	16. 4	19. 4
2. 2	5. 3	8. 4	11. 4	14. 4	17. 4	20. 3
3. 3	6. 4	9. 4	12. 1	15. 4	18. 4	21. 4

Review Exercise 1-33: Nationality Intonation Quiz

1. French	4. french	7. Canadian
2. restaurant	5. toast	8. French
3. French	6. horn	9. door

Review Exercise 1-35: Contrast of Compound Nouns

1. room	9. coffee	17. hair	25. guitar
2. dark	10. coffee	18. hair	26. photography
3. antique	11. chemistry	19. hair	27. photo
4. dealer	12. reaction	20. station	28. wedding
5. chair	13. sense	21. police	29. ceremony
6. video	14. cents	22. radio	30. wedding
7. video	15. sixth	23. orange	
8. coffee	16. grade	24. guitar	

Review Exercise 1-36: Description and Set Phrase Test

1. schoolkids / subway / downtown / field trip / urban living
2. local sheriff / bumper sticker / back bumper
3. homeowners / property taxes / federal government
4. small tremblers / earthquake / San Francisco
5. Geology Club / camping trip / Mount Hood
6. award ceremony / Hilton Hotel / two hours
7. Bob Smith / surfboard / stormy day / Diamond Head
8. boy scouts / pup tents / mountaintop / pouring rain
9. little late / babysitter / over night
10. sixth graders / comic books / chocolate milk

Review Exercise 1-51: Extended Listening Practice

1. wee thing keez gä duh geh do ver rit.
   We think he's got to get over it.

2. də zeh nee wən no hæo də geh də lye nə creh dit
   Does anyone know how to get a line of credit?

3. try də show wəm hæo də yooz thee yi ner net
   Try to show them how to use the internet.

Review Exercise 1-60

1. is there	6. didn't she
2. wasn't it	7. wouldn't she
3. do you	8. hadn't she / shouldn't she
4. would he	9. would she
5. can't they	10. had she

Review Exercise 2-4

1. ai thing kee zänizway.
2. hee püdi din'num brella stand.
3. wee bädidi nidalee.

Review Exercise 2-8

1. NickClark hopest' put[(t)]endollarzdown.
2. ButTommakeso muchjuice.
3. Bobzdäggätsomebones.

Review Exercise 2-9

1. Can you see[(y)]it through to the[(y)]end?
2. Be[(y)]available for the[(y)]other opportunity in my[(y)]office.
3. He[(y)]always wants to[(w)]offer to go[(w)]over it again.

Review Exercise 2-11

1. We're glad the cher homework's done.
2. Wüdjoo help me with this?
3. Didjoo missher old friends?
4. Where zhier brother?

ESL Teacher's Guide

This is a very practical, step-by-step guide to working with foreign-born adults. If you go through all the exercises, giving strong feedback, you should have results similar to the one you heard on Track 1.

CHAPTER 1: THE AMERICAN SOUND

Intonation, **voice quality**, **liaisons**, and **pronunciation** are the four pillars of the American Accent Training method. It's the way that children learn their native language, and they are the main elements that are unfortunately missing when adults study a foreign language. Without intonation and voice quality, a student is simply using English words in a non-English format. It is your task to make sure that the voice is properly placed and that the rhythm patterns become ingrained. *Voice quality* is a combination of vocal placement and cadence, which means a throaty sound and a stairstep intonation. *Intonation* is the pitch-change pattern used by native speakers. Within a word, a phrase, or a sentence, certain syllables are given more stress (accorded a higher pitch) than others. How this stress changes the meaning of a sentence, how it can move around in a sentence, and how it can reflect the speaker's intent—or even personality—is what you need to convey to your students. Use the Nationality Guides to let the students see the correlation between their intonation and pronunciation—where it's similar and where it's different. Also point out that every language has intonation, but it's most likely that they won't have realized that about their own language.

Asking Questions

In America, students are encouraged to ask questions; Asian students are not. Your students need to realize that not only are questions welcomed, but also that they **must** ask them. ESL teachers tend to talk too much. Limit yourself to 10 percent of the talking, and have your students do the other 90 percent. This means you only talk for six minutes in a one-hour class. Make the students do the work, not you.

The American Sound

The first step is to get the student to generate his voice from the correct place. It's not up in the head or forward in the mouth, but rather in the back of the throat with the air projected from the diaphragm. While working on the airflow and sound production, have the student start correlating the phonetic symbols with the actual spelling. One of the main goals is to get visual students oriented to the auditory aspects of English.

As you heard on Track 14, Eddie Izzard demonstrates moving his voice back and down to imitate the American sound. This essential throaty quality—*rhoticity*—is that solid **R** as in *hard* and *far*.

With a slight detour to the general pronunciation introduction later in this chapter, the first third of this program deals with voice quality and intonation. Even as you work through word connections and pronunciation, you'll find yourself coming back to vocal placement and cadence as the most important determinants of a standard accent.

Most intermediate-to-advanced students have studied a lot of grammar and have sufficient vocabularies. They need to understand, however, that their accent is actually more important than perfect grammar or an extensive vocabulary—after all, if the listener can't understand, what's the point of having a mastery of the pluperfect subjunctive? It's interesting to know that 25 percent of what we say consists of just nine words: *and, be, have, it, of, the, to, will, you*, and they are almost always unstressed. Of the hundreds of thousands of words that exist in English, the daily usage is about 1,000. Get your students to focus on high-frequency vocabulary.

Explain the difference between the intonation, or rhythm, of a sentence—the music or tonality—and the actual sounds of the individual words, or pronunciation, and demonstrate that rhythm has more to do with "sounding American" than the individual words do. Make the sound that Americans make when they say, *I don't know* (one step beyond *I dunno*) without enunciating the words. In this case, rhythm alone is communication. (See page 7.)

Getting Started

During the diagnostic analysis on page xi, ask why the student is taking an accent class. You can call us for advice at (800) 457-4255. In order to get students into the zone and to find out what they think their potential is, ask what they think they can achieve on a scale of 1 to 10. Make a note of the number. Ask where they think they are now and note that number as well. It's usually pretty accurate.

In order to give them confidence in what you will be doing, explain that they will be recorded at the beginning and at the end of the course, as well as intermittently throughout, and that after they have gone through the steps, they can't help but sound more American. If the students haven't had a diagnostic analysis, mention you will be integrating all four components of the accent (voice quality, intonation, liaisons, pronunciation), and you will be covering it all in detail. Things like *tense* and *lax vowels or voiced* and *unvoiced consonants* can all be dealt with as they come up in their respective chapters. If you are asked directly, of course, go ahead and answer. Start right in on the American speech music on page 7 and get the student to have the proper vocal placement. In the second exercise, you'll be approaching the American sound via nonsense syllables. This will circumvent the student's inclination to fall back on old habits and misconceptions. Have the student write down the five syllables: **bä bee bä də bäik**. It doesn't have to be phonetically accurate, and don't insist on the symbols. If they write **bah bi bah duh byk**, that's just fine. Have the student say it out loud as a regular sentence, and they will get bits and pieces before figuring out, **Bobby bought a bike**. The major take-aways are that the letter **O** sounds like *ah* and that the **T** between vowels turns into a **D**. This is the first step in guiding a student from spelling-based pronunciation to a phonetic understanding of pure sound. Next, have the student work on perfecting a go-to phrase, including vocal placement and facial position, to get into the American zone. Along these same lines, work on active listening, with the student responding to your scenarios with the various options on page 19. This segues directly into the non-verbal intonation exercise and the sounds of empathy. For Exercise 1-26, you can either work from Track 49 or, if you're confident, you can create the sounds yourself.

General Pronunciation

Here, you're diving straight into pronunciation, starting with an incredibly easy sound, *mmm*, which everyone can do. Have the student observe how and where the air comes out, the point of contact, and the vocality. This pre-answers a lot of questions that tend to come up, such as *What is a consonant?, What do you mean by voiced?, What's a nasal?* In Exercise 1-2, you'll have them take the baby step of adding the *ah* sound and some other bilabials, for a nice, clear *mah, pah, bah*. Repeat this several times, making sure that the *pah* and *bah* are sufficiently popped. You can have them hold their hand in front of their mouth to feel the air. Next, you're going to start combining pronunciation and rhythm with Exercise 1-3, using the physicality of snapping, slapping, or pulling. We'll delve more deeply into the different ways of making intonation in Chapter 1, pages 6–7, but for the moment, just make sure they are using **pitch** and not **volume**. Encourage them to lengthen the vowel duration a bit when the second syllable is stressed.

In Exercise 1-4, you'll circle back for the third time to pure sound. The reason we approach this from so many directions is that students are *very* invested in maintaining the correlation between spelling and pronunciation. We've even heard people pronounce the **L** in *would* and *half*! Have the student read the three sentences and focus on pronouncing them it exactly the way they're written. Quite often, they'll get very distracted trying to figure what the meaning is, but keep them laser focused on the sounds. In Exercise 1-5, they get to put it into regular English and in Exercise 1-6 to create the sounds while knowing what the meaning is. Your job is to make sure they maintain the **bä bläs diz jäb, skät tä də lät, dän bä də bäik** pronunciation.

Exercise 4-15 is a great reality check, and students are amazed at what rhymes and what doesn't. On pages ix–x, there is a very soothing exercise, almost like chanting the sounds in sequence. The first column should be 95 percent easy, with just a few predictable hiccups on **rä** and **thä**. Based on the nationality, you'll also need to work on **bä/vä** (Spanish), **fä** (Japanese), **dä** (Spanish), **pä/bä** (Arabic), **lä/nä** (Southern China), **vä/wä** (India/Pakistan), **fä/vä/wä** (German), and **sä/zä** (Spanish). Make sure that the vowel is clear and open, and you may need to have them double the vowel—**mä-ah**—to catch the musicality and the proper vowel duration.

The second column is a bit more problematic, both because **æ** doesn't exist in other languages and because it's a rather unlovely sound. It's so distinctly American, though, that you need to have them get comfortable with it early on. The third column is as easy as **ä** because everyone has an *eh* sound. Other universal sounds are *eeh*, *ooh*, and the **long A** and **long I**. It's quite a task to get students to distinguish *ih / eeh* and *ü / ooh*. The latter pair can be illustrated with the chicken (*ü*) and the fish (*ooh*) in Chapter 12, "Tense & Lax Vowels." Actually, *ih / ü* are very similar, as in *kick / cook*. The key is that there should be no lip rounding with *ü*. The long vowels **A** and **I** are actually diphthongs, and the task is to get students to produce both halves: *eh-ee* and *ah-ee*. This brings us to the neutral vowel, the schwa (**ə**), which students have a heck of a time distinguishing from **ä**. You need to contrast the two columns, side by side, *bä / bə*, *chä / chə*, *dah / duh*, etc.

The chart on page viii is important in that it helps with the lateral transfer of information. Rather than creating a sound from scratch, students can work from a nearby one in their own language. Chances are, when they read their character set, the vowels will be shorter than you want, so have them double them up. This is a good time to direct them to the Nationality Guides in the back of the book.

The chart on page x is similar to Exercise 1-6 in that they will be transitioning from pure sound over to spelling again. Make sure to hold them strictly accountable for each sound, in particular *the*, as it's the most commonly used word in English. This chart will give you a head start on the **TH** (more detail in Chapter 8). The main point is that although it's tempting to teach a breathy **TH**, it's actually popped in natural speech.

American Intonation

You've already introduced intonation in Chapter 1, and now you're going to introduce the concept of musicality and tone shift that can be visually represented by the staircase. One of the most important things that students know intuitively in their own language is the importance of pitch change and the effect of shortening a word. For some reason, however, that information does not transfer in the second language. Students tend to shorten their words, which makes them sound *curt*, *clipped*, or *abrupt*. Literally, each of these words just means *short*, but figuratively (and that's what accent is all about) they sound rude.

Let the students know that they are to use this book and audio set on their own and that your role is to listen and give them feedback. They also need to know that they will not be losing their accent—they will be learning a new one. This is an important psychological point since people are nervous about the effects of such a change. As they learn the accent, they will make it their own, and their thinking won't change as a consequence; it's just a skill like a new dance step. It comforts students to hear that even among Americans there are misunderstandings due to intonation and meaning. Once a student can accurately hear and use the difference between a compound noun and a description, a large part of the intonation work is done.

Three Ways to Make Intonation

Once they have the sounds in place, you're ready to get more specific with the intonation. Demonstrate all three ways, and then have the student focus on **pitch**, rather than on **volume**. Vowel duration is an extremely important component of intonation and is covered throughout the text.

Nonsense Syllables

Exercise 1-7 is extremely important. Students can disassociate from grammar, content, meaning, and vocabulary and simply focus on the pure sound and rhythm of English. Some students are staccato, some heavy on volume, some monotone, some misplace the stress points, and some sound like they're singing rather than talking. You know what it should sound like—keep modifying until the student sounds like you. Female teachers should deepen their voices a bit with male students.

In Exercise 1-7, there are two groups—one of purely nonsense syllables and a second of the transition from nonsense to sense. In the first group, have the student read each row across (1–4) for the same pattern with different sounds, then down (A–D) for the same sound with different patterns. The main point here is to capture both the musicality and the vocal placement. If the student is able to sound American saying **duh-duh-duh**, everything else can follow from there.

In the second group, have the student read column A (1–4). Make sure that **duh-duh-duh** and **ABC**, **123**, **Dogs eat bones** all sound the same in terms of voice placement, cadence, and musicality. Then go on to columns B, C, and D.

Staircase Intonation

The staircase is simply a visual metaphor to help students understand pitch. It is the same as a stress point, musical notes, or an accent mark. The primary rule of stress in English is that, given no counter indicators, such as contrast, nouns are stressed. Have the student read Exercise 1-8, giving a slight lift to each noun. In Exercise 1-9, have the student read side to side, contrasting the noun stress with the verb stress. This makes the test in Exercise 1-10 extremely simple.

Shifting the Stress Points

Intonation is the mainstay of the American Accent Training method. It is the way that children learn their native language, and it is the main element that is usually missing when adults study a foreign language. Intonation is the pitch-change pattern used by native speakers. Within a word, a phrase, or a sentence, certain syllables are given more stress (accorded a higher pitch) than others. How this stress changes the meaning of a sentence, how it can move around in a sentence, and how it can reflect the speaker's intent or even personality is what you need to convey to your students.

Duh-Duh-Duh

One of the first steps in the transition from the printed word to the sound of spoken English is to have students start applying an unmistakable intonation to all sorts of different expressions. Even when you walk the student through the importance of the American up-and-down, people will still want to underemphasize.

To get around this, after the student reads the **New Information** sentence **It sounds like rain** and it sounds flat and unmusical, have them replace most of the words with **duh-duh-duh**. Stress **RAIN** very heavily. **duh-duh-duh RAIN**. If **rain** is stressed loudly but unmusically, have them put it on two tone levels: **ray-een**.

This tone shift will help students with the idea of the staircase. Have them read the four sentences, and every time they lose the intonation and start stressing each word (**It.Sounds.Like.Rain**), go back to **duh-duh-duh**. Every time they lose the musicality, break the key word into two parts, put it on a little stair step, and make the pitch higher on the first step.

It sounds like **rain**.	duh-duh-duh **rain**
It **sounds** like rain.	duh-duh-duh **sounds** duh-duh-duh
He **likes** rain, but he **hates** snow.	duh-duh-duh **likes** duh-duh-duh,
	duh-duh-duh **hates** duh-duh-duh
The rain **didn't affect** his plans.	duh-duh-duh **didn't affect**
	duh-duh-duh

Translation

The next part of the intonation exercise is a translation. This again is twofold. In many English classes, native languages are implicitly or explicitly forbidden. Since language is such an integral part of an individual, it feels as if part of her or him is being denied or shut out. I think it is much preferable to use what you can of each language to show the student where his natural advantages lie. Most languages have a trilled **R**, which is instantly convertible to the American **T**. Let your students know what their strengths are, and you will have much more confident and teachable students.

Translation Summary

1. Translate the sentence.
2. Write it out on the board, phonetically or otherwise.
3. Students read them with their normal accents.
4. You read the sentences in an American accent.
5. Students imitate your accent.
6. Students read it in a native accent, emphasizing a word.
7. Other students guess which sound was stressed.
8. Explain the similarities or differences in intonations in different languages, such as the American staircase, the Indian upward glide, or the Swiss up-and-down.
9. Briefly discuss how this strong intonation feels to them.

Maybe in English, but in My Dialect . . .

Have the students translate the sentence **I didn't say he stole the money** into their own language or dialect. Have them say it at a regular speed and intonation so you can hear how different it is from English. Then, jot down the translation, phonetically or by normal ABC's, and read it back with an average American accent. It's a hugely important exercise to have the student imitate you, saying their own language with an American accent. They should feel like they're talking and chewing gum. For them to speak their own language sounding like an American is funny and unnerving, but it definitely improves their American accent in English.

Next, have the student read the sentence with a natural, native accent, but jumping heavily on a stressed word while you identify which word stood out. It may take a couple of tries here, but it is important to get them to realize that it is only the sound you are looking for, not the meaning of the sound.

After they can move the intonation around freely in their own sentences, ask if this is it similar to his or her native language?; does it feel natural to do it?; how did it feel? You will get a wonderful variety of answers as they start thinking about how they actually do it. At this point, students realize that they do the same thing in their own language and it is just a question of applying concepts that they already know and use to English.

Syllable Stress

This is a dense and important section, where you'll be working on making sure that the student's pitch is appropriate, in terms of placement, pitch range, and vowel duration. The one-syllable patterns contrast the single stairstep of the vowel in a word ending in a whispered consonant (unvoiced) with the double stairstep of a word ending in a voiced consonant. In the two-syllable patterns, you start to get into descriptions (stressing the second word—white house) and set phrases or compound nouns (stressing the first word—White House). Students often feel the need to have a set list of rules for syllable stress, but this is not typically a big problem. To assuage them, however, there is a Syllable Rules section on page 29. You will notice that Indians stress the first word in *beginning* and *component*, and the French like to stress the last syllable of just about everything, but this is minor compared with the rest of the intonation problems.

Complex Intonation

This chapter starts getting to the heart of the rhythm patterns, and you'll need to review it, both in exercises and in context while the students are speaking. You'll notice that the sentences are fairly short in **Goldilocks**, and there are two reasons for this. The first is that they need to master the basics, and the second is that this will be contrasted with *sentence balance* later on.

CHAPTER 2: WORD LINKING & PHRASING

Phrasing is pretty straightforward in that punctuation is such a strong guide. Tag endings are included on page 57 because students tend to under use them. They should practice with tags as both a query and an affirmation.

Word Connections

The point of this chapter is to get students away from sounding so staccato or robotic and into using the *wa-wa, nya-nya, woo-woo, bada-bada* sounds of spoken American English. The most important thing to stress is that, although students have learned to pronounce word by word, and, of course, that's how things are written, they have to regroup into sound groups rather than individual word groups. They have to listen for and hear whole phrases or they will miss the meaning. It's like when they say you can't see the forest for the trees—the students can't understand the meaning of the whole sentence because they are only listening for the meaning of each word.

They also have to stop intellectualizing every sound they hear—"mēt! What did that mean? Was it a noun (meat)? Was it a verb (meet)? An object? A subject?" By this time, the speaker has left the student in the conversational dust. The important thing to deal with is, of course, context. The identical sounds can be either logical or nonsensical: *I'm meeting Bob* or *I'm eating Bob*?

Have each student read the five sentences in Exercise 2-1. #3, **the D** will sound fine, but #4 will probably revert to **that he**. Bring this immediately to the students' attention and have each one concentrate on making #4 sound exactly like #3. Then, explain that certain sounds are just attracted to each other, like a magnet. There are four situations for connecting words listed just below Exercise 2-1. The first one is when a word ends in a consonant and the next one starts with a vowel—they automatically link up. Have the student read the three examples, preferably from the right-hand side.

CHAPTER 3: CAT? CAUGHT? CUT?

Exercise 3-3 takes a long time, but it lets students finally break through the spelling barrier of **A**s, **O**s, and **U**s. There are 8 æ, 5 ä, and more than 35 ə.

First, have students go through and ferret out the 8 æ sounds, writing the symbol over the words. It is better to do it first in pencil and then use a highlighter afterward because any mistakes result in pink on top of blue on top of green. A student reading after each color facilitates correction because that way they are not targeting too many sounds at once. Then, look for the 5 ä words, first in pencil, then in color. Finally, ə. This takes quite a bit of time, and it's better to review them line by line, rather than trying to say all of them out.

Cat? (8)

The æ sound is relatively scarce, but is highly noticeable and has such a distinctive sound that it is not difficult to train. It's just a combination of **ä** and **ɛh**. It sometimes helps to temporarily put in a small (ʸ) before æ, such as **keeyæt**, to make a huge exaggeration, which they can later relax into a regular æ. You should have them drop the jaw down (like **ä**) and then back (like **ɛh**) while pushing up the back of the tongue. Or have them say **ɛh** and leave the tongue in the same position while dropping the jaw.

Caught? (8)

The **ä** sound is easily cued to either *what you say to the doctor when he uses the tongue depressor* or the musical *lä-lä-lä*, so whenever they come to a word like *caught, thought, bought*, they can be cued with *kä-kä-kä, thä-thä-thä*, or *bä-bä-bä*, respectively. If a student is reluctant to fully pronounce this sound, have him put his hand under his chin to feel the jaw as it drops. The strong tendency will be to round the lips, because, after all, this is usually spelled with an **O**. Keep going back to the phonetics to break this habit.

Cut? (35+)

The schwa (a neutral vowel sound) is best done last since it is the most subtle and elusive of the three sounds, as well as the most common vowel sound in English. Because you eliminated the other two most likely candidates for confusion beforehand (æ and ä), the smoke screen is a little more readily penetrable. It is, in large part, due to the schwa that spelling is so difficult—the neutral vowel in poss**i**ble and pass**a**ble sounds identical, but needs to be spelled with appropriately different letters.

It is pronounced *uh*, which is the sound that is produced when you press on your diaphragm and don't change your mouth position at all. If it's a group that has meshed well, I have them press on each other's diaphragm so they can hear what neutral, unforced sound it is. The point usually comes up of the difference between ə and Λ (as in **a**bout and b**u**t) and ä and Ɔ (as in c**o**t and c**augh**t). For practical purposes, however, we will only use the first of each pair (ə and ä), the intent of the program being to get students to sound American, rather than phonetically "perfect," which, of course, Americans are not.

The schwa is the noise we make when we are thinking—*uh, um*; for Americans, it is an unconscious but ever-present sound.

Read Down

After the paragraph has been completely worked for all three sounds, in order to get a flow going of a single sound, I have the students read each sound group in Exercise 3-3, from 1–24 without stopping. Unless, of course, they fall back into the spelling trap and mispronounce, at which point we go back to basics with the original vowel sound, then add on the new consonants around it. For example, ä, **kä**, **caught** or uh, **k'**, **cut**.

Read Across

Once they can go through the entire list smoothly, basing pronunciation on the sound they know to be from the category, rather than from what spelling would indicate, we read across the rows, incorporating all five sounds.

Random Reading

As a review, we come back to this exercise and they pick words out at random, which I try to guess with no clues other than their pronunciation.

The æ, ä, ə Reading

There are three paragraphs in Exercise 3-4, 3-5, 3-6 for æ, ä, and ə respectively. The targeted sounds are underlined to help students realize three things.
1. How **many** of that particular sound there are
2. **Where** they are
3. How the **sound** relates to **spelling**

The Miracle Technique: Reverse Phonetics

The purpose of this exercise is to get your students away from the impression that they can't do it—"it" being to produce native-sounding speech. Stated or not, conscious or not, students have resistance to changing their pronunciation either from their native accent or from how they think the spelling indicates. You need to hone their skill in hearing and reproducing pure sound, in or out of context, and they need to abandon the spelling crutch.

In Exercise 3-7, you're introducing the concepts of pure sound, of ignoring spelling, of using any phonetic system. Let them know that they are going to write backward, but just two little sounds. Say *lie* and listen for the students to say back what they heard. They can write it *lie, ly, lye,* or *läi*. Then, have them repeat it after you, making sure they get both the *ah* and the *eeh* sounds. When both sounds are in place, have them read it back themselves and decipher what it says: *I like it*. Read the sentence using the rubber band or tapping on the stressed word (*like*) until everyone sounds quick and fluent. After you've finished Exercises 3-8 and 3-9, have the students create their own sentences, broken up into pieces. They should give you the pieces, back to front, and you then decipher them. Interestingly, in the beginning, as you read back, you'll have their accent. As they come to understand the rules, you'll sound more and more standard.

CHAPTER 4: THE AMERICAN T

Beddy Ba Da Bida Bedder Budder. This exercise leads students through the mysteries of what looks like a **T** but sounds like a **D**, or worse yet, like nothing at all. The sound of each **T** is determined by its position on the staircase (you knew it would be—you can't escape intonation). Here are four rules of thumb.

Top of the Staircase

First, they go through and notice all of the **T**s that are just **T**s, which are explained in Exercise 4-4 on page 68 of the student text.

Middle of the Staircase

Then they pick out the nine **T**s that are pronounced **D** (#4); this is easily explained using any language that uses an apical flap (trill) for an **R** (Spanish, Italian, Russian, Indian, Korean, Japanese, etc.) as what they use as the **R** sound in the various dialects. For example, if someone is having trouble with *ought to*, which Americans usually say in rapid conversation as *oughtta*, write *ara* on the board (or have them write it down, if you're on the phone) and ask them, with no coaching whatsoever, to pronounce it in their native language. Likewise with *bara*: *I bought a (bara) book*. Other pairs are: *bottom/baram*; *lot of/lara*; *ought to/ara*; *petal/per'l*; *could have/kura*; *caught a/kara*, etc. There are only a few exceptions to this rule: *politics*, *militant*, *crouton*, *futon*, etc.

Bottom of the Staircase

Last, they find the 7 **T**s that aren't really pronounced at all (#5, #6, #7). One of the most difficult things for students to do is get used to not letting final **T**s and **D**s be plosive. Tell them not to pop their final consonants, just hold the tongue in position and don't let the air out. They are used to expelling the air after **T**s, **D**s, **P**s, **B**s, etc. Use matches in class, and if the flame even wavers, they can see if they have gone too far. A less flammable way to test the **T** is for each student to hold his hand in front of his face to see if he can feel his breath. Remember to have them read the paragraph after each of the three selections to avoid overload.

The Held T before N

A difficult sound to produce is the **held T before an N**. The tongue goes to the **T** position, but the air is not released. Then, from the **T** position, an **N** sound is made. Not -**en**, just **nnn**. The sound rises quickly in pitch to the held **T** and then drops back down with the **N**. *Bitten* is pronounced *bi(t)n*. It is not pronounced *biTn* or *bi(t)ən*. On the other hand, the **D** sound before an **N** doesn't have the sharp pitch rise, contrasted in *written* and *ridden*. Commonly-used held-T words are *certain*, *gotten*, *forgotten*, *sentence*, *important*.

No T with N

In some commonly used words, the **T** just drops out completely since the **T** and the **N** are created so close together in the mouth (just behind the teeth). You'll hear this in *interview*, *advantage*, *percentage*, etc.

CHAPTER 5: THE AMERICAN R

This is one of those high-value sounds, and you are going to have to get your students to use the growly throat sound of the rhotic **R**, and not let the tongue touch any other part of the mouth, particularly the alveolar ridge. The hand trick on page 75 works really well. You can also have them put a spoon on their tongue while saying *race*, *berry*, and *car*. The spoon will impede the tongue tip from reaching up and forming a consonant, instead of the more liquid vowel-type sound that is the American **R**.

CHAPTER 6: THE EL

The El: A Diphthong Consonant

The **L** presents all kinds of interesting problems. It's hard to get students to appreciate what a big, round sound it is, with the back of the tongue dropped way down while the tip is firm and anchored to the top of the mouth behind the teeth. The American **L** is **ə + L**. Indians and Russians tend to make the **L** far too quick, and too heavy. Spanish speakers make it too quick and short. Chinese speakers just leave it off the end of words. Students need to put the **L** on the two-tone double stairstep, with the second half being **ə**l.

Even when the **L** is silent because it's a voiced consonant, it has the effect of lengthening the previous vowel. Here is a five-step technique that works well.

Final El

1. Have them talk without removing the tip of their tongue from the alveolar ridge.
2. Use a mirror to make sure that the bottom of the tongue is visible.
3. Hold the nose shut to make sure that the air doesn't escape through the nose, which results in an **n**-like sound.
4. Have them add a final, tiny schwa to finish off the **L** sound.
5. Connect the final **L** to a following vowel whenever possible (tell a story > te lə story).

CHAPTER 7: REDUCED SOUNDS

This is part of intonation, but instead of focusing on the peaks, you'll be looking deep into those murky valleys. Students tend to overpronounce, so you have to be vigilant about not letting them get away with it. You may find yourself unsure about what "proper" speech is, but because this program is more descriptive than prescriptive, you'll need to focus on strong intonation, letting the schwas fall where they may.

Grammar in a Nutshell

Along with the Miracle Techique, this is a Desert Island exercise. If all you had was a sheet of paper with these two exercises, you could get a lot of English teaching done. It covers intonation, voice quality, linking, pronunciation, phrasing, and grammar. The only tricky part is when the students write their own sentences. To have as much linking as possible, follow the rules in Exercise 7-8.

CHAPTER 8: TEE AITCH

If the tongue is too relaxed and protruding, not only does it not look good, it also doesn't feel good or sound right. The tip of the tongue is tense and hardly protrudes as it darts quickly out and back. Contrast **th** with **s**, **z**, and **d**, using a mirror. For the voiced **th**, have a student practice on a word like *then*. Have him say *den* and then with the exact same feeling, say the **d** sound with his tongue slightly between his teeth. This should come out a good voiced *then*.

For an unvoiced **th**, do the same thing with **s**. Start with *sing*, move the tongue tip forward and say *thing*. They almost can't do it wrong. A good thing about highlighting all of the **th**'s is that a student can see how frequently used the sound is, thereby allowing him to realize that even that one small sound will leave him sounding accented if he neglects it. Bear in mind that, in every word-count study, *the* is the most commonly used word in the English language, making up 6 percent of all utterances. Hence, with this single word pronounced wrong, 6 percent of a student's speech is flawed.

If students have trouble with the **th** paragraph, go to Exercise 9-2. Have them read **A Surly Sergeant**, replacing all of the **s**'s with **th**'s. They should sound like Daffy Duck on a good day.

When they go back to the regular **th** paragraph, it's a lot easier. Another strange technique that works is to have students read the paragraph completely silently, but mouthing the words—and focusing on every **th**. A mirror or a partner helps, too. Also, in Exercise 8-1, mark the 10 voiced and 2 unvoiced **th**'s. Voiced sounds are easier than unvoiced sounds for English speakers to make, so the more common sounds tend to be voiced: *the, then, this*, etc.

CHAPTER 9: S OR Z?

This is just getting used to **z**'s in **s**'s clothing. For a general rule, students can be told that the final consonant, voiced or unvoiced, of a word determines whether the plural **s** or third person singular **s** is voiced or unvoiced. This topic is very important for Spanish speakers.

CHAPTERS 1–9: REVIEW AND EXPANSION
Psycholinguistics

Have the student listen to the before/after audio on Track 209. The purpose of this is to get them in the frame of mind that *it's just an accent*. To find out if your students are all-at-oncers or step-by-steppers, play Track 212, **Please call Stella**, and have them mimic the sound. If they sound pretty much like they already do, or fixate on what the actual words are, you've got *steppers*. If they capture the essence of the sound, you've got *oncers*. Follow up on this with Review Exercise 2 (page 113) to see how they respond. This is actually a quick triage to see who is flexible and who might be more stubborn and resistant to change. Follow up on the Stella mimicry by having the student imitate you saying, *There was a time when people really had a way with words*. Their mimicry should include the vocal quality, rhythm, and as much pronunciation as possible. (These words were chosen because they are very high frequency.) Circling back to pure sound in Review Exercise 4 (page 115), have the student read *gäddit*. Make sure the **ä** is clear and open and that it's a quick, flicked **D** in the middle. Stress the first syllable. Have the student repeat at least ten times or until it sounds just right. As you correlate in Review Exercise 5 (page 115), you may notice some backsliding with the **O** in *got* rounding up a little. In that case, go back to the phonetics and make sure that the vowel is nice and open and the lips aren't at all rounded. The next step is super important, particularly for the empiricists in your class. They need to actually go out and use this phrase with actual Americans. They can use it as either a statement: **Got it**; an exclamation: **Got it!**; or a query: **Got it?** Have them bring back the real-life experience of how it turned out. This is an important discussion and will lead to a better understanding of how to interact with Americans while applying the techniques.

Ask your students how many times a day they have to repeat themselves and make of note of this as their What Factor. The goal is, of course, to get it down to zero.

CHAPTER 10: MORE REDUCED SOUNDS

Most students will pronounce *good, güd*, as **güd** as in *smooth* (as well as *could, should, stood, look, took, book, cook, put, push, pull, wool*, etc.). In order to get rid of the pronounced lip movement in **ū**, work with **bic/ bək / book** and **lick / lək / look** groups, which makes the throat work more than the lips. Read across **u / i / ü / ə / r**, feeling the difference between the first-column words with strong, visible lip movement and the second- and third-column words with rear tongue and throat movement and almost no lip change whatsoever. *Ih* and *eeh* are usually paired as tense and lax vowels, but *ih, ü*, and *ə* are much closer, with just the tongue shifting back.

You'll have to explain to your students that it starts getting subjective here. Because **ü** is a soft, lax, or reduced vowel, it can very easily slip over into being a schwa. Therefore, some people may say either:

There's a lot tü learn,
There's a lot təlearn,

They're both correct, but a full **tü** sounds overpronounced. It's a similar case before a vowel. To start out, it's probably better to have students make a **ü** and a glide before a vowel for clarity.

. . . that I'm easier tü(w)understand

When they are comfortable with the sound, the concept, and their own intonation, they can later reduce it further.

. . . that I'm easier dənderstand

If you put used to in the middle of the sentence, it quickly reduces to **usta**. Not at the end of sentence, however. It sounds abruptly Southern.

I ustə live in LA.
more than I used tü.

CHAPTER 11: V AS IN VICTORY
V Is Just a Voiced F

Just as you re-paired for the American **R**, it's a good idea to relieve students of a common misconception that **b** and **v** are related. At this point, review the pairs **f/v** and **p/b** and **w**. Indians reverse the two sounds.

For some reason, though, when pressed, students come up with an over-exaggerated **v** sound that involves biting their lips too far. I explain that native Americans don't put their teeth outside of the bottom lip, but rather draw the lip up and press the front teeth against the inside of the lip. Since most people have little difficulty with **f** (except the Japanese and Koreans), again we work from unvoiced to voiced, physically holding the lip in place against the teeth, if need be. The final surprise for them is the **v** of *of*.

CHAPTER 12: TENSE AND LAX VOWELS

So far, you've been through most of the vowels with **Cæt? Cät? Cət?** & **How Much Wüd?**, including the tense/lax vowels **ū/ü**, **o/a/e**, and **i** presented in Chapters 3 and 10.

Remember, tense vowels cause facial movement; lax vowels play up and down the throat and do not cause facial movement.

Part of the problem is that students don't double up on the sound, so when you come to any of these sounds, have the students put them on the little two-step staircase.

CHAPTER 13: THE RIDGE

This section groups all of the sounds that take place at the alveolar ridge, and it's a surprisingly large number. As you have the students contrast the sounds, they should notice that the main difference is how the air comes out: popped (**ch, j, t, d**); hissed or buzzed (**s, z, sh, zh**); or glided (**n, l**).

CHAPTER 14: GRAMMAR IN A BIGGER NUTSHELL

This is an expansion of the "Grammar in a Nutshell" section of Chapter 7, and it's a good review for students so they can realize how much progress they've made. They typically struggle with that section, but after going through this, when you take them back for a review, they see how easy it's become.

CHAPTER 15: PRACTICAL APPLICATION

This is to transition students to the real world. For some reason, they think they should stay with a textbook much longer than they really need. Explain that once they have the tools, they should start actively applying the techniques to materials that interest them, be it podcasts, audiobooks, or talk radio. They will want to use printed material, but orient them more toward audio.

CHAPTER 16: NASAL CONSONANTS

Fortunately, this is an easy, self-explanatory chapter. There are three nasals—lips (**m**), tongue tip (**n**), and glottal (**ng**).

CHAPTER 17: THROATY CONSONANTS

By the time you get here, you are reviewing sounds that have already been introduced, so like with "The Ridge," you are getting them to focus on a particular area while noticing vocality and air flow.

CHAPTERS 1–17: REVIEW AND EXPANSION

This is the second of two reviews in this book. The explanations are omitted so you can circle back and reinforce the concepts in order, just working with the actual exercises.

Index

Downloadable Audio Track Breakdown by Chapter

Introduction: Tracks 1–7
Chapter 1: Tracks 8–92a
Chapter 2: Tracks 93–120
Chapter 3: Tracks 121–131
Chapter 4: Tracks 132–147
Chapter 5: Tracks 148–157
Chapter 6: Tracks 158–176
Chapter 7: Tracks 177–193
Chapter 8: Tracks 194–197
Chapter 9: Tracks 198–207
Chapters 1–9 Review & Expansion:
   Tracks 208–256

Chapter 10: Tracks 257–272
Chapter 11: Tracks 273–280
Chapter 12: Tracks 281–289
Chapter 13: Tracks 290–305
Chapter 14: Tracks 306–310
Chapter 15: Tracks 311–313
Chapter 16: Tracks 314–318
Chapter 17: Tracks 319–328
Chapters 1–17 Review & Expansion:
   Tracks 329–452

Get access to the downloadable audio for *American Accent Training* at:

http://barronsbooks.com/media/AAT8934